Michigan Football

From the Pages of The Michigan Daily

A HISTORY OF THE NATION'S WINNINGEST PROGRAM

TRIUMPH
BOOKS

814 North Franklin Street
Chicago, Illinois 60610
www.triumphbooks.com

This book is available in quantity at special discounts for your group or organization. For further information, contact:

Triumph Books LLC
814 North Franklin Street
Chicago, Illinois 60610
(312) 337-0747
www.triumphbooks.com

A special edition hard cover version of the book is sold exclusively by The Michigan Daily and available at www.michigandaily.com.

Printed in China
ISBN 978-1-60078-765-2

The Michigan Daily is published daily during the school year and weekly during the summer term. The paper is produced in the Stanford Lipsey Student Publications Building located at 420 Maynard. Content published in the newspaper can also be found on www.michigandaily.com.

Cover photo by Jed Moch.
Cover illustration and design by Sarah Squire.

This book is dedicated to all the writers, photographers, designers and Daily staff members who have left a piece of themselves at 420 Maynard.

TABLE OF CONTENTS

BLOCK "M" FOR GAME TO EXCLUDE ALL WOMEN

2500 SEATS IN WEST STAND GIVEN OVER TO FORMATION OF HUGE LETTER

In order to make the block "M" at next Saturday's game strictly maize and blue in color, it has been decided that absolutely no women will be allowed to sit in that section reserved for it. In past years it has always been noticed that the various colors that the women wore in the "M" tended to detract from its effectiveness. It is the desire of the committee this year to due away with this.

The block "M" will be formed in the west stand. Tickets for seats in this section have been stamped on the back with a large "M" by the Athletic Association and mailed out to men students only. This block will include 2500 seats in all.

Members of Sphinx, junior literary honorary society, who are supervising the formation of the "M" will be at the stand in Ferry field to see that no women bearing "M" tickets are admitted. These tickets are supposed to be held by men only and any women who come with them will be turned away. The committee urges all women who have these tickets to exchange them immediately.

CHEERING SECTION NOT PLANNED FOR SPARTAN CONTEST

There will be no cheering section for the game this afternoon, according to an announcement by the committee of the Student council in charge of the section. This announcement was necessitated because of the misunderstanding which seems to exist in some quarters regarding the dates of the games at which the cheering section will function. The section will be used only at the three home games which follow this one, the Ohio State, the Navy, and the Minnesota games.

Attention is also called by the committee to the fact that students who have applied for seats in the cheering section are responsible for their seat in that section for all three games, and should make application for their seat for the remaining home games at once. Some students who signed to sit in the cheering section have ordered only their ticket for the first home game and the committee has not yet received the application for the other games.

After the seats for all of the games have been ordered in the cheering section, arrangements may be made with the committee to sit outside of the section at one home game.

Stadium wreckers de luxe or a Michigan charioteer resting his steed of tin 'ere setting out on his pilgrimage to Columbus.

Football Saturday -- Better than Faygo red pop

Three University alumni and an Eastern Michigan University graduate from Saginaw kick-off the football season with a tailgate picnic before yesterday's game.

Excitement bubbles at football festivities

Festivities started well before game time yesterday as students and tailgating alumni soaked up the sun, tossed the frisbee, ate the food, and sucked down an early-afternoon beer.

By 10:30 a.m. parking lots surrounding the stadium were packed with tailgaters. Michigan fans from Ohio, Indiana, Illinois, and every corner of the State of Michigan were all spouting the proverbial optimism for which Wolverine fans are famous.

AND PLAYING the defending national champion and number-one ranked University of Miami Hurricane further charged the spirit of the pre-game celebration.

The throng seemed to divide into three types:

• The partiers, like freshman Lorenzo Henderson who set his priorities as "having a good time, partying, and the most important thing — winning the football game."

When asked if the Wolverines were her number one priority, one fan said "sex and food are important but I think they're two and three." Another woman explained that in her hometown of Lake Angelus, Michigan, "weddings are postponed for Michigan football."

FLIP THOSE CARDS:

Hail Achievements of Block-M

By MARILYN KORAL

The illustrious Block-M freshmen, semi-mascots and sometime-sole-supporters of the team on rainy Saturdays, have survived attempts by Michigan State saboteurs and other stumbling blocks to emerge "better than ever this year," in the words of Mervin Sharfman, '64, who handles the group.

"Our block is as good if not better than any Big Ten football block," Sharfman arrested.

While other blocks like that of UCLA proudly flip cards spelling "Beat California" at the Rose Bowl (it was felt that Cal Tech intriguers were the culprits), the University block only makes minor errors such as displaying a Confederate Flag when the band was supposed to be playing "Dixie," but decided not to.

Pressure of Studying

Besides, Sharfman insists, blocks like UCLA have 5,000 participants to Michigan's 1200 and practice three times per week while Michigan cannot due to "the pressure of studying."

Sharfman explained that this is only the second year that the block has been seated in the end zone. It traditionally performed on the 10-15 yd.-line. However, this had to stop because fraternities would buy whole blocks of tickets and then refuse to co-operate in the half-time performance.

The block is now 90 per cent freshmen, mainly because of the poor choice of seats. Attendance is the biggest problem, and when the 1,000 minimum necessary for operation of the stunts do not show up, the leaders are forced to recruit boy scouts and other bystanders.

Portrayal of David

Artists from the Wolverine Club design the stunts in conjuction with themes planned by the band a week before every game, taking into consideration the opposing team (such as an ear of corn for Nebraska and a portrayal of David standing on top of Goliath for the Army game) and the possibility of special weekends such as Homecoming.

MARGARET MYERS/Daily
LSA first-year student Dylan Brock stands in his ceremonial J. Crew boxer shorts. Brock wears the same shorts during every game, whether or not he has a ticket to sit in the stadium. (Dec. 10, 1997)

The Michigan football program is seen through a million lenses, but none is quite like the pages of *The Michigan Daily*. *Daily* staffers live at the intersection of journalist, fan and student. They are invested in covering the team. They understand, instinctively, what Michigan football players go through because they also pour their hearts, energy and time into an extracurricular activity — not for fame or money, but out of pure passion for their craft.

That is why the book in your hands is special. It is not a promotional tool for the athletic department, a memoir from a coach or player, or even a retrospective by a great reporter. It is an as-you-go, as-they-lived-it history of Michigan football. It will give you a feel for how the great teams, players, coaches and games were viewed in the moment on campus.

Like most alumni, I spent four of the best years of my life attending the University of Michigan and following the football team. I often wonder how my experience would have been different in another era. What was U-M like when Fielding H. Yost built the program? Or when the Mad Magicians won the 1947 national title? Or when Anthony Carter made his famous catch against Indiana? This book holds the answers.

When Bo Schembechler coached his first game at Michigan in September 1969, students were more caught up in a Vietnam War protest and the new artificial playing surface at Michigan Stadium than in the fortunes of the team. It was the *Daily*, not the big newspapers of the day, that captured Bo's challenge in a single sentence: "Politics and Tartan Turf were, at 1:30 yesterday, the major attractions in the Michigan Stadium for the 70,183 not-so-screaming fans that came to drink away a Saturday afternoon."

The *Daily* has been close to the action for every era of Michigan football. Bo once got in trouble for pushing a writer from the *Daily*. One of his protégés, Lloyd Carr, once walked into the Student Publications Building, put his feet up on a desk, and waited to chastise a sports editor for the *Daily*'s coverage of a player's arrest.

But mostly, *Daily* writers, photographers and editors have made a much more favorable impression. Not long before Bo died, I sat in his office and listened to him talk fondly about somebody from his early days at Michigan. But he wasn't talking about a player or a coach.

He was talking about Robin Wright, a former *Michigan Daily* football writer who became a famous journalist. Schembechler had recently heard Wright give a talk about the Middle East, and he told me, with his eyes open wide, that Wright really knew her stuff.

By that point, Wright had established herself as one of the best foreign correspondents of the past 40 years, and I doubt she needed the validation of a retired football coach. But I don't think Bo meant it that way. He just thought it was so great that a reporter who covered him for the *Daily* had reached such heights.

> **[The Daily] is where I worked the hardest, stayed out the latest, got paid the least and laughed the most. I figured out what I wanted to with my life at the Daily, not just because I found a profession. The Daily is where I figured out who I am.**

Wright is not the only *Daily* writer to reach the top of her profession. Others have won Pulitzers, broken major national stories and written bestselling books. And in most cases, those success stories did not just start at the *Daily*; they happened because of the *Daily*.

Ask a typical *Daily* alum about his time in the Student Publications Building, and he will smile like you asked him about the time he dated a supermodel while flying to the moon and watching Michigan beat Ohio State. The place means that much to us. It is a classroom, a studio, a co-ed fraternity/sorority, a careers office and an unofficial dating service.

The *Daily* is where I met my wife and many of my best friends. It is where I worked the hardest, stayed out the latest, got paid the least and laughed the most. I figured out what I wanted to with my life at the *Daily*, not just because I found a profession. The *Daily* is where I figured out who I am. I'm sure there are hundreds of *Daily* alumni I've never met who feel the same way I do.

MICHAEL
ROSENBERG
Roses Are Read
Final Column

Distant return

ANN ARBOR, Mich., April 11, 2006 — Went back to the alma mater today, went back to school. Went back, way back, all the way back to my freshman dorm room. Knocked on the door and out came a kid wearing a "Pearl Jam Reunion Tour" T-shirt. I asked him if he saw the band in concert, and he said he hadn't — his parents did, and they bought him the shirt. He said he hated Pearl Jam. He said he was only wearing the shirt because he was almost out of clothes, he needed to do laundry, and who was I anyway? I quickly walked away.

I took a stroll on the Diag, stood on the 'M,' stared at the buildings. Some of the buildings looked familiar, some I swear I've never seen before. I remember when I was a student here, when the place was under construction. The construction was finished long ago. Now students walk to class without any concept of what was here before. Not that they care, or should. I passed by the kiosks, which, as always, were filled with fliers of every color. I stepped closer and read the fliers, which touted MSA parties I had never heard of, bands I had never heard of, even bars I had never heard of.

Surprisingly, I actually saw somebody I recognized. A friend who graduated with me. Kind of a slacker, as I recall. He looked the same as I remembered, with a young female student next to him — except that he was wearing a tie and teaching the student history. He's a professor now. He was holding office hours.

The University has changed since it was an odd mixture of flannel shirts and strange and textbooks and e-mail and beer — none of which I really enjoyed at the time, except the beer. None of them are part of my life anymore, except the beer, occasionally.

In time, we chose our majors, settled in with our own groups of friends — we "found ourselves," as they used to say. But despite our separate paths, mutual experiences connected us. Most of us still remember where we were when Chris Webber called timeout, or what we thought of Hash Bash or where our favorite spots to study were. We still remember certain moments, and we still remember who was with us at those moments. Those friendships were unlike any before or since, friendships we knew would last forever.

They didn't.

I don't keep in touch with my college friends much anymore. The inevitable factors of time and space have wedged between us, whittled away at the connections. It isn't anybody's fault. It just happened.

That's why I came back here, I confess. I haven't been back much lately — not enough, anyway. The more time passed, the fewer reasons I had to come back here. And the more I wanted to.

So here I am, wandering around the few square blocks where my days once unfolded. I walked along the same streets — State Street, Washtenaw, Tappan, Wash U., if you can believe that.

This town has evolved since the days when we couldn't have enough coffee shops or pizza places. In a desperate attempt to find something that hadn't changed, I went up to Michigan Stadium. I remember walking there on crisp autumn Saturdays, when the old stadium was filled with seemingly everyone I knew. Today the stadium was locked, of course — they don't play football in April. I knew it would be locked. A cool breeze blew, affecting me and me alone as I stood against the chain-link fence. It felt weird, eerie, so I left the stadium. Feeling hungry, I went back to my favorite sandwich place.

It's a store now.

I almost gave up, almost gave up on salvaging anything from my visit. This is somebody else's school now, I thought. I started heading back to my hotel room.

That's when I saw it — the same restaurant I used to go to with friends late at night, the kind of place I wouldn't be caught dead in today. I stared through the window as students passed by me. I went inside, and the place was still recognizable, thank God. The decor was the same. The menu was the same. The people were different, but the crowd was the same. I sat down and ordered the usual.

I hope I contributed, in some small way, to the rich tradition of the *Daily*. For more than a century, the University of Michigan has had one of the nation's most storied football programs and one of its finest college newspapers. The football team produced some of the great moments in the school's history, and the *Daily* captured them. Now you get to enjoy them. I think Bo would agree: These *Daily* writers, they knew their stuff.

Michael Rosenberg

January 2012

Michael Rosenberg is a senior writer for Sports Illustrated, former columnist for the Detroit Free Press, and author of "War As They Knew It: Woody Hayes, Bo Schembechler and America in a Time of Unrest." He was a Michigan Daily staff writer from 1992 to 1996 and the Daily's editor in chief as a senior. He covered University of Michigan football during the 1994 season.

On my first day as a freshman at the University of Michigan, my mother summoned her inner interior designing talents and did her best to decorate my Mary Markley dorm room.

At a book store on State Street, she purchased an oversized laminated poster of what looked like a small Midwestern city crammed into one spot above a sprawling hash-marked field. She purchased, and later helped hang in my dorm room, a poster of Michigan Stadium.

While the poster hung in the center of my dorm room, the actual stadium and the teams that played in it turned out to be the centerpieces of our college experience.

Almost any student who walked among the maize-and-blue masses of Michiganders along State Street, to Hoover, to the corner of Stadium and Main, through the iron gates and into the stadium, became a convert. From the shock-and-awe moment they first entered it, they were transformed.

Sitting in the mosh pit known as the student section became the easiest way to accelerate the friendships that are formed at school. Strangers became acquaintances. Acquaintances became friends. And friends became friends for life.

Even now, the names of my freshman classes elude me. Football facts do not.

Back in November 1985, in yet another tight game between Ohio State and Michigan, quarterback Jim Harbaugh play-action faked to running back Jamie Morris, then delivered a perfect strike to wide receiver John Kolesar, who raced 77 yards, right toward the student section in the corner of the endzone with the decisive touchdown during the Wolverines' 27-17 victory.

More than 25 years later, those feelings still are as fresh as tomorrow. Students from those sections can still see Kolesar running our way. We can still feel friends jumping on our backs. We can still remember celebrating Michigan football that day, along with all the others to come. Students from 2011 understand. They saw Roy Roundtree catch a 16-yard touchdown pass from Denard Robinson with two seconds left to beat Notre Dame, 35-31.

While our freshman classes fade further into our memories, football is the subject few forget. Students mark their time at the University not by the classes they take, but by the football teams they followed and the men who coached them.

Incoming students now will be a part of the Brady Hoke era, which they expect to last longer and turn out better than the Rich Rodriguez era. Yet all eras are measured against the ones from 1969-1989, when Glenn "Bo" Schembechler became the standard for Michigan Men. These men, and the teams that they led, provide a timeline for the memories by which we recall our school years.

The Diag might be at the center of campus, but football is at the center of the school. At a university that has produced people responsible for more than 130 Olympic medals, 26 Rhodes Scholarships, 18 Pulitzer Prizes, seven Nobel Prizes and one United States presidency, none are more celebrated for their achievements at U-M than Tom Harmon, Desmond Howard and Charles Woodson — the only three men in Michigan's history to win the Heisman Trophy.

> 66 **Michigan is our family, and its stadium is the (big) house we grow up in. For better or worse – and does anyone really recall much bad at all? – they are ours for life.** 99

As accomplished as Michigan's Ross School of Business is, as prestigious as Michigan's Law School is, its football program is historic.

"Hail to the Victors," which student Louis Elbel wrote after Michigan pulled out a last-minute victory over the University of Chicago that resulted in a league championship in 1898, has been proclaimed by some as the greatest college fight song ever written.

Michigan Stadium is the largest college football stadium in the nation, one of the largest football-only stadiums in the world and the only place known as The Big House.

And the school's maize-and-blue colors — seared in our minds — are as heartfelt and recognizable as red, white and blue. They are a part of the school's history and a part of ours as well.

Few realize it at the time, but when the University of Michigan admits an applicant to the school, it also grants entry into

The Schef's Specialty
BY ADAM SCHEFTER

A time to say so long

Now, I am in in the unenviable position of having to say good-bye to the finest years I've ever known.

So this is my good-bye column. My chance to try to express what it means to have the best four years of my life come to a close. What it means to have to say good-bye to the friends that I love so dearly. What it means to have been lucky enough to have had four years at the best school in the country.

In the past, I have often heard adults say that they would give anything to have one more year at college. Can I consider myself an adult and say the same thing?

I've certainly done everything possible these past few months to prolong my final year.

I have walked down State Street slower than I ever have, staring nostalgically at trees that I once sat under, eating Steve's ice cream, taking in all that a sunny day in Ann Arbor has to offer. I have lied on the hammock on the porch of my house and gazed out at Church Street, replaying a road trip to Chicago or a fraternity football game that was salvaged in the final minutes.

Yet, like I imagined, none of this has made a difference. The days have picked up speed, almost like watching Leroy Hoard breaking through the line of scrimmage and into the open-field against USC in this year's Rose Bowl.

In the song *America* by Simon and Garfunkel, there is a line that puts this passage of time into perspective:

"*Michigan seems like a dream to me now.*"

And today, my alarm clock is going off, louder than ever before. But this time, unlike so many other mornings at college, there is no snooze button to press. Time to get up. Say good morning to the real world. Sure was the fastest dream I've ever had.

They say you always remember your first kiss. Well, your first day at college is just as memorable. Lasts longer, too.

I remember my mother and I arriving at my dorm, Mary Markley. Unpacking all my belongings into a tiny, square-shaped room and going to eat dinner at the Real Seafood Co. to relax my nerves.

From then until now, I have accumulated memories that make a college experience, especially a Michigan one, unforgettable. They thought they had a lot of memories to discuss in *The Big Chill*.

Hah. I could talk their ears off.

There was Michigan wide receiver John Kolesar pulling in a 77-yard touchdown pass against Ohio State and running right at the frantic student section. Spring break trips. Florida and Coppertone. Acapaulco and Corona. Jamaica and reggae. Venezuela and riots. Cooking dinners. Dinner dates. Laughs. Parties. Barbecues. Intramural championships. National championships. More laughs.

Life doesn't get any better than that.

Never mind the times of being buried in the library and being forced to learn an entire semester of accounting. Never mind the times of waking up the morning after a big party at your house that looks like only Neanderthals attended. Not to mention simply waking up the morning after a big party.

This is not what you remember.

But now, I am forced to face reality: the past is gone, the present is fleeting and the future is frightening.

Graduation is staring me right in the face. I don't think I have ever wanted to turn my back on something more. Who wants to give up a grown-up life without grown-up responsibilities?

Next year, I will be without my best friends, Dave, Gregg, Jeff R., Jeff W. and Sam, who have been my best buddies since my first year at school. I will be without football Saturday's; without long Christmas and summer breaks; without thousands of people, all close in age, all ready to have a great time; without late nights with long conversations; late nights with munchies; and just late nights.

And who will ever forget any of it?

There are certainly enough memories to fill my car for a long and lonely ride home. Just like I was warned. Just like I witnessed.

You know, I never did like saying good-bye.

Instead, I say, so long.

---

a not-so-exclusive nationwide football fraternity.

The fraternity includes hundreds of thousands of people who gather on Saturdays in the fall — and for years to come. They come together to follow and support a Michigan football program that often winds up stamped into their soul.

Football becomes a unifying force to bring friends back together. Sometimes it happens at a sports bar in another city, far from Ann Arbor. Other times it is with an actual reunion of college friends in Ann Arbor, where old memories are relived and new ones are created.

Michigan is our family, and its stadium is the (big) house we grow up in. For better or worse — and does anyone really recall much bad at all? — they are ours for life.

It was impossible to realize it at the time, but the first poster purchased at Michigan turned out to mean more than a Picasso could have. Inside that stadium, some of our most endearing memories were created.

There were players charging out of the tunnel and jumping up to touch the Go Blue banner. There were wins over archrivals like Ohio State and painful losses to powerhouses like Miami. There even was our graduation ceremony in that stadium, which marked the end of our rights to those student section seats. But as one chapter ends, another begins.

Students became professionals, professionals found spouses and spouses celebrated parenthood. And yet as much as lives changed, some facets didn't. Michigan still brings everyone together, usually on Saturdays, usually for some big game. Only now, it is not about the game so much as what happens around the game.

It's an excuse for Michigan friends — lifelong friends — to get together. It's a chance for them to hand down the traditions that were once handed to them.

Now their children dress for the occasion, wearing the same maize-and-blue colors their parents did, cheering the same school their parents did. They have become converts. One day they will understand, if they don't already, that Michigan football is not about the X's and O's so much as it is the bonds that are formed.

Yes, there are other fine universities and outstanding football programs. Yet anyone who has been a part of Michigan football believes there's no stadium and no program like the one in Ann Arbor.

By now, the picture of Michigan Stadium my mom bought me on my first day at school — that hung neat and centered in my freshman dorm room — is long gone. But the pictures in my mind never will be.

Adam Schefter

January 2012

Adam Schefter is ESPN's NFL Insider. He was a Michigan Daily staff writer from 1985 to 1989 and a sports editor from 1988 to 1989. He covered University of Michigan football during the 1988 season and graduated in 1989.

Tucked on the second floor of 420 Maynard, hundreds of heavy, bound books contain thousands of frayed and yellowing newspapers. The volumes — once neatly lined on rows of shelves in chronological order since 1890 — were piled on chairs and tables and scattered in corners throughout *The Michigan Daily* newsroom by the time this book was finished.

Generations of *Daily* editors have understood the historical value of the archives and often tossed around the idea of connecting the *Daily* and Michigan football in a book. For some reason, the four of us latched on to this idea and turned it into a reality with very little understanding of the massive project we were about to undertake.

The production began about a month after Michigan coach Brady Hoke took over a football program that hadn't won a BCS bowl in more than a decade. As a new era surfaced, we thought there was no better time to show how the past had shaped the present — to reflect on the key coaches who helped build the program into what it is today and the players who proudly wore the winged helmet.

The process of making this book was slow and not always pretty. We spent countless hours, weekends and summer nights nose deep in the collection of the bound volumes to find the stories and pictures that define the football program's 132 years. Page by page, we became Michigan football historians and got a sense for the development of American culture and print journalism in the 20th century.

It wasn't simple. We knew how to make a daily newspaper, but producing a coffee table book with a distant deadline was a foreign concept. We lost articles and mismatched photos with captions. We searched for headlines and photos sometimes only knowing the year it was published. And yet, some gems were included in this book only because we stumbled upon them accidentally at 3 a.m. — when everything was funnier than in broad daylight.

We spent upward of 13 hours a day in the *Daily* newsroom the week before this book's deadline. It was crunch time — just as though it were 1 a.m. on *Daily* production nights. But these were not the average production nights when we had eight pages to produce, not 180.

We started this book as *Daily* editors and finished as alumni of one of the oldest and most respected student-run institutions on campus. The experience was a history lesson, a business lesson and an initiation into the real world for four young journalists.

This journey also helped us say goodbye to 420 Maynard. Even if we made 10 more books (don't worry, we won't), we wouldn't be able to repay the *Daily* for all it has given us.

The second floor of the Stanford Lipsey Student Publications Building, with the bedlam of students covering breaking news and the lingering smell of coffee, will hold a special place in our hearts forever. For those who are *Daily* alumni, we hope this book reminds you of all the times you missed class to chase a story. For the rest of our readers, we hope this book gives you a shared appreciation for a newspaper that has chronicled the history of Michigan football and transformed the lives of thousands of college students.

We hope you enjoy *Michigan Football: From the Pages of The Michigan Daily*.

Chantel Jennings, Nick Spar, Sarah Squire, Stephanie Steinberg
2011 *Michigan Daily* editors

All content in this book is from *The Michigan Daily* archives except for designated photos from the Bentley Historical Library and text in blue boxes that was included for clarification and context. Some text has been edited for legibility and spacing reasons. All other stories and photos, including grammatical and spelling errors, appear exactly how they were published in the *Daily*. Date tags refer to the date of publication.

MARISSA MCCLAIN/Daily

This book was largely produced by *Michigan Daily* staffers Chantel Jennings, Nick Spar, Sarah Squire and Stephanie Steinberg. Chantel was a sports writer and editor from 2007 to 2011. Nick was a sports writer, co-managing sports editor and managing editor from 2008 to 2011. Sarah was a managing design editor and web development manager from 2009 to 2011. Stephanie was a reporter, news editor and editor in chief from 2008 to 2011. The four editors designed each page and scoured the 122 years of *Daily* archives to find the best stories, headlines and photos that represent the greatest moments in Michigan football.

A large thank you goes to managing photo editor Marissa McClain for editing photos, designers Alex Bondy and Emily Cedar for designing pages, managing sports editor Stephen J. Nesbitt for researching football coaches and news editors Bethany Biron and Joseph Lichterman for gathering content for decade feature pages. Thank you to the *Michigan Daily* staff members who contributed their time and ideas to this project — including sports writers Everett Cook, Ben Estes, Michael Florek, Kevin Raftery and Neal Rothschild, designers Sara Boboltz, Melissa Dulic, Hermés Risien, Katie Williams and Anna Zielinski and managing photo editor Jed Moch for taking the picture of Michigan Stadium on the cover.

Thank you to the Board of Student Publications for supporting this project; Adam Schefter for the introduction; Michael Rosenberg for the foreword and publishing advice; The Bentley Historical Library for the use of photos; Bentley Historical Library archivists for their help; the Office of Public Affairs for providing tuition and endowment data; 2010 Editor in Chief Jacob Smilovitz for passing on the idea for the book and providing feedback; Greg Dooley, Gary Kicinski and Todd Schafer for reviewing each page; the parents of *Michigan Daily* staffers who supported this book and their children's work at the *Daily*; the editors at Triumph Books for partnering with the *Daily* and believing in this book.

Most importantly, thank you to the former *Michigan Daily* writers, editors, photographers and designers whose words, photos and designs fill these pages and make this a one-of-a-kind book about Michigan football.

1973

ARE YOU A

Drunk ?   Debaucherer ?   Degenerate ?

IF SO, TRY THE

DAILY SPORTS STAFF

*"No matter how bad you are,
we'll make you worse."*

NOV. 20, 1943

HERE TODAY...

... By HARVEY FRANK

WOMEN are strange creatures. Now that they have gone into many of the fields that men formerly kicked them out of, they claim to have acquired new skills. Marion Ford, a woman, the Daily's managing editor, is one of the new usurpers in the field of sports writing.

Naturally, just to show her how inferior she really is, the male members of The Daily sports staff half-heartedly invited her to join the board of experts in picking the winners of the Saturday gridiron battles.

Everything has gone just as was unexpected. In the first week's poll Black Marnie tied for first place with Fred Delano, Michigan's athletic publicity director, getting 15 out of 20 selections right. And she improved on her pace last week by missing on only two games, edging out three other experts by one tilt. That leaves her with an .825 percentage for two weeks, .050 points, two games difference, ahead of the rest of the field, including that guy Concensus.

While the other experts claim that they use scientific and mathematical means to arrive at their conclusions, Marnie brags that she just guesses. (We're coming in to see you about dropping our math course, tomorrow, Dean Walter.)

MAY 26, 1966

Join The Daily, and Attend All The Best Parties in Ann Arbor

SEPT. 19, 1957

Daily Sport Staff Seeks Tryouts

Do you know the difference between a pass ball and a punt? Then The Daily sports staff wants you.

The sports staff, a clandestine crew of 19 men and one woman, (probably the last of her breed), is beginning another year's search for new members.

Nowhere else can a sports-minded student find all these advantages in one package: a top campus activity on the top college newspaper, association with the people that make the Michigan and national sports news, choice seats at many sporting events, and the knowledge that he is serving over 20,000 people on the campus.

No experience needed except a hunger interest in sports — all sports. We train our members from the bottom up.

NOV. 23, 1918

MICHIGAN DAILY ISSUES EXTRA IN RECORD TIME

COMPLETE STAFF ORGANIZATION FROM FIELD TO LINO- TYPE

(By James C. J. Martin)

"Football Extra! All about the football game!" cried the newsboys this afternoon.

"How did The Daily get out an extra one minute after the game?" queried one of the gridiron fans coming up State street from Ferry field.

Well, patient reader, this is the way it is accomplished.

Special stories are assigned by the editors several days before. They are then written up by members of the staff, set by the linotype man, proof read, corrected slugs—lines of type that have been reset—inserted, and put in the forms. Pages two and three ar then "slapped on the press" and "run off," which is otherwise known as printed.

Now comes the exciting part of the adventure. After the fourth page is already in the forms, the great machine is in readiness for the remainder of the task of getting out the extra. A Michigan Daily man is stationed in the press stand on Ferry field and dictates a running story over the telephone, which is connected to one of the telephones in The Daily office. A man at a typewriter in The Daily pounds out the story as the other man dictates it from the field.

Four men carry the copy from the typewriter in The Daily office to the linotype man who sets the story up as quickly as it gets to the machine. The story is then taken from the linotype machine and set in the forms piece by piece.

As the game nears the close the force carrying copy from the typist to the linotypist in The Daily office works with feverish haste. One minute before the whistle blows closing the contest the "ribbon"—72 point type—is put in the forms, which are in turn taken to the press.

The second the game ends the typist in the The Daily office tells one of the "copy runners," who in turn informs the linotypist and the pressman. The forms are then locked, the "juice" turned on, the papers fed through the press, and the printed extra rushed to the front office, which is immediately sold to newsboys, who in turn, sell them to the fans returning from the game.

That's the way The Daily gets out its football extra. Each year the extra staff makes an attempt to beat the record of those who have gone before them. The record for speed of production is now held by the 1917 M. A. C. extra staff who succeeded in getting the paper on the streets in 55 seconds after the final play was made.

Pizza and politics at 420 Maynard

By NADINE COHODAS

A lot of snazzy things happen around the clock at The Daily.

At 2:03 a.m., for example, one may find an intense bridge game going on amid half-assembled news stories from the Associated Press and the decarbonated vestiges of the country's only nickel cokes (Greedier staff members play poker.)

Or a cursory glance around the 420 Maynard St. office at 8:15 p.m. is likely to reveal a brief struggle between two hungry staff members over the last piece of a half sausage, half anchovies pizza from the nearby Greek pizza restaurant.

But much of the time, we spend our hours publishing six newspapers weekly from September to April and five a week during the summer.

Although The Daily is a college newspaper, we also print national or world stories. The Daily is the only morning paper in Ann Arbor and has the latest deadline in the state.

However, the bulk of Daily stories come from the campus or the city and are written by Daily staff members of all shapes, sizes and abilities.

Some people say there's no substitute for experience, but any interested student can work on The Daily although he may never have worked on a newspaper before.

If you can hold a pencil, read from left to right, apply rubber cement on paper in a straight horizontal line, we can use you. (If you can type, you get a free kiss from the editor of the appropriate gender.)

There is plenty to do here, and you can work your way literally from the bottom up. All trainees, regardless of previous experience, start their Daily careers in the shop on the first floor proofreading stories for the next day's paper and then move to the second floor for more advanced work.

420 Maynard is really a very nice place. Although we have lots of paper, pencils, glue, nickle cokes, and four telephone lines to boot, we can't promise Mae West.

But when you get to Ann Arbor, why don't you come up and see us some time?

The Michigan Daily vs State News
10   9
October 8, 2010
Ann Arbor, Michigan
(Final in 2OT)

JILLIAN BERMAN AND TONY DING/Daily

The Michigan Daily staff plays Michigan State's newspaper, *The State News*, the weekend of the Michigan-Michigan State game.

PLAY & BY-PLAY

—By AL NEWMAN—

Second Sight . . . Predictions . . .

* * *

DON'T be disillusioned when we make the startling statement that sports writers are not gifted with second sight. We have never met one who was, and we never expect to find one thus endowed. What's more, if we should meet such a person we would immediately characterize him as a very dumb cluck, indeed.

He would be wasting his time pounding a creaky old typewriter in some fly-blown newspaper office when he might be living in the lap of luxury merely by indulging in games of chance for the odd bit of silver. He might apply his foreknowledge of events to lift himself from his journalistic limbo.

Despite this state of affairs, sports writers in general are very very fond of predicting the outcome of this and that. It is a great weakness of the breed. Still, there is no denying that it is fun predicting things especially when the predicter does not have to shell out some of his own hard-earned cash to back up his judgment.

Thus, we have decided to run a sports staff Concensus on the larger football games of each Saturday. Each of the five juniors on the staff will pick his own list of winners in these selected games, and the result of the vote, or concensus, will run in this column. The percentage of each man will be taken and at the end of the grid season the individual winner will be awarded a fur-lined bicycle or a barb-wire bathtub or something equally useful.

1890
1891
1892
1893
1894
1895
1896
1897
1898
1899
1900
1901
1902
1903
1904
1905
1906
1907
1908
1909
1910
1911
1912
1913
1914
1915
1916
1917
1918
1919
1920
1921
1922
1923
1924
1925
1926
1927
1928
1929
1930
1931
1932
1933
1934
1935
1936
1937
1938
1939
1940
1941
1942
1943
1944
1945
1946
1947
1948
1949
1950
1951
1952
1953
1954
1955
1956
1957
1958
1959
1960
1961
1962
1963
1964
1965
1966
1967
1968
1969
1970
1971
1972
1973
1974
1975
1976
1977
1978
1979
1980
1981
1982
1983
1984
1985
1986
1987
1988
1989
1990
1991
1992
1993
1994
1995
1996
1997
1998
1999
2000
2001
2002
2003
2004
2005
2006
2007
2008
2009
2010
2011
2012

TEAM PHOTOS

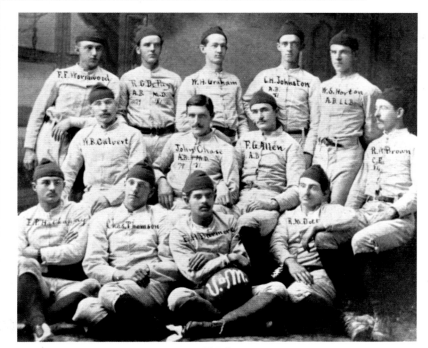

1880

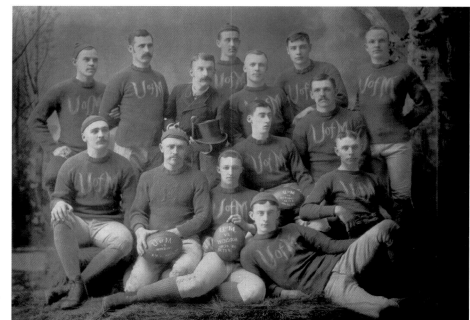

1885

1890

1895

MICHIGAN COACHES

(1879-1890) No coaches 23-10-1	**(1891)** Frank Crawford 4-5-0	**(1892-1893)** Frank E. Barbour 14-8-0	
(1894-1895) William McCauley 17-2-1	**(1896)** William D. Ward 9-1-0	**(1897-1899)** Gustave Ferbert 24-3-1	**(1900)** Langdon "Biff" Lea 7-2-1
(1901-1923, 1925-1926) Fielding H. Yost 165-29-10	**(1924)** George Little 6-2-0	**(1927-1928)** Elton E. Wieman 9-6-1	**(1929-1937)** Harry Kipke 46-26-4
(1938-1947) Fritz Crisler 71-16-3	**(1948-1958)** Bennie Oosterbaan 63-33-4	**(1959-1968)** Bump Elliott 51-42-2	**(1969-1989)** Bo Schembechler 194-48-5
(1990-1994) Gary Moeller 44-13-4	**(1995-2007)** Lloyd Carr 122-40-0	**(2008-2011)** Rich Rodriguez 15-22-0	**(2011-)** Brady Hoke 11-2-0

RETIRED JERSEYS

11
- **Francis Wistert, tackle** (1931-1933)
- **Albert Wistert, tackle** (1940-1942)
- **Alvin Wistert, tackle** (1947-1949)

47 **Bennie Oosterbaan, end** (1925-1927)

48 **Gerald Ford, center** (1932-1934)

87 **Ron Kramer, end** 1954-1956

98 **Tom Harmon, halfback** (1938-1940)

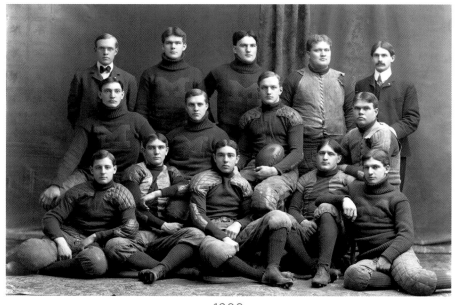

1900

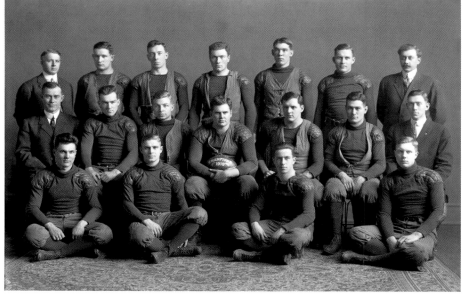

1910

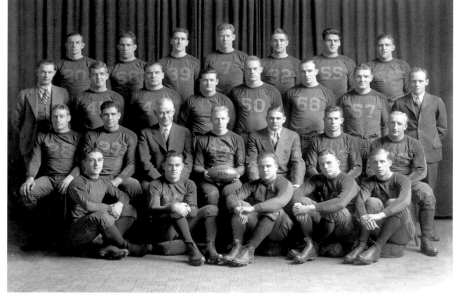

1930

1960

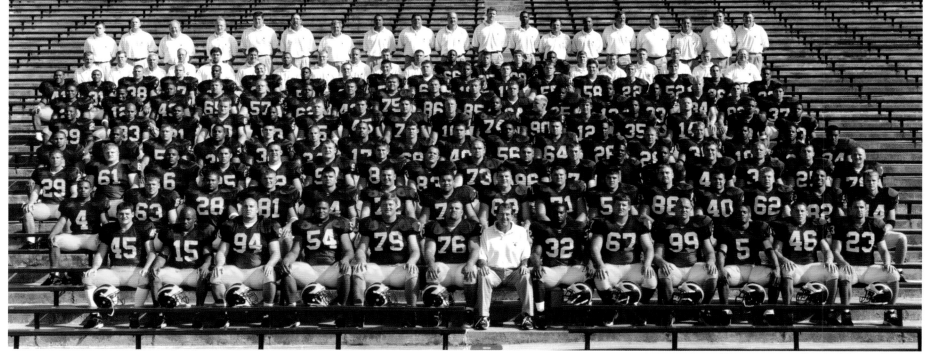

2000

Photos courtesy of Bentley Historical Library

FROM THE PAGES OF THE MICHIGAN DAILY

1890
1891
1892
1893
1894
1895
1896
1897
1898
1899
1900

1890–1899

1890
1891
1892
1893
1894
1895
1896
1897
1898
1899

Michigan defeated Racine College, 1-0, in its first football game on May 30, 1879 — 11 years before the first issue of *The Michigan Daily* was printed.

SEPT. 29, 1890

U. of M. DAILY.

OCT. 2, 1890

JIMMY IS GONE.

THE PATRIARCH JANITOR OF THE MAIN HALL

Loses His Position after Twenty-Seven Years of Faithful Service.

Jimmy Ottley, the janitor of the Literary department, has stood in the Main hall at chapel time with the mail bag in his hands for 27 years, and everybody supposed he would continue to do so for the rest of his natural days. Not so. When chapel services were resumed this morning Jimmy was missed from his accustomed place. He has made his last appearance in a Latin play.

APRIL 23, 1891

OH, HORRIBLE!

A Curling Iron In Nearly Every Student's Room.

The Chicago Tribune published, recently, an interview with Elisha P. Bowen, of Cincinnati, O., in which Mr. Bowen charges that nearly all the male students at the U. of M. use curling irons with which to curl their hair. That the charge is utterly without foundation, it seems hardly necessary to say. It is as false as it is ridiculous. This is what Mr. Bowen is credited with

saying :

"The artificial curls were not worth seeing," said Mr. Bowen, "but I could not help discovering them. At first I thought the curls were natural, and would have come away with that impression had not one of my sons exploded the secret. I noticed that nearly every young man I passed on the street had pretty, curly bangs. The boys there wear caps and always take good care that they are tilted back on the head. They do this so the curls can be seen and admired."

FEB. 22, 1892

SPECIAL EDITION.

EX - PRESIDENT CLEVELAND'S

ADDRESS TO THE STUDENTS.

"Sentiment in our National Life" the Theme Discussed by the Brilliant Statesman.

OCT. 19, 1893

THE GREAT AFRO-AMERICAN.

A few Facts of Interest Regarding Mr. Douglass.—A Great Orator and Statesman.

When the lecture association invited Frederick Douglass to come to Ann Arbor to lecture, he responded by a very happy letter, in which he said that he felt greatly honored by the invitation and recollected with pleasure the cordial reception he received by the students of the University of Michigan a number of years ago.

Mr. Douglass's interesting and remarkble life has been written so many times that it is familiar to every student of American history and politics, but that everyone who hears the venerable gentleman tonight may know something of him, we give a short sketch of the most important events of his career.

JAN. 26, 1899

DON'T DO IT.

President Angell Does Not Think That the University Should Leave Ann Arbor.

When President James B. Angell heard of the plan of removing the University of Michigan to Detroit, he expressed his disapproval in vigorous terms. "Perfect nonsense" he declared; "every once in so often someone will think up some absurd plan like this. The university is

here, and I'm in favor of letting it stay here to the end of time."

He even said that Ann Arbor is a better place, anyhow, setting aside the undesirability of moving, and that the advantages so much talked of are small in comparison with the disadvantages.

The only department with any special leaning toward the scheme seems to be the medical. Some of the doctors admit guardedly that the hospital training would be much improved.

AS OF 1890...

19-9-1
MICHIGAN FOOTBALL PROGRAM RECORD

0-0
VS. OHIO STATE

0-0
VS. MICHIGAN STATE

3-0
VS. NOTRE DAME

0-0
VS. MINNESOTA

2,299
ENROLLMENT

$20
IN-STATE TUITION

$30
OUT-OF-STATE TUITION

$1,131
ENDOWMENT

NO HEAD FOOTBALL COACH

James B. Angell
UNIVERSITY PRESIDENT

NOTABLE GRADUATES

1878 Clarence Darrow, American lawyer

1883 William Mayo, Mayo Clinic founder

1893 George Jewett, first African-American varsity football player

Vol. I. No. 11.   UNIVERSITY OF MICHIGAN, SATURDAY, OCTOBER 11, 1890.   PRICE 3 CENTS.

EXTRA.

U. OF M. VS. ALBION.

A Brisk Game at the Fair Grounds this Afternoon.

THE U. OF M. WINS BY A SCORE OF 56 TO 10.

Albion Handicapped by the Loss of Both Half Backs.

At 1 o'clock rain threatened to put a stop to the game, but at 3 the clouds parted and the sun shone brightly. U. of M. won the toss and chose the north goal.

Van Nortwick, '93, acted as umpire for the U. of M. F. E. Allen, Albion, was referee. About 350 were present.

Game opened by Albion with a pass to end rusher, who carried the ball nearly to our 25-yd. line. A series of good runs, aided by Albion's blocking, brought it to the 10-yd. line. Snell failed to kick goal from field. Albion followed and Anderson got the ball, making a touchdown—4 points.

Another rush carried the ball to Albion's 25 yard line, whence it is advanced 15 yards more by a V, with Grosh behind it. At this point Landon was put off the game for slugging Malley, and Parmeter took his place. Two more rushes carried the ball over the line 4 points. Malley bluffs on the punt-out, and the ball is down 6 yards. It is then rushed over the line again, but Jewett fails to kick goal. Score—Albion, 4; U. of M., 8.

Jewett ran beautifully for 30 yards, but Grosh lost the ball after a 10-yd. run. Albion rushed through centre for 10 yards, and then kicked. Dygert tried to run, but was down on our 30-yd. line, whence Grosh carried the ball beyond centre. Jewett brought the ball to the 25-yd. line, and Grosh, with the V, took it over. Jewett kicked goal. Score: Albion, 4; U. of M., 20. Time was called before any more points were made with the V, took it over. Jewett kicked goal. Score: Albion, 4; U. of M., 20. Time was called before any more points were made

The try at goal failed; but the ball was rushed over and a goal kicked from the touchdown. Score—Albion, 4; U. of M., 30. Ball is taken to center of field and kicked after three downs.

Dygert gets it. Abbott and Jewett advanced it to the 15 yard line, and Jewett carries it over. No goal.

Prettyman runs to 25-yd. line, and on the next play Jewett makes a touchdown. The try at goal fails, but Sutherland gets it and takes it over. No goal. Van Inwagen follows the ball and gets it, making three touchdowns in succession, with no goals. Albion, 4; U. of M., 56.

Albion gets the ball and kicks. It is down at the 25 yard line and then is rushed to the 5 yard line and lost. Albion kicks, Jewett advances the ball, but in the scrimmage Dygert and Van Inwagen are hurt. de Pont and Payne take their places. We lose the ball, and two good runs by Albion carry it across our line. Goal. Albion, 10; U. of M., 56.

After a good deal of rough play Jewett made two good runs to the 25 yard line, but time is called just before the ball goes over. Albion, 10; U. of M., 56; Albion was handicapped by the loss of both her half backs, who were disqualified for rough tackling.

After a good deal of rough play Jewett made two good runs to the 25 yard line, but time is called just before the ball goes over. Albion, 10; U. of M., 56.

Michigan's 56-10 victory over Albion was the first football game the *Daily* covered, and was the season opener in the Wolverines' 12th season.

At 1 o'clock rain threatened to put a stop to the game, but at 3 the clouds parted and the sun shone brightly.

— *The Michigan Daily*

Yells and Songs.

U. OF M. RAH! RAH!! RAH! RAH!!
U. OF M. RAH! RAH!! RAH! RAH!!
ROO! RAH!! ROO! RAH!!
MICHIGAN MICHIGAN RAH! RAH!! RAH!!!

— 1 —

Who can? We can!
Michigan, can! can!
Beat Chi-ca-go !!!

— 2 —

Who made that play?
Who saved the day?
——— ! 'twas ———!!

— 3 —

1-2-3-4-5-6-7-8-9-10-11-12,
That was the score!
Come, boys, this year and make it
more!!

— 4 —

Who trains Chicago?
A. Alonzo Stagg!
What do we say of him?
"He's a warm rag!"

— 5 —

Ye-e-e-e! Ki-yippi, Ki yan!
What's the matter with Michigan?
She's O. K.! Who's O. K.?
The team that's going to win today!!

— 6 —

Go-it-Chica! Go-it-Chica!
Go it as hard as you can!!
We'll make you sweat,
Now you can bet!
We boys from Michigan!!

— 7 —

Dickory! Dickory! Dock!!
The mouse ran up the clock!
The game's begun,
There'll soon be fun!!
Dickory! Dickory! Dock !!

(Air: Ta-ra-ra Boom-de-aye.")

Eleven men from Michigan,
Come here to do you spick and span;
You'll always see us in the van,
We sturdy sons of Michigan.

CHORUS.

Rah! Rah! Rah! boom-de-ay!
Rah! Rah! Rah! boom-de-ay!
Here is the U. of M.
To do you up again;
Rah! Rah! Rah! boom-de-ay!
Rah! Rah! Rah! boom-de-ay!
Here is the U. of M.
To do you up again.

Eleven men from Chicago,
Try to show what they don't know;
If you don't believe it's so,
Just get on to how they blow.

Elbel, 1900.

(Air: "Comin' Through the Rye.")

If a body meet a body
Comin' round the end,
If a body meet a body
Need a body bend;
Every line-up has its smash-up
All save Michigan,
She's the noblest and the boldest,
Hail to Michigan.

If Chicago bucks the center
There'll she'll find us strong,
If she tries to plunge through tackle
There'll she'll find she's wrong;
Every line may fall before her
All save Michigan,
She's the noblest and the boldest,
Hail to Michigan.

Now we'll cheer for Michigan,
The finest of the fine,
A-rushing round with half-back plays
And bucking through the line;
Every team has felt our prowess
We of Michigan,
We're the noblest and the boldest,
Hail to Michigan.

—Marshall, 1900.

Two years before Louis Elbel composed Michigan's official fight song, "The Victors," the *Daily* unveiled some of the yells and cheers heard at Regents Field during home games.

(Air: "The Golden Hair was Hanging
Down Her Back.")

The U. of M. is in Chicago, a football
game to play,
And we'll wave the maize and blue
agoing back;
'Tis the last game of the season, 'tis
on Thanksgiving Day,
And we'll wave the maize and blue
a going back.

CHORUS.

Chicago, Chicago, They used to play
the game
Before they strike Old Mich'gan they
are fly;
But alas! and, alack! Our line and
our backs
"We'll get them" where the chicken
got the axe.

And when the game is over we'll be
champions of the west,
And we'll wave the maize and blue
agoing back
Our players we'll be heroes and Chicago knows the rest,
And we'll wave the flag of victory
going back.

EGAN, '99 L.

THE YELLOW AND BLUE.

Sing to the colors that float in the
light;
Hurrah for the Yellow and Blue!
Yellow are the stars as they ride thro'
the night,
And reel in a rollicking crew;
Yellow the fields where ripens the
grain,
And yellow the moon on the harvest
wain;
Hail!
Hail to the colors that float in the
light;
Hail to the ribbons that Nature has
spun;
Hurrah for the Yellow and Blue!

Here's to the college whose colors we
wear;
Here's to the hearts that are true!
Here's to the maid of the golden hair,
And eyes that are brimming with
blue!
Garlands of blue-bells and maize in-
tertwine;
And hearts that are true and voices
combine;—
Hail!
Hail to the college whose colors we
wear;
Hurrah for the Yellow and Blue!

—Charles Gayley.

(Air: "The Red, White and Blue.")

O. Ann Arbor, the gem of the nation,
The home of true sport, pure and
free,
The shrine of each rooter's devotion,
The West offers homage to thee.
"Thy mandates make heroes assem-
ble"
When the oval is brought into view,
Thy banners make foes all to tremble
When borne by the yellow and blue.

Chorus:—

When borne by the yellow and blue,
When borne by the yellow and blue,
Thy banners make foes all to tremble
When borne by the yellow and blue.

"The wine cup, the wine cup bring
hither
And fill you it true to the brim;
May the wreaths they have won never
wither,
Nor the star of their glory grow
dim;"
May our warriors in battle ne'er
waver,
"But they to their colors prove true;"
The team and Ann Arbor forever—
Three cheers for the yellow and blue.

Chorus:—

Three cheers for the yellow and blue,
Three cheers for the yellow and blue,
The team and Ann Arbor forever—
Three cheers for the yellow and blue.

—O. H. H., '98.

The U. of M. Daily.

VARSITY TAKES A BRACE

Ohio State University Defeated by a Score of 34 to 0.

Michigan had no trouble defeating the Ohio State University representatives in Saturday's game. Two halves of 20 and 15 minutes respectively were played and the score was 34 to 0. It was not so much Michigan's strength as Ohio's weakness that brought about the score. The visitors lined up with three of their best players absent, while Michigan put her best team in the field. While the form of the varsity team was not on the championship order it showed an improvement over that of the Saturday before that was most encouraging. The interference was better, the playing snappier and the defensive work stronger than ever before. In the line, the work of Caley at guard was especially strong. Caley opened holes of the biggest kind in Ohio's line and made interference that repeatedly enabled the backs to make long runs.

Bennett, Teetzel and Ayres on the ends were stronger than ever , but still somewhat weak on defensive work. All of the backs played great ball. Hogg bucked the line hard and went around the ends for consistent gains. Stuart, who played for the first time, has the longest runs to his credit, due to the way in which he followed the interference. Pingree made several good gains and a dash of 50 yards across Ohio's goal was annualled by Parker's off-side play. Talcott at quarter also played for the first time and did well. His passing was surer than any he has shown in practice In the first half a high wind favored Ohio, but they had only two or three opportunities to take advantage of it as Michigan kept possession of the ball through almost the entire half. All of Michigan's points were made in this half.

The Wolverines earned an easy win in their first meeting with future archrival Ohio State.

The line-up follows:

Michigans.		Ohios.
Teetzel	L. E.	Engelsberger......R. E
Lehr	L. T.	Rloss......R. T
Snow	L. G.	Urban......R. G
Savage	C.	Jones......C
Caley	R. G.	Mackay......L. G
Jutner	R. T.	Miller......L. T
Bennett	R. E.	Schribber......L. E
Talcott	Q. B.	Saxby......Q. B
Stuart	L. H. B.	Purdy......R H.B
Hogg	R. H. B.	Benedict......L.H. B
Hannan	F. B.	Hawkins......F. B

Substitutes — For Michigan: Ayers for Teetzel. Baker for Jutner. Pingree for Stuart. McLean for Hogg. For Ohio Baker for Jones. Culbertson for Urban.
Touchdowns—Stuart (3), Hannan. Hogg Pingree. Goals froine touchdowns—Hogg, 5 Pingree.
Officials—Knight, Princeton; Wilson, Ypsilanti.

> **While the form of the varsity team was not on the championship order it showed an improvement over that of the Saturday before that was most encouraging. The interference was better, the playing snappier and the defensive work stronger than ever before.**
>
> — *The Michigan Daily*

ON THE SIDELINES

OCT. 27, 1897

New Button a Beauty

The Athletic Association buttons arrived last evening and. the design proves to be the handsomest yet offered by the association. The back ground is of blue and the "M" yellow.

The accompanying cut shows the button as it is Members of the association may get one by presenting their association tickets at Palmer's drug store on State st.

1898

CHAMPIONS OF THE WEST.

Michigan Earns Title by Defeating Chicago 12 to 11

STAGG'S VETERANS BEATEN

In One of the Greatest Gridiron Battles Ever Seen in the West

The greatest game of football ever played on a western gridiron was played on Marshall Field Thanksgiving day, and Michigan won it, and with it the undisputed title to the Western Championship. She won it because she had the best team and played the best game. By hard consistent team work she wrung the prize of victory from Stagg's veteran, victory-flushed giants.

The toss was won by Kennedy and he chose the north goal giving Michigan the kick-off. Caley made a poor kick-off of 20 yards. Chicago was unable to advance the ball past Michigan's stonewall defense and Herschberger was compelled to punt. Michigan soon lost the ball on a fumble, as did Chicago immediately after. Chicago gained some distance by trick plays till she lost the ball and Michigan began her march down the field for a touchdown. By constant, but small gains the ball was advanced to Chicago's 8-yard line where Michigan lost it on a fumble. Herschberger punted on the first down, but Michigan compelled him to kick sidewise with no gain. The ball was brought in on the 8-yard line where Michigan had lost it. Widman was sent around the end for the first touchdown. Snow easily kicked goal.

Kennedy kicked off to Street who returned 25 yards. Chicago held for the first time in the game and Caley was compelled to punt. Herschberger returned the ball 4 of the 35 yards. Twice the Chicago backs hit our line without budging it and then Herschberger made the sensational kick of the day. From the 45-yard line he sent the ball square between the goal posts, so high and far that it would have been an easy goal 5 or 10 yards farther away. Time was called with the ball in Michigan's possession on their own 17-yard line. Herschberger started the second half with a 50 yard kick-off which was returned 15 by Street. Caley punted for 35. Chicago was unable to gain and punted. Caley punted in return and Chicago was downed on her 42-yard line. From this point she advanced steadily through the line to the center of the field where she lost the ball on a fumble. Michigan advanced the ball for first down twice, but failed to gain on the next two downs. Widman was given the ball for a mass on tackle. Chicago's ends were drawn in the Michigan mass back of Widman was being pushed back when Widman twisted out sidewise and made a sensational sprint of 45 yards for a touchdown. Three of Chicago's fleetest tacklers were after him but could neither reach him or crowd him out of bounds. He sprinted on until Hamill caught him with a diving tackle, but he shook himself loose and crawled over the goal line. After several exchanges of punts Chicago secured the ball on Michigan's 25-yard line. From this point she advanced the it steadily forward for a touchdown by desperate, diving rushes in which Slaker carried the ball and Cavanaugh and Kennedy interfered. The game closed with Michigan advancing the ball on the 50-yard line.

> **The greatest game of football ever played on a western gridiron was played on Marshall Field Thanksgiving day, and Michigan won it, and with it the undisputed title to the Western Championship.**
>
> — *The Michigan Daily*

CAVANAUGH'S DIRTY WORK.

With the exception of Cavanaugh, both teams played a straight, clean game. He tackled roughly all the time and tried to knee players several times. But he committed one offense for which he might clearly have been ruled out of the game.

McLean caught one of Herschberger's punts that went out of bounds and the big, burly center tackled him when about a yard out, and brutally tried to throw him against one of the posts on the side lines. There was no excuse for tackling at all as the ball was out of bounds, but the attempt to strike McLean's head against the fence was an act of brutality of which no one but Cavanaugh could have been capable. It will be well for Chicago when she puts a bridle on the unrestrained brutality of her center rush. In striking contrast to Cavanaugh's acts was the work of Captain Kennedy who was playing the game of his life to win. Kennedy was all over, while playing fiercely, his game was ever of the cleanest kind, as was that of the other players.

91-29-3
MICHIGAN FOOTBALL
PROGRAM RECORD

1-0
VS. OHIO STATE

1-0
VS. MICHIGAN STATE

5-0
VS. NOTRE DAME

3-2
VS. MINNESOTA

3,308
ENROLLMENT

$30
IN-STATE TUITION

$40
OUT-OF-STATE TUITION

$231,809
ENDOWMENT

Langdon "Biff" Lea
FOOTBALL COACH

James B. Angell
UNIVERSITY PRESIDENT

NOTABLEGRADUATES

1905 Ralph Rose, Olympic
shot putter

1905 Lawrence C. Hull,
University's first Rhodes
Scholar

1906 Alexander Ruthven,
future University president

OCT. 13, 1904

MICHIGAN UNION.

REASONS FOR ITS EXISTENCE—AIMS TO FURTHER MICHIGAN
SPIRIT—ALUMNI INTERESTED—CLUB HOUSE PLANNED.

APR. 19, 1907

BOOKER WASHINGTON PLEASED AUDIENCE

Expressed Views on Solution of the Race Question – Asserted That the Negro Is Wonderful Race.

Booker T. Washington, president of Tuskegee Industrial Institute, Alabama, gave his solution of the race question last night before the Students' Lecture Association in University Hall. He urged first, industrial education for the black race; and second, a recognition of the reciprocal duty of one race toward the other. He declared that although the problem is one of the greatest moment, he had every confidence that in time it would gradually be settled amicably. He pointed out that in all history there is no instance of a race advancing with such enormous strides as have the negroes within the last forty years. He made a special plea to his hearers to lend a helping hand to the lower race whenever possible, and aid him in doing all that could be done to uplift his brethren.

The audience which heard Mr. Washington was large and enthusiastic. Again and again the speaker's words were broken by great bursts of applause.

President James Burrell Angell, who lays down his duties as president of the University next June.

FEB. 18, 1909

PRESIDENT'S RESIGNATION IS ACCEPTED BY REGENTS

Doctor Angell Withdraws From Executive Position, But Is Offered
Chancellorship of University, to Take Effect at End
of Year—Successor Not Determined.

OCT. 8, 1903

CHANGES IN RULES.

Summarized for the Benefit of the
Daily Readers in Response to a
Student's Query.

The changes made in the football rules this season tend, in the main, toward obviating the so-called "Mass play," which has in the past caused so much adverse criticism.

The most important change in the rules provides that, when the ball is put in play between the twenty-five yard lines, there must be at least seven men on the scrimmage line, and the player first receiving the ball (the quarterback), may carry it beyond the line of scrimmage, provided that in doing so, he crosses the scrimmage line at least five yards from the point where the ball was put in play. So that the umpire may rapidly calculate this distance it is recommended that, between the two twenty-five yard lines, the field be marked off by additional lines, five yards apart and parallel to the side lines.

Another important change affects the fullback. Formerly, the fullback, after kicking the ball beyond the line of scrimmage, might put the other men on side by running ahead, or might himself secure the ball. To prevent his doing this, it was necessary for his opponents to attack him and oppose his advance. This attack always seemed to the spectators unnecessarily brutal and hence the rules this year read that the man who, standing back of his own line of scrimmage receives the ball and then kicks it beyond the scrimmage line, may not put his men on side by running ahead, nor himself touch the ball, until it has been touched by a player on the opposing side.

The rule regarding the changing of goals has been altered so that it is now clear that the teams shall change goals after every try-at-goal following a touchdown, and after every goal from the field, and that at the beginning of the second half, the teams shall take opposite goals from those assumed at the beginning of the first half.

Also, after every goal from the field, the side just scored against shall have the option of receiving the kick or of having their kick-off. This last is of advantage to a team which is being badly beaten or pushed down the field.

Another important alteration of the rules forbids players to wear sole leather headgears or such as shall be judged by the umpire to be dangerous to other players.

1901-'23-'25-'26

APRIL 6, 1901

YOST TAKES CHARGE

Michigan's New Head Coach Inspires Enthusiasm at Once—Will be Here Only Until Spring Vacation —Returns Early in Sept.

Coach Yost arrived Thursday night and was out with the football men yesterday. He will stay only till the spring vacation, which means that there will be practically just one week of training.

Coach Yost said: "I will drill the men in the minor points of the game such as catching the ball, falling on the ball, and intereference. I will be back next fall very early as a new squad of men need a lot of 'roughing in.' "

When asked what style of play he would use Yost said that he had talked with Capt. White and Keene Fitzpatrick and that they had come to some agreement. It seems that while the Yale style, with which Keene Fitzpatrick is familiar, will be used somewhat, Yost will try his own style of play which proved so successful with Kansas, Nebraska and Stanford, at which schools he was head coach.

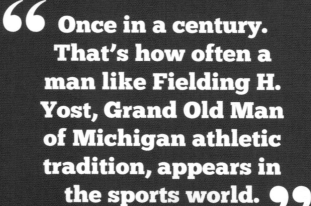

> " **Once in a century. That's how often a man like Fielding H. Yost, Grand Old Man of Michigan athletic tradition, appears in the sports world.** "
> — *The Michigan Daily*

Coach Yost Is Making Friends

Coach Yost put the foot ball squad through some formations and signals Tuesday, and his ideas coincided almost precisely with the style of play which Michigan used before Biffy Lea introduced his methods. The interference will be more compact, and will go up the field more directly, instead of shooting across and waiting for individual men to bowl over opponents. Manager Baird thinks he has found a gold nugget of 24-carat quality in Yost, and shows a great deal more enthusiasm over him than he ever did over Biffy Lea.

OCT. 31, 1903

THE GREATEST COACH.

Yost's Record Proves Conclusively His Claim to the Title—Has Never Lost a Championship —His Career in Brief.

The most famous football coach the world has ever had is Fielding Harris Yost, who is known as "Hurry Up," because of the rapid style of play which is shown by every football eleven which he trains. This really wonderful teacher of the game of the gridiron has never coached a losing team.

In six years coaching Yost has a record of having developed six champion teams.

Yost's first year at Michigan is an epoch in Western football. He developed a team that scored a total of 550 points, while his own goal was never seriously threatened. It was a record unequaled in football annals. The next year, 1902, he almost duplicated the preceding year's record, for his team scored 644 points, while opposing elevens scored 12 points on fluke plays.

This year Yost has his hardest problem. Seven of his best men of last year graduated and left only five veterans as a nucleus for a team. But with such a hard task before him it appears Yost has accomplished it.

The Yostmen outscored opponents 2,821 to 42 in Yost's first five seasons.

From 1901 to 1905, Yost led Michigan to 56 straight games without a loss.

YOST COINS NEW POSITIONS

"Set Backs" He Calls Them and They Are Placed Behind the Scrub Forwards to Reinforce the Reserve Line Against the Varsity Rushes.

YOST WILL STAY HERE.

Greatest Coach in the World Will Direct the 1904 Eleven—Michigan Men Are Enthusiastic Over His Decision—Has Never Coached a Loser.

WILL SAPP/Daily

Twelve-year-old Maurice Gould is telling his friends today how he played football with Michigan's grand old man of sports, Fielding H. "Hurry-Up" Yost. And here's the proof— Maurice, a 104-pound fellow who plays sandlot football over by Mack Junior High School, sneaked into the Wolverines' secret practice the other day. When Coach Yost walked onto the field the youngster caught his eye and in a few minutes the two were tossing passes to one another. Maurice fumbled and when Yost kneeled down beside him to show him how to handle the ball the Daily photographer caught this unposed picture. (Oct. 19, 1940)

OCT. 1, 1940

Michigan Honors 'Grand Old Man' With Celebration

Once in a century.

That's how often a man like Fielding H. Yost, Grand Old Man of Michigan athletic tradition, appears in the sports world.

On the evening of Oct. 19, night of the Illinois homecoming battle, students, alumni, and friends of the University of Michigan will gather at a gigantic testimonial dinner, feting the 69-year-old Athletic Director who has devoted 40 years of enthusiastic service to the University.

Upon reaching his seventieth birthday April 29, Yost will step down from his present post of Athletic Director, thus climaxing a long career as coach and in an administrative capacity.

The story of the "Grand Old Man" since he first became connected with the University in 1901 is almost synonymous with the history of Wolverine athletics. The feats of his point-a-minute gridiron juggernauts just past the turn of the century are indelibly inscribed in Maize and Blue

SEPT. 20, 1927

Yost Has Produced More All-America Football Stars Than Any Other Coach

(By Alfred L. Singer)

With his resignation as head football coach at the University of Michigan, Fielding H. Yost, the grand old man of football, carries with him the enviable record of having produced more All-American players than any other coach in the history of the game.

Since Yost first took up his coaching duties at Michigan more than a quarter of a century ago thirteen of his men were picked for that mythical team by the late Walter Camp, regarded as the greatest authority on the game, and two were later chosen by Grantland Rice whose team immediately became universally recognized as succeeding as official the ones previously chosen by Camp.

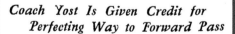

The Daily Palo Alto Says "Great is Michigan and Greater is Yost Who Made Michigan."

Coach Yost Is Given Credit for Perfecting Way to Forward Pass

When the forward pass was first attempted in football, all old timers laughed at it, and freely predicted that as a scoring play it would never be taken seriously by any of the big universities. They argued that it was a very good play for a small opponent to attempt on a stronger brother, but that any attempt to introduce it at any of the big universities was decidedly out of the question.

FIELDING H. YOST, Michigan head football coach from 1901 to 1929 and athletic director from 1929 to 1941, will celebrate his 75th birthday at his home in Ann Arbor, today. (April 30, 1946)

SEPT. 24

REGULAR PRACTICE BEGUN.

Coach Yost and His Charges Tendered an Ovation on Regents Field. 35 Candidates out for Business and 1,000 Rooters in the Bleachers.

Thirty-five men turned out this afternoon on Regents' Field for the first regular football practice of the season for Michigan. The work was a great surprise to the thousand students who occupied the grand stand and bleachers and there was also a big surprise in the way the rooters themselves turned out. At no time so early in the season last year did so many students watch practice. Intense interest is shown in football this year.

Coach Yost is electrifying the University. His boundless good nature, his ever-ready wit, his straight forwardness and determination all go to make him an idol for hero worshippers. The coach has not only won the hearts and convictions of his men, but he is at the same time a hard master. Yost's rule thought, is the kind that does not gall. He works with his men.

For three long hours this afternoon he kept his men on the running jump and he worked as hard as they did. Did a mass play appear slow there would come a hoarse cry of "Hurry up," and down the field would come the coach, his red legs flying and an old grey, felt hat's wide brim flapping about his ears.

"Hurry up!" is going to be Coach Yost's title. It struck the students today and hit the right spot. If Michigan hurrys up she will win is the sentiment. No names could be given by Michigan students more worthy their dashing coach that his own favorite cry of "Hurry up!"

> **'Hurry Up!' is going to be Coach Yost's title. It struck the students today and hit the right spot. If Michigan hurrys up she will win is the sentiment.**
>
> — *The Michigan Daily*

1901	MICH		OPPONENT
SEPT. 28	55	0	Albion
OCT. 5	57	0	Case
OCT. 12	33	0	Indiana
OCT. 19	29	0	Northwestern
OCT. 26	128	0	Buffalo
NOV. 2	22	0	Carlisle
NOV. 9	21	0	Ohio State
NOV. 16	22	0	Chicago
NOV. 23	89	0	Beloit
NOV. 28	50	0	Iowa
JAN. 1	49	0	Stanford (Rose Bowl)

SEPT. 24

New Rules for Rooters.

Manager Baird and Coach Yost have issued a special request to the student body relative to crowding on the field during Varsity practice.

This both hampers coaching and embarrasses the movements of the players and must hereafter be discontinued. Spectators at Regents' Field are expected to take places in the stands or bleachers and on no account to step inside the side ropes. The trouble which this caused the coaches last year serves is an object lesson.

ON THE SIDELINES

A CALL.

To All Loyal Michigan Students.

On Friday, at 4:15 p. m., in University Hall, will occur the first university singing meeting. It is a duty every student owes to Michigan's victorious football team, and to his university to come out and join in the singing. The Daily-News has done all within its power to make the first meeting successful, and it now remains for the student body to take advantage of the opportunity offered and to show its apreciation by atending not only the first but such subsequent meetings as may be held.

> ## " Hereafter the 'Varsity will wear the latest confection in fall bonnets in the remainder of the games played this season. The lids are of a durable material, sole leather, and will have the effect of cannon balls on the opposing line. "
>
> — *The Michigan Daily*

OCT. 16

BONNETS FOR THE 'VARSITY.

Coach Yost Will Use Leather Headgear On His Men—First Secret Practice of the Season Yesterday.

Coach Yost has added another innovation to his list. Hereafter the 'Varsity will wear the latest confection in fall bonnets in the remainder of the games played this season. The lids are of a durable material, sole leather, and will have the effect of cannon balls on the opposing line. The scrubs will not be made to suffer, however. Only in 'Varsity contests will the new coiffures be used. The experience of the Yale coaches in employing the heavy headgear during the progress of regular practice with the reserves serves as a lesson as to the proper use.

The stunt is a new one in the case of a Michigan eleven. Michigan has heretofore been a shin-guardless and unarmored team and the sight of the Wolverine forces swathed in their leather headpieces will be greeted with surprise by the student body.

Michigan
vs.
O. S. U.

At Columbus, Ohio

Saturday Nov. 9, 2:15 p. m. on University Field.

ROUND TRIP FARE $2.40.

ADMISSION, (including reserved seat in the bleacher) $1.00.

JAN. 8

550-0

The Season Ended Brilliantly

By Winning From Leland Stanford the Michigan Team Proved Itself the Greatest Scoring Team the World Has Ever Seen.

(Paste this account in your Michigan Daily-News Football Yearbook.)

The greatest event of the Michigan vacation period was the football game at Pasadena on January first when Michigan defeated Stanford University by the decisive score of 49-0. This score is said to be quite in proportion to the general superiority of Michigan over the great team of the far west, but it does not tell the story of Stanford's desperate but futile effort against defeat. The Association Press dispatches were general in character, so the Michigan Daily-News will only give a detailed account of the game.

The game was played under the auspices of the Tournament of Roses Association and the conservative estimate places the attendance at eight thousand. "The enormous crowd sees the Michigan back-breakers make monkeys of the Stanford footballists," is the significant comment of the Los Angeles Daily Times.

Technically speaking, Michigan lost no prestige in the Stanford game. The team successfully kept Stanford out of Michigan territory. Stanford was unable to break the record of fifteen yards as the longest gain made against Michigan during the year. None of the Michigan players were compelled to leave the field. Sweeley place-kicked the only goal from field for Michigan outside of Shorts' successful attempt in the Carlisle game, during the season. Michigan's sacred goal line was never in danger. In the gathering dusk, with ten minutes yet to play, Captain Fisher came to Captain White and said: "If you are willing, we are ready to quit," and, at the expense of one or two more goals, Michigan granted his request.

JAN. 19

Team Measurements, an Instructive Comparative Table.

The showing is a remarkable tribute to the game of football as a developer of the human body. Football is not a developer of one part at the expense of another. The football man is uniformly developed in every part. Rowing is great for the back and legs, baseball especially brings out certain muscles, but the gridiron is where the whole man is brought into play.

The progress that is made by this one year of gym work is remarkable, but the football men surpass even this to a surprising degree. In appearance the gridiron man is neither a giant nor a muscular monstrosity. He is simply broad in the shoulders, strong in the limbs, and generally "fit." His health is splendid.

Following are the averages. In the first column for the average student after a year of gymnasium work, and in the second column for the 'Varsity football man:

		Per. Ct.		Per Ct.
Height	68.3	60	69.8	85
Weight	139.0	50	179.	99
Shoulders	16.5	70	17.9	100
Chest, trans.	11.7	82	12.1	90
Chest, ant. post.	7.7	80	8.8	100
Neck	14.0	60	15.4	100
Chest, muscular	35.6	30	40	90
Chest, natural	34.0	55	38.4	99
Chest, expanded	35.9	54	40.4	99
Chest, contracted	31.1	58	36.9	105
Waist	29.1	58	33.4	99
Hips	36.2	70	39.5	99
Right arm, down	10.8	80	12.8	105
Right arm, up	11.8	55	14	99
Right forearm	10.4	55	11.7	99
Left arm, down	10.6	80	12.6	105
Left arm, up	11.6	55	13.8	105
Left forearm	10.3	65	11.5	99
Right thigh	208	65	23.5	97
Right calf	13.9	55	15.4	97
Left thigh	20.6	65	23.4	99
Left calf	13.9	60	15.3	97
Lung capacity	242.0	35	270	80

1902

OCT. 26   **MICHIGAN 86** / **OHIO 0**

MICHIGAN 86, OHIO 0

O. S. U. Snowed Under—Their Great Hopes Pounded to Pieces in First Few Minutes of Play

What will we do,
What will we do,
We'll rub it into O. S. U.
That's what we'll do.

Thus sang the Michigan rooters yesterday afternoon in answer to the old Wah-hoo yell raised proudly by 2,000 wearers of the scarlet and gray.

And rub it in they did with both hands and feet by the absolutely un-hoped for score of 86 to 0.

The Ohio rooters began to arrive at 9:30 a. m. and special train followed special train at short intervals until the whole city was thronged with the excursionists. They overran the campus in all directions and pene-trated into every building including the Anatomical Laboratory.

Shortly after 1 o'clock the crowd began to stream out toward Ferry Field and by a quarter past two every inch of available room on the big stands and bleachers was occupied, the late comers being forced to stand up along the wire fences enclosing the field.

The O. S. U. rooters filled the whole east half of the south bleachers and part of the grand stand while the sup-porters of Michigan swarmed on both sides of the field.

The rooting before the game was by far the best ever heard on Ferry Field, song answering song, and yell answering yell in never ending suc-cession Michigan seemed to have a shade the best of it principally on account of their forces being on both sides of the field where they could applaud each others efforts.

The O. S. U. band and the Michigan band took turns at working up the enthusiasm and at 2:15, when the Michigan men trotted on the field fol-lowed almost at once by the Buckeyes the excitement was at the highest pitch.

ON THE SIDELINES

A FOOTBALL ROMANCE

Couple Wed on a Wager—He Won and She Lost at Thanksgiving Day Game

One of the most romantic weddings that ever interested Toledo society was announced last Saturday.

Edwin R. Thomas and Miss Nettie Backus are members of Toledo's wealthiest families and move in the most exclusive set. Mr. Thomas and Miss Backus came with a jolly party to this city on Thanksgiving day to see the Michigan-Minnesota football game.

Miss Backus became an ardent ad-mirer of the stalwart Minnesota play-ers, while her escort, for the sake of merriment, held up Michigan as a winner. As the game progressed the couple began to wager, and Mr. Thomas suggested that Miss Backus become his wife immediately should Minnesota lose the game. The young folk had long been sweethearts and their wedding was to take place early next spring.

Miss Backus accepted the challenge, and the score—Michigan, 23; Minne-sota, 6—tells the rest of the story. The ceremony was performed accord-ing to agreement, and Mr. and Mrs. Thomas left for Chicago on a short honeymoon. The other members of the party returned to Toledo, but the story did not become public until last Saturday.

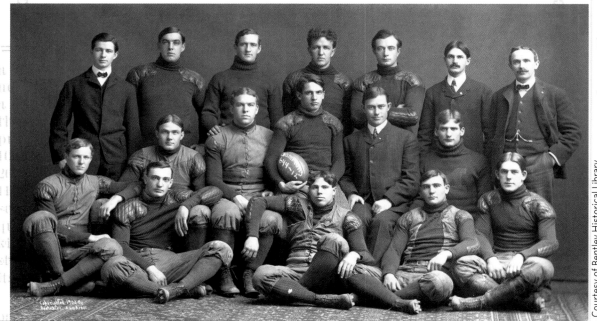

MICHIGAN FOOTBALL 1902 TEAM--CHAMPIONS OF 1901-1902

OCT. 9   **MICHIGAN 119** / **M.A.C. 0**

MICHIGAN 119, M. A. C. 0

Another Spectacular Game—Many Long Runs—Lawrence Kicks 19 Out of 20 Goals

---

NOV. 2

CHAMPIONS

Michigan Earns Clear Title to Two Years Championship by Defeating Badgers in Hard Fought Game

MICHIGAN AND CHICAGO

Are the Only Two Undefeated Teams in the West—Scores Made so Far This Season

Michigan made a long stride toward the championship of the west Saturday by defeating what everybody considered her most formidable opponent by the score of 6 to 0. She meets yet two formidable teams, Chicago and Minnesota, and two teams on which she ought to fatten her score, Iowa and Oberlin. On points scored the teams now stand:

	Opponents	Games
Michigan	430	6	7
Cornell	235	26	8
Illinois	232	27	8
Yale	223	12	9
Minnesota	214	6	6
Chicago	199	6	9
Wisconsin	177	17	6
Harvard	157	17	9
Pennsylvania..	139	35	10
Ohio State....	132	91	6
Princeton	128	5	7
Iowa	99	45	5
Notre Dame...	77	33	6
Northwestern..	58	33	6
Indiana	55	123	5

1902	MICH		OPPONENT
SEPT. 27	88	0	Albion
OCT. 4	48	6	Case
OCT. 8	119	0	Michigan Agric.
OCT. 11	60	0	Indiana
OCT. 18	23	0	Notre Dame
OCT. 25	86	0	Ohio State
NOV. 1	6	0	Wisconsin
NOV. 8	107	0	Iowa
NOV. 15	21	0	Chicago
NOV. 22	63	0	Oberlin
NOV. 27	23	6	Minnesota

MICHIGAN 21, CHICAGO 0.

Wolverines Vanquish Maroons in a Fiercely Contested Game on Marshall Field

Sweeley Kicks Two Field Goals—Heston Makes a Touchdown after 85 Yard Run -Chicago Could Not Score

CHAMPIONS OF THE WEST!

Maize and Blue Waves Triumphant—With Total of 644-12—Michigan's Claim is Undisputed

Michigan, the greatest football aggregation in America, put the finishing touches to a glorious season Thanksgiving Day in the greatest game ever seen in Michigan, before the largest crowd ever assembled in the state to witness the game. It was a game to settle the championship of the west, which Michigan claimed last year, but her title to which was then disputed. But this year there are none to dispute. One by one she has met her big rivals and easily vanquished them all.

And the credit belong to Yost. Yost is the greatest football coach in America. He has never coached a team which lost.

Michigan won yesterday because she knew more about football than her opponents, because she played faster, because she was more versatile, because she had team work, because she had Fitzpatrick to keep her men in condition to play and because she had Yost, with his hurry up orders. She has met heavier teams than herself and vanquished them.

 Michigan won yesterday because she knew more about football than her opponents, because she played faster, because she was more versatile, because she had team work ... because she had Yost, with his hurry up orders. "

— *The Michigan Daily*

ON THE SIDELINES

ATTEMPTED BRIBERY

Ann Arbor Man Offered Halfback Heston $500 to Throw Game To Minnesota

According to the Washtenaw Times of last evening, Martin Heston, Michigan's great halfback, was approached the day before the Minnesota game and offered $500 cash if he would manage by some means or other to throw the game to the Gophers. The motive for such an unmanly act is at once obvious, for the Ann Arbor man intended betting $2,000 on Minnesota providing he could get Heston to turn traitor and turn the game in Minnesota's favor.

Evidently this man did not know the kind of a man he was dealing with. Heston not only promptly turned down the offer but gave the tempter such a roast for the insult to his manhood that it is not likely that the fellow will ever again attempt another such proposition to a Michigan man.

When Heston was seen yesterday regarding the matter he said "I do not care for and publicity about it, but I will say that an offer of that kind was made me. I will not state who the man is or what is his business." The fine playing that Heston did for Michigan in that game well showed his contempt for such an offer, and no one there present could be found who would say that Heston did not play one of the fiercest games he ever exhibited on Ferry Field.

1903

MICHIGAN 6 - MINNESOTA 6

The Wolverines And Gophers Struggle For Three Hours And The Result Is a Tie. Greatest Game In Western Football History.

Yesterday's football game was the momentous event of the year in the football world. It was not only a game between the two strongest of the Western universities, but it is generally conceded to be the Western championship game.

The result of the game, a tie, between Michigan and Minnesota, leaves Michigan still claimant for honors as Western champions for the season of 1903. The probabilities are that the outcome will necessitate a post-season game to definitely settle the championship, because neither Minnesota nor Michigan have as yet been defeated.

Too much can not be said for the good work of Michigan's team, her coach and her trainer.

The men stood their twenty-hour ride better than was really to be expected, arriving in the best of health and spirits. They felt deeply the confidence that their classmates placed in them and went out to win, notwithstanding the difficulties necessarily incurred in playing on hostile grounds and in the presence of some thirty thousand hostile rooters.

The work of the team as a whole was wonderful, and the individual playing of Heston, Graver, Maddock, Longman, Norcross and Hammond has given them prominent places on Michigan's list of football heroes.

University Hall was crowded yesterday afternoon. It is estimated that above four thousand students were present to hear the telephonic reports of the game. Enthusiasm was at its highest pitch, but dominating over all was a gentlemany and sportsmanlike feeling. When a Minnesota man was obliged to retire from the game he received as hearty nine rahs as her own men when they made a particularly good play.

Only once was any antagonistic feeling shown, that was when it was announced that the Minnesota rooters had overrun the field so that the game could not be continued.

As to the result of the game Michigan is elated. She feels now the more confident that she can defeat any of the Western college teams, and happy in the thought that the Western championship is ours again this year.

History of Brown Jug Rich with Action

By PHIL DOUGLIS

An outdated, worthless piece of crockery goes on the line again Saturday, as Michigan and Minnesota vie for the fabled Little Brown Jug.

The ancient crock symbolizes a rivalry in its 51st year, for it was back in 1903 that a powerful Yost squad left its waterjug on the bench after a 6-6 tie.

The Minnesota groundskeeper, old Oscar Munson lugged it to the Minnesota gym after the game, and there it sat, labeled "Michigan Jug — Captured by Oscar — Oct. 31st, 1903." Across the top of the crock, then painted a motley white, was the inscription "Not to be taken from the Gymnasium."

Minnesota officials then wrote to Michigan, telling them "We have your jug—come on up and get it." The men of Yost did just that six years later, winning the crock by a 15-6 count.

The tremendous rivalry that grew out of the 30c water container is packed so full of unforgettable games that it would take a book to adequately describe them all.

> **Before more than thirty thousand spectators, the greatest football game ever was playing in the West, was contested yesterday afternoon on Northrop Field, Minneapolis. The weather was all that could be desired, not overly cool for the rooters, and not too warm for good playing.**
>
> — *The Michigan Daily*

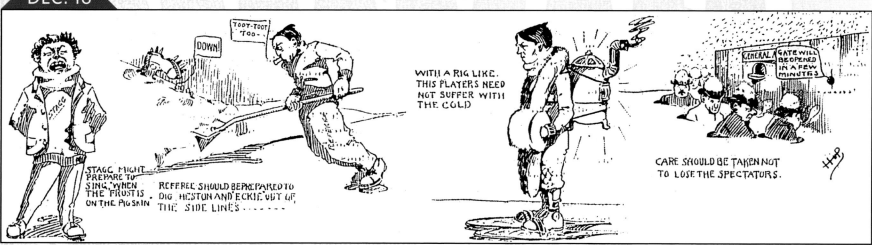

STAGG MIGHT PREPARE TO SING WHEN THE FROST IS ON THE PIGSKIN

REFEREE SHOULD BE PREPARED TO DIG HESTON AND ECKIE OUT OF THE SIDE LINES

WITH A RIG LIKE THIS PLAYERS NEED NOT SUFFER WITH THE COLD

CARE SHOULD BE TAKEN NOT TO LOSE THE SPECTATORS.

1903	MICH	OPPONENT
OCT. 3	31	0 Case
OCT. 8	76	0 Albion
OCT. 10	79	0 Beloit
OCT. 14	65	0 Ohio Northern
OCT. 17	51	0 Indiana
OCT. 21	90	0 Ferris State
OCT. 24	47	0 Drake
OCT. 31	6	6 Minnesota
NOV. 7	36	0 Ohio State
NOV. 14	16	0 Wisconsin
NOV. 21	42	0 Oberlin
NOV. 26	28	0 Chicago

NOV. 15   MICHIGAN   16
           WISCONSIN   0

MICHIGAN 16 WISCONSIN 0

The Fiercest Game Ever Played on Ferry Field Resulted in a Score of 16 to 0---Hammond Makes two Place Kicks

WON DECISIVE BATTLE.

Michigan Won Most Exciting Football Game Ever Seen On Ferry Field—Longman's Line-bucking a Feature—Championship Contest Was Free From Rough Playing.

In a contest which taxed the powers of the players to the utmost, the Michigan football team yesterday met and defeated the remarkably strong players from the University of Wisconsin by the decisive score of 16 to 0. The Wolverines were aided by almost perfect weather conditions and the organized rooting of the largest crowd gathered on Ferry Field this year. Yesterday's mighty struggle was in many respects the most exciting game ever played here, and the first half was especially productive of good football.

The two teams were almost evenly matched in weight, but the superior training and physical condition of the Wolverines was apparent from the start. The game was remarkably free from rough tactics and the best of feeling was evident among the players. Yost's choice for fullback was vindicated by the wonderful line-bucking of Longman. Time after time the fullback was called upon to make a first down, and rarely did he fail to do so. Hammond's place kicks, which netted ten of Michigan's 16 points, were remarkably accurate, and on defensive work the Chicago lad starred James, despite his sprained wrist played a steady game, and his back-field tackling was all that prevented the Badgers from scoring on more than one occasion.

Coach Curtis was far from disheartened when seen at the Cook House last night. "Michigan beat us fairly and demonstrated her superiority, although a score of 6 to 0 would have been more accurate. Michigan will defeat Chicago by seven touchdowns. The first half made me feel proud of my team," he said.

Coach Yost wears a broad smile of contentment. "Wisconsin played a strong game, but the second half showed the real Michigan spirit Longman's work was little short of marvelous, and Hammond's defensive work was one of the features," he said. "The best football game ever seen here," is the verdict of everyone of the 10,000 rooters who witnessed the battle.

The crowd commenced coming on the field at noon and a steady stream of enthusiasm blocked the gates. The arrangements for handling the crowds were perfect. Ideal weather conditions prevailed, with the exception of a strong wind quartering across the field from the northwest. The standing bleachers were packed early. Michigan yells followed each other in rapid succession, varied by an occasional song. Wisconsin was not heard until the faithful bunch of rooters took their seats. At 1.40 the U. of M. band came on the field and their advent was greeted by a loud burst of applause.

YOST.

ON THE SIDELINES

A MICHIGAN BAND.

Permanent Organization of Student Musicians to be Formed—Fred Day, Formerly of Fisher's Orchestra, Is Pushing the Project.

"By the time of the Minnesota game the University of Michigan will have as good a band as any college, if the students are willing to push the project."

The above statement was made to a representative of the Daily yesterday by one of the promoters of the band question.

Nearly all of last year the University was without a band and the need was then sorely felt, and it is not the desire of all true Michigan supporters that the same thing should occur this year. "A band is a necessity," seems to be the sentiment of the student body, and already a few have commenced to exert their efforts toward the formation of one.

A DRUM MAJOR APPOINTED.

U. of M. Band will have a Drum Major—Band will play at Albion and Beloit Games.

"The U. of M. Band will have a drum major before its next appearance," said Band Master Day to a representative of the Daily.

This is an entirely new departure from anything which has ever been tried here but it is the new thing which the students desire. A drum major is as essential to a good band as a captain to a company of soldiers. As their leader and director he relieves the band master of many of the small things which have to be attended to but which he cannot properly see to if he plays an instrument. The drum major also gives a certain grace to the band which is lacking without him. He is a necessity and all will be pleased to know that the U. of M. band is not behind the times.

WILLIAM M. HESTON.

DEC. 13

HESTON CHOSEN.

Michigan Half-back Only Western Man on Camp's First All-American, Maddock, Redden and Graver Have Places on Third Team.

1904

ON THE SIDELINES

"THE VICTORS."

Probably the most inspiring of Michigan's football songs is "The Victors." It was dedicated to the victorious team of '02 and at once rose into the greatest popularity. This march will be sung and played by the 'Varsity musical clubs at all of its concerts and will be the prominent musical number at the Michigan club house banquet. The piece has been ordered by the band and will be played from now on at the Saturday games while the football men are marching on the field. The verse of the song is difficult but everyone should at least be familiar with the words. The chorus has a fine martial swing, is quite simple, and if learned and sung by the student body to the band accompaniment as the team enters the gridiron, it would add materially to the spirit shown at the games. The words are printed below:

Now for a cheer, they are here, tri-
  umphant;
Here they come with banners flying.
In stalwart step they're nighing, with
  shouts of victory crying
On! Hurrah, hurrah, we greet you now
  —Hail!
For we their praises sing for the glory
  and fame they bring us.
Loud let the bells then ring,
For here they come with banners flying.
Here they come. Hurrah!

CHORUS.

Hail to the victors valiant;
Hail to the conquering heroes;
Hail, Hail to Michigan,
  Leaders and best.
With pride we hail the victors, val-
  iant,
Hail to the conquering heroes,
Hail, Hail to Michigan,
  The Champions if the West.

We cheer them again, we cheer for
  Michigan,
We cheer with might and main.
Hail to the victors valiant,
Hail to the conquering heroes,
Hail, Hail to Michigan,
  The Champions of the West.

OCT. 16

FEW FOOTBALL FIGURES.

The newspaper reports of injuries to college football players seem to be greatly exaggerated.

About one college man in ten in the country plays football.

About one player in thirty-five is injured sufficiently each season to necessitate loss of time from college duties.

The opinion of college officers regarding the value of the game is about 17 to 1 in its favor.

NOV. 4

HARD PRACTICE

Yost Makes Men Work Hard for Two Hours and a Half—End Position Still Open—Regular Backfield Out of Scrimmage.

Yesterday the football squad had one of the hardest practices of the season. For two hours and a half the men practiced on the charging machine and dummy, sprinted, ran relays, practiced punting and goal kicking, ending with signal practice and scrimmage.

JAN. 22

FOOTBALL MOST POPULAR.

Report of Financial Secretary Shows That Football Receipts are Much Greater than Baseball or Track.

The report of the financial secretary which was read at the meeting of the athletic association yesterday furnishes an interesting commentary upon the relative popularity of the different branches of athletics at Michigan. While about $16,800 was taken in at the football games last fall, only a trifle over a thousand dollars was received from the baseball games, while the track meets brought in over two thousand. While the big Chicago game is responsible for a large share of the football receipts, yet these figures still prove the oft repeated assertion that football is the popular game at Michigan, and from the showing of the figures below it would appear that track meets are more popular than baseball games.

The report of the financial secretary is as follows:

RECEIPTS.

Football	$16,802.06
Baseball	1,032.04
Track	2,012.27
Interscholastic	259.53
General	3,118.11
Total receipts	$23,224.01

DISBURSEMENTS.

Football	$8,990.14
Baseball	2,521.41
Track	2,245.62
Interscholastic	437.51
Tennis	124.14
Golf	61.73
General	5,468.81
Office	399.96
Permanent improvement fund	146.55
Total disbursements	$20,395.87
Cash on hand Jan. 16, 1904	$6,319.88
Receipts during year	23,224.01
Total	$29,543.89
Disbursements during year	20,395.87
Cash on hand Jan. 20, 1905	$9,148.02

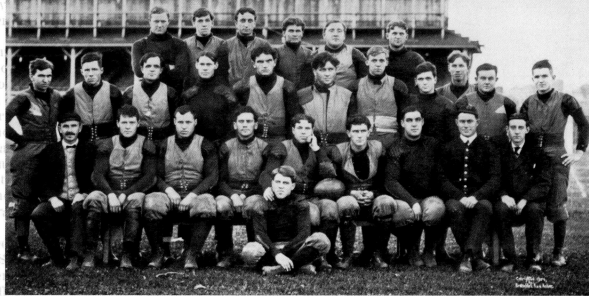

Courtesy of Bentley Historical Library

Top row, left to right—Assistant Coach Cole, Stuart, De Pree, Magoffin, Graham, Patrick. *Second row*—Weeks, 11. Hammond, Small, Briggs, Schultz, Love, Garrels, Clark, Rheinschild., Ted Hammond, Becker. *Bottom row*—Trainer Fitzpatrick, Tom Hammond, Curtis, Shulte, Heston (Captain), Longman, Carter, Coach Yost, Student Manager Montgomery, Norcross.

NOV. 13 — MICHIGAN 22 / CHICAGO 12

MICHIGAN IS CHAMPION!

Wolverines Win First Honors for the Fourth Time--Maroons Fight Gamely to Stem the Tide of Defeat---Score: Michigan 22; Chicago 12.

For the fourth time, the University of Michigan football team is the western champion. Before the largest crowd ever assembled at a football contest in Ann Arbor, the yellow and blue warriors put away Stagg's maroon-clad aspirants by a score of 22 to 12. It was only after the fiercest kind of a struggle, however, that Michigan won for the men from the Midway played as a Chicago team never played before.

ON THE SIDELINES

The Daily ran a special "Souvenir Extra" printed on yellow paper with blue ink the day after Michigan beat Chicago.

SOUVENIR EXTRA
The Michigan Daily
MICHIGAN IS CHAMPION!

1904	MICH		OPPONENT
OCT. 1	33	0	Case
OCT. 5	48	0	Ohio Northern
OCT. 8	95	0	Kalamazoo
OCT. 12	72	0	P&S* (Chicago)
OCT. 15	31	6	Ohio State
OCT. 19	72	0	A.M.S.** (Chicago)
OCT. 22	130	0	West Virginia
OCT. 29	28	0	Wisconsin
NOV. 5	36	4	Drake
NOV. 12	22	12	Chicago

*College of Physicians and Surgeons **American Medical School

NOV. 29

YOST'S LETTER

The Greatest Football Coach Not Impressed by the Yale-Harvard Game—Thinks Michigan Could Defeat Eastern Elevens.

The following letter to the Daily from Coach Yost needs no comment:

West Point, Nov. 22.
The Michigan Daily.
Ann Arbor, Mich.

I would like to say a word or two that might be interesting to readers of the Daily. Last Saturday I witnessed the Yale-Harvard game at New Haven. It was a game devoid of anything sensational, in fact, just the opposite. In the first place, the playing of both teams was very slow. Not only were the plays brought off at long intervals but the execution was slow. It seemed to be a game of push ball. The punting was not good. Yale punted eleven times for an average of 33 yards and Harvard punted fourteen times for an average of 32 yards. This is counting kick-offs. In our game we kicked five times for an average of 38 yards and we thought that very poor. Chicago's average was over 50 yards.

During the game the ball was fumbled twelve times, five by Yale and seven by Harvard.

The style of game as shown Saturday by Yale and Harvard is not nearly so interesting as the games played in the west. There is not near the dash and go to it.

From what I have seen already of the game as played in the east, I would be confident of a victory for Michigan were they to meet an eastern eleven. F. H. YOST.

DEC. 17

YOST FOR NEXT FIVE YEARS!

Manager Baird Announces at Football Banquet that Yost Will Coach Michigan Teams for Five Years More—Banquet Was a Hugh Success.

DEC. 20

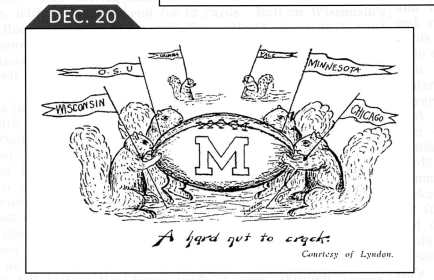

A hard nut to crack.
Courtesy of Lyndon.

1905

> " **In every backwoods school and four corners academy where husky young fellows meet together at the national game, a copy of Yost's book must be had.** "
>
> — *The Michigan Daily*

SEPT. 28

YOST'S FOOTBALL TEXT=BOOK MAKES BIG HIT

Commendatory Notices From Every Sporting Expert in the Country—Orders For Copies Pouring in From All Sides.

That Fielding H. Yost is the greatest football coach in the country few will deny. But that he should come forward as the author of the best text-book ever written about the sport is at once a surprise and a revelation. Yet, the author of "Football for Player and Spectator" is the same forceful personality who five years ago picked up a broken and disheartened collection of players and welded them into a team which time after time has beaten the best teams in the west back to the ropes.

The book is undoubtedly the product of its author. One can feel back of it the force, the energy, the resolution of "Hurry Up" Yost. "Hurry up, hurry up" might well be the motto of the book.

Already the book is being sold far and wide. Orders have come in from all parts of the country. In every backwoods school and four corners academy where husky young fellows meet together at the national game, a copy of Yost's book must be had. For the book is practical. Yost does not merely theorize. He tells how to train and diet; he explains formations and plays by diagrams and copious illustrations; he tells how to tackle or avoid being tackled, how to use the stiff arm, how to use the hands in the line, how to pass

FIELDING H. YOST.

—*From Yost's Football Book.*

and hold the ball, how to punt and drop kick. He explains the duties of each member of the team and their place in every play.

The Ann Arbor Press (formerly Parker & Snyder) printed the book. It contains over eighty good halftone illustrations, including pictures of all the principal athletic fields of the country; and to illustrate various formations, he has had pictures taken of the champion-

ship team of 1904. The familiar figures of Tom Hammond and Willie Heston appear as illustrations of line bucking or end running.

Over 3,000 copies of the book have been sold already, and a second edition will soon be necessary. Every sporting paper in the country is loud in the praise of his book and there is no question that it will increase the wide reputation he has already won.

NOV. 19   MICHIGAN 12   WISCONSIN 0

MICHIGAN, 12; WISCONSIN, 0.

Wolverines Make Two Touchdowns Against Badgers--West Bleachers Collapse But No One Is Seriously Injured--Over Seventeen Thousand People in Attendance Michigan Team Comes Out of Game in Good Shape.

True to expectations, the annual Wisconsin-Michigan football game yesterday resulted in one of the greatest football contests ever played in the west, and after the gamest struggle ever seen on Ferry field, Wisconsin went down to glorious defeat by a score of 12 to 0. Michigan scoring one touchdown in each half, and Tom Hammond kicking both goals. On straight football Michigan greatly outplayed Wisconsin and the score hardly represents the relative merits of the two teams. The phenom-

enal work of Melzner in running back punts and kick-offs, however, as well as his excellent drop-kicking attempts, kept Michigan on the defensive during the last twenty minutes of the second half, and so close did Wisconsin come to scoring on three separate occasions that nearly every Michigan rooter experienced a sense of relief when the time keeper announced the end at 4:40, after the gathering darkness began to make it somewhat difficult to see across the field.

DEC. 5   MICHIGAN 0   CHICAGO 2

CHICAGO WINS WESTERN FOOTBALL CHAMPIONSHIP

Michigan Meets First Defeat in Years--Score Is 2 to 0 Garrels Out-punts Eckersall--Curtis Ruled Out of the Game For Alleged Rough Playing.

JAN. 23

CONFERENCE RESOLUTIONS CAUSE GREAT INDIGNATION

Students Demand Retention of Coach Yost—Mass Meeting Will Be Held This Week.

"We must keep Yost!"

That was the sentiment on the campus yesterday. The storm of indignation that arose when it became known that the action of the conference would probably bar the great coach was a magnificent tribute to the popularity that Yost has won during his connection with the university.

JAN. 24

REGENTS MAY SAVE FOOTBALL

Hope of Saving Football Not Yet Lost—Regents Dean and Hill Favor Retention of Yost.

Several major changes to the game of football were proposed in a series of athletic conference meetings spearheaded by University President James B. Angell in January 1906. Provisions included prohibiting non-faculty members like Fielding Yost from coaching, shortening the season by five games and banning many parts of the game that critics considered violent. The changes proposed by Angell and others caused an uproar on campus, but the approved changes were less drastic than those proposed.

Three Thousand Students Protest

JAN. 25

UNIVERSITY HALL—WHERE MICHIGAN STUDENTS WILL ASSEMBLE TONIGHT TO PROTEST AGAINST CONFERENCE RESOLUTIONS.

CONFERENCE ADOPTS MORE LIBERAL RULES

Professional Coaching Is Retained—Three Year Rule Not to be Retroactive.

Chicago, Mar. 10 (Special).—Substantial modifications of the drastic measures originally adopted were made by the members of the football conference at their second meeting yesterday. Michigan won the points for which she was contending, and as a result the professional coach is to stay and the three-year rule is not to apply to athletes who have already competed three years.

The most important modification adopted by the members of the conference reads as follows:

Rule 10 in the former recommendations shall be changed to read: "No football coach shall be maintained excepting he is appointed by the university governing body and upon the recommendation of the faculty and the president," instead of "No coach shall be maintained who is not a member of the university faculty."

MICHIGAN DEFEATS O. S. U.

| OCT. 20 | MICHIGAN | 6 |
| | OHIO STATE | 0 |

Hard Fought Contest Won in Last Few Minutes of Play---Score 6-0---Loell Plays Star Game.

Columbus, O., Oct. 20.—After being held scoreless until the last few minutes of play, the Michigan football team rallied and by a terrific onslaught carried the ball within striking distance of Ohio's goal, when Garrels scored a field goal from the 35-yard line. Two minutes later Gibson downed a high pass for a punt behind his own goal line for a safety, making the final score 6 to 0.

After the first half had ended with the score 0 to 0, the maize and blue supporters were encouraged, for their team had kept Ohio State on the defensive during nearly the entire half. When, however, in the second half, Michigan would carry the ball well into Ohio's territory, only to lose it without scoring, they began to fear. Twenty-five minutes had passed and the score was 0 to 0 with only five minutes of play left and visions of a second Chicago surprise became more and more prominent.

| OCT. 28 | MICHIGAN | 28 |
| | ILLINOIS | 9 |

ILLINOIS OUTCLASSED

But Scores First Touchdown Since 1903 on Michigan --- Championship Form Displayed.

> "The biggest home game of the year was contested on the worst day that Ann Arbor has seen this fall. But both teams were out for blood. ... The six thousand spectators could not but decide that Michigan had completely outplayed the Illini at every stage of the game."
> — *The Michigan Daily*

OCT. 7

The Last Big Game Played on Old Ferry Field---Michigan vs. Wisconsin.

JAN. 13

CONFERENCE SHOWS NO MERCY TO MICHIGAN

Students Will Probably Rise in Rebellion--Conference Cripples Athletic Teams--Bars Seven-Game Schedule.

Michigan loses Captain Garrels, Ramey and Stewart from the track team.

Michigan loses Captain Magoffin, Graham, Hammond and Patrick in football.

Michigan loses Wendell and Carruthers in baseball.

Michigan is refused seven football games, and is told to be content with five.

The western conference in session at Chicago yesterday dealt Michigan a terrible blow. Startling results are now expected. If anything like the old Michigan spirit prevails among the students, a mass meeting will in all probability be called next week to petition the University senate to withdraw from the conference. This last merciless attack is generally regarded on the campus as the straw that will break the camel's back. It is generally considered as the height of absurdity that Michigan's athletic development should be guided by colleges like Northwestern, for instance, which abolished football five years ago.

APR. 12

CONFERENCE WILL MEET IN SPECIAL SESSION

Michigan's Status in Big Nine to be Determined Next Week—Saturday's Game Postponed.

Athletic relations with Chicago are at a standstill. The game scheduled for Saturday has been postponed, pending the result of the special meeting of the Western Conference, probably to be held sometime next week, at which Michigan's status in the organization will be determined. Judge Lane and Coach Stagg telephoned this report to Manager Baird last night.

If the Conference decides that Michigan's attitude is justifiable, the game will be played later in the season.

Team manager Charles Baird and coach Fielding Yost removed Michigan from the Big Nine Conference after the conference had enacted a number of rule changes. For example, athletes were given only three years of eligibility, and the season was reduced to five games. As a result, Michigan was prohibited from playing Big Nine teams and instead took on schools such as Ohio State, Michigan Agricultural College, Penn and Cornell.

OCT. 3

RE-ENTER BIG NINE? "NO," SAYS LANE

Chairman of Board of Control Denies Knowledge of Any Action—Baird in Like Statement.

APR. 25

WHAT THEY THINK AS TO CONFERENCE

Prominent Students and Others Express Opinions on Athletic Situation.

Many angles of the Conference situation are revealed in the following interviews obtained by THE DAILY yesterday:

Prof. J. P. McMurrich, of the Athletic Board of Control: "Michigan is now under obligations to certain universities of the Western Conference. This is the highly undesirable position into which Michigan has forced herself. For it is due to the friendly attitude of several of the colleges that Michigan has been allowed to remain in the Conference, after having broken its rules.

"If we had cut loose from the Conference, we would have had eight enemies upon our backs and been deprived of western games indefinitely. We are not out of the Conference and can enter into athletic relations with western schools as soon as we are willing to abide by Conference rules.

"Michigan's natural field is the west—to go east is practically an impossibility. After next year we will have just reason for remaining out of the Conference. The retroactive rule upon which Michigan has defended her actions will have virtually lost its effect, so it is likely that athletic relations with the west will then be resumed."

John Garrels: "The Conference situation is no different from what we must have expected it to be; and it could not be better. Our relations with the east have not been altered in the least. As for the Conference itself, we are only temporarily affected. As soon as Michigan sees fit to conform to the regulations of the organization her status will be the same as before. Havoc has been wrought with the baseball season, but that is rather due to the lateness of the board's action than to anything else, for a new schedule might have been arranged earlier in the season."

> **Everywhere on the campus and at the various boarding houses and clubs this is the leading topic of conversation.**
>
> — *The Michigan Daily*

The Michigan Daily

NOV. 7 MICHIGAN 3 NOTRE DAME 11

MICHIGAN OVERWHELMED BY NOTRE DAME ELEVEN

Varsity Unable to Withstand Onslaught of the Catholics----Err in Judgment at Crucial Time ----Score 11 to 3.

Notre Dame defeated Michigan 11 to 3. the Wolverines losing because of the bad judgment of Wasmund in calling for a place kick near the close of the second half, the score 5 to 3 against Michigan, with the goal but ten yards away and with but one yard to go to secure a first down. Allerdice's attempt was blocked. the ball rolled to midfield, was secured by Notre Dame and a minute later Ryan made the Catholics' final touchdown. Borleske received a broken collar bone in the early part of the game and will be out for the rest of the season.

Michigan scored first in the middle of the opening half. Allerdice making a pretty place kick for three points. Two minutes before the close of the half Notre Dame rushed the ball down the field with forward passes and long runs by Miller and Ryan and after being twice held for no gain on the one-yard line the ball was sent across for a touchdown, Vaughan failing to kick goal.

Capt. Allerdice, who assumes responsibility for selection of plays used in Notre Dame game.

EXTRA.
U. OF M. VS. ALBION.

(Special to the Michigan Daily.)
Franklin Field, Philadelphia, Nov. 13. —Michigan triumphs by 12 to 6 score. Tonight the Maize and Blue of Michigan waves in victory over the Red and Blue of Pennsylvania and the Quakers, battered and bruised by Michigan's tremendous plunges, feel the sting of defeat that Michigan felt for three successive years.

Guided by the master hand of Wasmund, who proved the star in a game where many were prominent, the Wolverine eleven trampled over and around the Quakers, outplaying them in every department of the game and securing two touchdowns by brilliant play where old Penn could count but once.

Wasmund, playing his last game for Michigan, outplayed the veteran and much-touted Miller, returning punts in classy manner, gaining ground with amazing regularity and running the team with the snap and vigor that characterized Michigan teams in the days of "Boss" Weeks.

Indeed, the team that overwhelmed Penn today on Franklin Field, in its precision and accuracy, was more like the machines of Yost's golden days than any Michigan team since 1904. Every man helped every other, they spoiled Penn's pet plays, they broke up the Quakers' forward passes, they blocked the Penn tacklers, in short they played a game that no team in the country could equal.

MICHIGAN WRECKS PENN!

NOV. 13 MICHIGAN 12 PENN STATE 6

ALL ANN ARBOR IS AGOG

Led by the Band the Celebration Will Continue Today.

UNIVERSITY OF MICHIGAN FOOTBALL TEAM.
Left to right—Top row: Smith, Benbrook, Otis, Clark, F. Lawton, Edmunds, Freeney. **Middle row:** Yost, Lawton, Conklin, Ranney, Borleske, Magidsohn. **Bottom row:** Allerdice Wells, Watkins, Wasmund, Rogers, Bertrand.

JUNE 24, 1913

Hill Memorial Auditorium
Will Be Dedicated Tomorrow

APRIL 17, 1912

TWO SEA CAPTAINS WERE OLD FRIENDS

Capt. Sealby Acquainted With Capt. Smith and Part of Crew of Ill-Fated Titanic.

LOSES A DETROIT FRIEND.

Captain Inman Sealby, '12 law, former commander of the ill-fated Atlantic liner Republic, was well acquainted with Captain E. J. Smith of the Titanic, the ship which sank off Cape Race with great loss of life, early Monday morning.

In speaking of Captain Smith last evening, Captain Sealby said: "He was one of these noble, attractive men whom no one can help but like and respect. I have known him personally for twenty years and I regard him as one of the finest men who ever took a vessel across the Atlantic.

"When I was in the employ of the White Star Line, Captain Smith was my ideal of a seaman. He was not only popular among the officers but also with the sailors. I often went to him for advice and thought of him as a staunch friend.

JAN. 9, 1918

WILSON OUTLINES TERMS UNDER WHICH UNITED STATES WILL ACCEPT PEACE; IS ANSWER TO GERMAN CHALLENGE

Washington, Jan. 8.—America's program of war and peace with definite terms upon which the nations, great and small, fighting together against the German world domination are ready to lay down their arms, was given to the world by President Wilson today through an address to congress, in joint session.

This program, based upon the righting of wrongs and the safety of peace loving peoples, desiring to live their own lives, the President committed the United States to fight and continue fighting until it is achieved. Thus, he pledged the country to the Allied policy of no separate peace. "We cannot be separated in interest or divided in purpose," he said. "We stand together to the end."

AUG. 10, 1915

SECOND WOMEN'S HALL OPENS SOON

Martha Cook Dormitory with Capacity of 150, will be Ready in Fall

JAN. 17, 1919

PROHIBITION WINS NATIONAL VICTORY NEBRASKA VOTE

UNITED STATES TODAY BECOMES FIRST GREAT NATION WITHOUT LIQUOR TRAFFIC

APRIL 5, 1917

SENATE PASSES WAR MOTION

1910

CHAMPIONS OF AMERICA

EXTRA.

In a scintillating exhibition of modern football the Wolverines completely bewildered the much touted Gophers Saturday afternoon and by administering a decisive beating to the powerful Norsemen placed themselves on the topmost pinnacle of gridiron success. The score, 6 to 0, about represents the respective ability of the teams.

It was the most wonderful football game ever staged on Ferry field and one of the hardest fought. The triumph for Michigan, her men, and her methods was complete. The heavy, powerful Gophers who had swept the West fought desperately but the brilliantly conceived and splendidly executed offensive tactics of the Wolverines were utterly beyond their power to stop. Today Michigan stands with western supremacy unquestionably hers and in consequence of the Yale-Harvard tie score yesterday she may well claim that her eleven is the greatest in the land.

WILD CELEBRATION FOLLOWS VICTORY

Madly Enthusiastic Thousands Make Evening One of Revelry

FORMAL PROGRAM IS SUCCESS

STATISTICS OF BATTLE.

On straight football:
Michigan gained...... 137 yards
Minnesota gained...... 128 yards
On forward passes:
Michigan gained....... 115 yards
Minnesota gained...... 20 yards
First downs:
Michigan 11
Minnesota 6

Michigan punted 18 times for a total of 739 yards, averaging 40 yards to a punt.

Minnesota punted 25 times for a total of 999 yards, averaging 40 yards to a punt.

Michigan was penalized 30 yards.

Minnesota was penalized 10 yards.

Michigan used the forward pass successfully five times out of ten.

Minnesota used the forward pass successfully twice out of four times.

Courtesy of Bentley Historical Library

UNIVERSITY OF MICHIGAN FOOTBALL TEAM, 1910.
Top Row—Thomson, Magidsohn, Cole, Wenner, Hulbert, Edmunds, Clark, Mitchell, Daniels, Spice (Student Manager)
Middle Row—Cornwell, Quinn, Wells, Benbrook, Conklin, Lawton, Bogle.
Bottom Row—Siple, Pattengill, Picard, McMillan, Borleske, Cooper.

MICHIGAN FOOTBALL

MICHIGAN DEFEATS CORNELL 20—7

WOLVERINE WARRIORS RETRIEVE SEASON'S RECORD BY TRIUMPHING OVER CORNELL—20-7

ON THE SIDELINES

DEC. 11, 1912

FOOTBALL MEN MAY LOSE ONE HOUR'S CREDIT

Under Ruling of Attendance Committee in Law Department, Absences on Trips Count Against Players.

MEN IN LAW DEPARTMENT FEEL RULE WORKS INJUSTICE

Similar Absences are Excused by Attendance Committees of Other Departments.

Football men in the law department are somewhat dissatisfied with the devious workings of the attendance committee. According to the rule in that department, if a student is absent during the semester a sufficient number of times to constitute an equivalent of missing one class per week, that student will be deprived of one hour's credit. It has developed that the absences of football men while away on trips are treated as ordinary absences and count toward the deduction of credit. The men feel that this is hard upon them, inasmuch as they have missed their classes while working for the university, and they think that their absences should not be counted against them in deducting credit.

CAPACITY CROWD FILLS STANDS FOR BIG GAME

"Bottles" Thomson, full-back, Captain Michigan, 1912, who played his last game with the Wolverine aggregation today.

> " Here's a toast to Coach and Team,
> Hearts are happy and eyes a-gleam;
> Here's our school in a bumper high,
> Seize it foaming, and drain it dry.
> Cornell drinks to down her fate,
> **Michigan drinks to celebrate!** "
>
> — *Michigan cheer*

MICHIGAN 9   M.A.C. 0

LINE PLAYS REAL FOOTBALL IN DOWNING AGGIES BY 9-0 COUNT; MAULBETSCH AND SPARKS STAR

SPARKS' DROP KICK FOR FIRST SCORE RESULTS FROM HIGH PASS

22,000 SPECTATORS AT GAME

Niemann, Peach, Dunne and Rehor Play Brilliantly in Line

And lo! The Aggies fell!

Michigan's Varsity pushed the Farmers right off the top of the proud and elevated pedestal that they have occupied for the past season and the resounding thump as they struck the cold, soggy ground was music in the ears of the majority of the 22,000 spectators who defied the elements and saw one of the most interesting battles that has claimed a Ferry field setting for many a moon.

Oh yes, the score was 9 to 0, but this is merely an incidental and superfluous detail.

Michigan's victory is more or less directly attributable to this newest of football stars whose position in the gridiron firmament was rather firmly and convincingly established yesterday afternoon—Mr. Sparks, if you please—and if he maintains the pace that he set yesterday, ere long his name will be writ in capital letters and they'll start naming babies and pullman cars and cigars and delicious fifteen cent sundaes after him. And well they may.

Pat Smith Halts M. A. C. Player

Michigan Agricultural College underwent several name changes before becoming Michigan State University in 1964.

FOOTBALL RESULTS ..

West

Northwestern, 10; Chicago, 0.
Minnesota, 81; South Dakota, 0.
Wisconsin, 13; Haskell, 0.

East

Cornell, 19; Bucknell, 0.
Princeton, 33; Lafayette, 0.
Pittsburg, 30; Syracuse, 0.
Pennsylvania, 13; Penn State, 0.

ATHLETIC BOARD VOTES 8—1 FOR RE-ENTERING CONFERENCE

PETITION REGENTS TO TAKE ACTION ALLOWING SENATE COUNCIL VETO POWER OVER BOARD'S ACTIONS LEADING TO RETURN TO BIG NINE

GOVERNING BODY EXPECTED TO TAKE UP RESOLUTIONS AT MEETING THIS MORNING

Michigan will compete with members of the western intercollegiate conference as soon as the schedules at present arranged have been played out, if the board of regents, which meets this morning, adopts the resolution framed at yesterday afternoon's special session of the athletic board. A petition will be laid before the Regents today, outlining the present difficulties in securing proper competition and presenting the advantages to be gained by a return to the conference.

The vote taken on the athletic board yesterday showed eight in favor and one opposed to a return to the conference. Judge Murfin of Detroit, who was looked upon as the one possibility to vote against a return, explained that out of defense to the wishes of the Detroit alumni he would vote in the affirmative. James Duffy, alumni member from Bay City, cast the sole ballot against the resolution. No reason was given for the action of Mr. Duffy.

DATE HISTORY OF CONFERENCE

1895—Organized at the suggestion of President James B. Angell of Michigan.

1905—New rules made necessary following numerous football fatalities.

1906—Adopt one-year residence rule, reduction of number of games, abolition of training table adopted.

1907—Regents indicate to board in control desire to withdraw. Board votes against such action.

1907—Makeup of board in control changed.

1908—Board in control votes 5-3 to withdraw.

1910—"Boycott" rule passed to keep Minnesota a member.

1912—Athletic captains ask that Michigan be returned.

1913—Board in control votes for return, 6-5. Senate council concurs. Regents oppose following unfavorable action of student body.

1917—Board in control votes for return, 8-1.

WHEN OLD FRIENDS MEET

CROCKETT -17

Return to Conference Will Require Slight Changes in Michigan Rules

If Michigan returns to the western conference, five existing Michigan rules will have to be changed slightly, with a few additional modifications in eligibility requirements. There are a number of particulars in which Michigan's rules will not have to be changed, contrary to the current opinion.

Michigan will not have to play any stated number of conference teams in football or any other sport. She will not have to play a single conference team if she does not wish to. Her athletic coaches will not have to be faculty members. She can still take part in eastern intercollegiate track meets under eastern rules. Her athletes can still eat together at training tables.

OCT. 11

OPPOSITION BEING SOUGHT BY ELEVEN

Mt. Union Forced to Cancel Because of Quarantine Over S. A. T. C.

YOST OPTIMISTIC THAT GAME WILL BE PRODUCED; PREPARING

Usher and Fortune to Play in M. A. C. Game; Northwestern to Be Here Nov. 2

Quarantine made it impossible for the Mount Union gridders to hold their date with Yost's eleven at Ferry field for Saturday. The students' army training corps at that school is being held in detention according to reports pending the passing of the influenza epidemic.

Despite the conditions that necessitated the cancellation, the Mount Unionites are accredited with having one of the best teams in years. If they would have met the Wolverines, critics are of the opinion that some intresting things might have taken place, yet there would have been no doubt of Michigan taking the long end of the score.

GOETZ

Proving to be one of the wonders of Coach Yost's war time eleven, Goetz is responsible for the victory of the Wolverines over the Ohio State team, yesterday.

First to get under kicks, first to intercept passes, and first to block any attempts of the opposition, to kick, Goetz usually gets what he goes after. In the Chicago game he proved a star. In the Syracuse game he was better. The M. A. C. contest proved him a reliable man, and yesterday's contest proved him one of Michigan's best grid warriors.

OCT. 18

YOSTMEN TO PRACTICE DESPITE FLU EPIDEMIC

TRAINING WILL KEEP MEN IN SHAPE TO RESIST THE DISEASE

Despite the fact that the Michigan Aggie game has been postponed because of the epidemic scouring the country, the Wolverines will not stop their practice. Coach Yost will keep his gridders on the field, giving them the necessary training to keep them in shape for the grid game, and at the same time will do his bit in combatting the epidemic.

Since the men will be kept in the best physical condition, and being in the open air continually, their liability to contract the disease will be low.

The coach will keep the men on the field running them through scrimmages, signal practice and regular work. Taking advantage of the absence of a game this Saturday, it is probable that he will give the men another of his famous blackboard talks, made scarce by the war time conditions. Since practice began this season, the hour and a half allotted to football work by the S. A. T. C. officials has been but a short time for the work, thus cutting out the blackboard talks altogether.

Theories advanced to explain the reason for prohibiting outdoor mass meetings are to the effect that officials fear the prolonged cheering at the games would weaken the throats of the spectators, thus making them more susceptible to the disease.

OCT. 16

SOME GAME!!!

"If you want to see a fighting football game come out and watch the Wolverine-Aggie contest at Ferry field this Saturday."

That is what Coach Yost said last night about the biggest game to be played in the month of October. The star contest of the month will be one of the most interesting of the year, between the University of Michigan and the Michigan Agricultural college, two of the bitterest of state rivals.. Furthermore, the coach says that the Farmers have one of the strongest teams in the history of their school, this season, and that it is going to take some work to win from them.

From the above, it can be readily seen that the clash between the two rivals will be of the variety exhibited when Nebraska traveled from their far western fortress to take Michigan into camp and claim the championship of the west.

The Wolverine-Aggie game is the only one of worth scheduled during the month, according to the Michigan mentor, and it will be an opportunity, not only to see a great football game, but to help keep the record of the Maize and Blue spotless!

IT TAKES THE MEN BEHIND THE MEN BEHIND THE GUNS TO MAKE A VICTORY POSSIBLE, AND THAT MEANS THAT MICHIGAN WILL HAVE TO GET BEHIND HER GRIDDERS, WILL HAVE TO TURN OUT FULL FORCE AT THE GAME, AND YELL FOR ALL YOU ARE WORTH.

OCT. 24

VARSITY GRIDIRON SCHEDULE WRECKED BY FLU EPIDEMIC

There will be no football games for the Michigan team for at least two weeks as the result of an order issued yesterday by the state board of health, putting the ban on all public gatherings of any kind, to be held in the state within the next two weeks. This period, it was announced was the shortest that the board would consider.

The 1918 season was curtailed due to World War I travel restrictions and the Spanish influenza pandemic. Michigan won the national championship this season with a 5-0 record after Illinois declined Michigan's offer to play a postseason game to settle the championship. Most news outlets recognized Michigan as the champions, since Illinois suffered a non-conference loss.

DEC. 1

WOLVERINES TAKE FINAL GAME OF '18 SEASON BY WINNING FROM OHIO STATE BY TWO TOUCHDOWNS IN LAST QUARTER

1918	MICH	OPPONENT
OCT. 5	33	0	Case
NOV. 9	13	0	Chicago
NOV. 16	15	0	Syracuse
NOV. 23	21	6	M.A.C.
NOV. 30	14	0	Ohio State

DEC. 3

FOOTBALL SEASON ENDS PROVING BIG SUCCESS

YOSTMEN DISBANDED FOLLOWING LAST GAME OF YEAR WITH O. S. U.

With but one score recorded against them and no defeats, Coach Yost's war-time eleven has completed the season of 1918 in record breaking shape.

At the close of the Ohio State game at Columbus, Saturday, the hurry up coach announced that he was greatly pleased with the way the season had turned out. He stated also that the men showed up even better than he had expected.

Yostmen on Long End

Out of the five teams played during the season, the Yostmen not only conquered all of them, but also piled up a score of 96 points allowing the opposition but six. M. A. C. was the only team that had a chance to cross the Maize and Blue goal line during the entire season.

Claims to the Conference championship were passed up by Coach Yost when the Illinois eleven, the only other contestant for the honor, disbanded its team, apparently fearing to meet Michigan.

Despite this however, Michigan fans and eastern critics are of the opinion that the Wolverines are rightfully entitled to the honor.

DOC MAY   COACH YOST   ASST. COACH DOUGLASS

THE MEN WHO ARE MAKING THE MICHIGAN TEAM

JAN. 13, 1923

MICHIGAN TAKES INITIAL ICE TILT FROM WISCONSIN

OCT. 22, 1921

MICHIGAN WOMEN PLAN BUILDING

ORGANIZATION TO BE CALLED UNIVERSITY OF MICHIGAN LEAGUE

Exterior view of the proposed University of Michigan League Building. The Womens League inaugurates a drive for $1,000,000 for the erection of this building next week.

JULY 22, 1925

SCOPES DECLARED GUILTY; MINIMUM FINE IS IMPOSED

Defendant Loses Evolution Trail

—————

BAIL FOR AN APPEAL IS FIXED AT FIVE HUNDRED DOLLARS

NOV. 10, 1923

DEDICATE NEW YOST FIELD HOUSE WITH CEREMONY BEFORE GAME TODAY

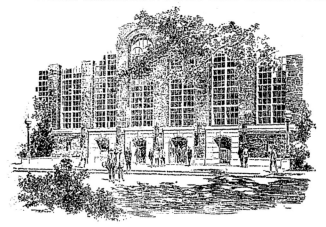

Conceded to be the largest field field house in the country, the new structure on Ferry field is the culmination of long efforts towards obtaining a suitable structure for the housing of Michigan athletes and athletic activities. The building is named after Fielding H. Yost, director of intercollegiate athletics, who for 22 years has piloted the Varsity teams.

MAY 25, 1929

REGENTS MAKE 1817 FOUNDING DATE

Centennial Celebration Plans Entirely Cancelled

By the action of the Board of Regents in meeting yesterday afternoon, the University is 20 years older today. Official recognition was given to the date 1817 as the year in which the University was founded and this date is to supplant 1837 on all official documents and the University seal.

OCT. 25, 1929

Stock Market Sets Record in Sales; Prices Hit Bottom in Frantic Session

MAY 22, 1927

AMERICAN AVIATOR LANDS NEAR PARIS AFTER EPOCHAL VOYAGE SIX HOURS AHEAD OF SCHEDULE

AS OF 1920...

225-55-12
MICHIGAN FOOTBALL PROGRAM RECORD

13-1-2
VS. OHIO STATE

11-2-1
VS. MICHIGAN STATE

8-1
VS. NOTRE DAME

6-3-1
VS. MINNESOTA

8,472
ENROLLMENT

$44
IN-STATE TUITION

$64
OUT-OF-STATE TUITION

$549,489
ENDOWMENT

Fielding H. Yost
FOOTBALL COACH

Harry Hutchins
UNIVERSITY PRESIDENT

NOTABLE GRADUATES

1923 Thomas Dewey, two-time presidential candidate and *Michigan Daily* editor

1925 Arnold Gingrich, founder of *Esquire* magazine

MINNESOTA HUMBLED

1922 GRIDIRON SEASON FORMALLY OPENS AT A DOZEN COLLEGES AND UNIVERSITIES

Bushnell 4/22

GOPHERS CRUMBLE UNDER DRIVING OF POWERFUL YOSTMEN

DEAN OF GRID MENTORS

COACH FIELDING H. YOST—
THE GRAND OLD MAN OF FOOTBALL

HUGE CELEBRATION TO GREET VICTORS TOMORROW NIGHT

Michigan's championship football team will receive the greatest welcome ever accorded a Wolverine team, when they arrive at the Michigan Central station tomorrow night. The Student Council this morning authorized committees to begin the work which will make the celebration a memorable one in the football annals of Michigan.

A huge fireworks display, the Varsity Band, a torchlight parade and a monster bonfire will greet the victorious Wolverines as they leave the train. They bring with them two things. First and foremost the championship of the Big Ten Conference, and second the cherished Jug.

For these two reasons Michigan will greet her "Champions of the West."

> " In these hurrying days when the little jugs are fast disappearing from our midst, it would seem to the uniformed person that there is something radically wrong with two universities when they put all of their forces and tactics into a battle where a little brown jug is at stake. "
> — *The Michigan Daily*

1923	MICH		OPPONENT
OCT. 6	36	0	Case
OCT. 13	3	0	Vanderbilt
OCT. 20	23	0	Ohio State
OCT. 27	37	0	M.A.C.
NOV. 3	9	3	Iowa
NOV. 10	26	6	Quantico Marines
NOV. 17	6	3	Wisconsin
NOV. 24	10	0	Minnesota

OCT. 7

RAGGED PLAYING FEATURES 36-0 TRIUMPH OVER CASE

OCT. 9

SPECIAL TRAINS TO RUN TO IOWA, WISCONSIN GAMES

RAILROAD COMPANIES DESIRE 200 STUDENTS TO IN-SURE PLAN

RATES FOR TRIP; IOWA $20.30; WISCONSIN $15.16

Reserved Tickets Attainable at Union; Sale to Continue Several Weeks

> " *Displaying a scintillating offense which was preponderously open, and an unpenetrable defense, Michigan's Varsity football team wiped out the only blemish of last year's record, a scoreless tie game, by defeating Vanderbilt, the champions of the South, this afternoon.* "
>
> — Ralph N. Byers, *The Michigan Daily*

OCT. 20

BUCKEYES VANQUISHED
WOLVERINES DRAW BLOOD WITH SCORE IN SECOND PERIOD

ON THE SIDELINES

SPORT STATISTICS FEATURE PROGRAM

Filled with photographs and information, the Athletic Program for the Michigan-O. S. U. game made its appearance yesterday on the campus. The pamphlet contains President Marion L. Burton's welcome to the guests of the University for the occasion, together with a picture of the president.

Full length photographs of the coaches and captains of the opposing teams are other features of the book. Statistics of the teams and records of past games form the major portion of the program.

Makes Touchdown

Herb Steger
Who made Michigan's second score late in the third quarter with a beautiful catch of a pass from Uteritz.

Jap Quarterback Makes W-M Team Formidable One

Ichya Matzu

As quarteback on the William and Mary grid team Matzu has come to be regarded as one of the ablest football players in the East. He also enjoys the distinction of being the only Japanese on an eastern college team Although he weighs but 144 pounds, he makes up for this deficiency by brilliant playing and an unbeatable spirit.

---

25 TICKET SCALPERS NABBED AT FERRY FIELD

Scalping was again prevalent before the game this afternoon. Both students and professional scalpers were active particularly at the entrance to Ferry field. For two hours prior to the game the sale of tickets at exorbitant prices were being consummated.

A corps of city police and private detectives in the employ of the Athletic association were kept busy up to the start of the game in making arrests. Arrests made by private detectives were turned over to the city police officials and a special car was kept in service between the entrance to Ferry field and the city jail. More than 25 arrests were made during the early part of the afternoon.

"This is in keeping with the policy of the Athletic association in its effort to stamp out scalping on football tickets", said Harry A. Tillotson this afternoon.

NOV. 10

LEATHERNECKS FALL BEFORE FAST PLAY OF WOLVERINE TEAM

NOV. 18

INJURED LIST GROWS AS VARSITY DOWNS BADGERS

YOSTMEN OVERCOME EARLY LEAD AND REMAIN IN BIG TEN RACE

NOV. 25

MICHIGAN DEFEATS MINNESOTA AND TAKES CONFERENCE TITLE

Game Sidelights

Captain Kipke had the better of his punting duel with Martineau throughout the game. In the first half Kipke averaged 45 yards while the Gopher leader averaged 35. In the second half their respective averages were 43 and 25.

Minnesota made seven first downs to Michigan's six, three of the Wolverines being made by passes in the second period.

Minnesota failed to complete a single pass in nine tries. Michigan attempted the same number, completing three for a net gain of 46 yards.

All of Michigan's successful passes came in four plays in the second quarter, when the Wolverines started their march down to and across the Gophers goal line.

MICHIGAN KEEPS TITLE

MICHIGAN WINS, 7 - 6

70 YARD DRIVE DOWN FIELD GIVES GOPHERS SCORE IN FIRST HALF

By Wilton A. Simpson

MEMORIAL STADIUM, Minneapolis, Nov. 20.—Michigan retained its leadership of the Western football Conference by winning the last of its five Big Ten games, defeating the powerful Minnesota eleven here this afternoon.

Today's victory was the second time the Wolverines downed the Gopher team this year. Michigan won the first game 20 to 0, at Ann Arbor at the opening of the season. Michigan entered today's battle rated as the under-dog, but mustered every bit of its strength to gain the victory which decided the Conference title in favor of the Yostmen.

The little Brown Jug will return to Ann Arbor, to rest on the shelves of the Field house, where it has been since the Wolverines brought it home from the Northland in 1920.

The playing field, which has been covered with three feet of hay since Sunday, was in good condition just before game time. Coach Yost assisted scores of workmen in clearing the gridiron.

The temperature was well below freezing but a strong sun made conditions more tolerable for the spectators.

A wind swept across the field from the west giving the defender of the west goal a kicking advantage.

VARSITY LOSES SEVEN

Today's battle with the powerful Minnesota team marked the final appearance of seven members of the 1926 Wolverine football squad as wearers of the Maize and Blue. Captain Friedman, Flora, Lovette, Dewey, W. Weber, McIntyre, and Heston comprise the list, and four of these departing athletes were in the starting lineup that faced the Galloping Gophers.

Scoops Up Fumble

Benny Oosterbaan

Michigan end, proved that he is caliber for the all-American selections of 1926 by scooping up a fumble on his own 40 yard line in the fourth quarter and running 60 yards to a touchdown. Friedman's place kick for the extra point gave the Wolverines a 7-6 lead.

The Coveted Brown Jug

"Shorty Almquist"

Minnesota quarterback, who was injured in the first quarter of the battle today, and was carried from the field on a stretcher. Almquist piloted the Gophers well during the opening period, sending his eleven through the Wolverine team for consistent gains.

Kipke Will Definitely Stay Here

DEC. 16, 1933

Coach Makes A Statement Before Boarding Train For New York

Increase In Salary For 1934 Assured

Claims Assistant Coaches Do Not Receive Enough Credit For Work

Coach Harry G. Kipke, in a statement made public yesterday, said definitely that he will remain as chairman of the coaching staff at Michigan next year. Kipke made the statement shortly before he boarded a train at 6:30 p.m. for New York where he will speak on the All-America broadcast Friday evening.

In his statement Kipke said that he had been assured of an increase in salary by the Board in Control of Athletics, the raise to go into effect next year. It is rumored that the Board's decision on the increase was reached before any agitation was begun to get Kipke at Yale or Dartmouth.

"I like it here at Michigan", Kipke declared in part, "and I am willing to continue coaching here, even for less money than might be had elsewhere."

It is Kipke's opinion that the rest of the coaching staff does not get enough credit for its work. In view of this Kipke said that he would petition the Athletic Board for increases in salary for these men.

The amount of the raise Kipke will get was not revealed, but it is supposed it will be a substantial amount. His present salary has been estimated between $4,500 and $6,500, but authoritative sources place it at $5,924.80.

Kipke since taking up his duties here in 1928 has been one of the most successful of the young coaches, winning or tying for four Conference titles in five years and winning the national championship under the Dickinson rating system for two consecutive years.

During this time he has been one of the lowest salaried coaches in the Big Ten, although he has been able to bolster his pay in the last year by endorsing athletic goods, writing magazine articles and speaking on radio programs.

SEPT. 18, 1934

Kipke Says Team Will Lose Three Games This Year

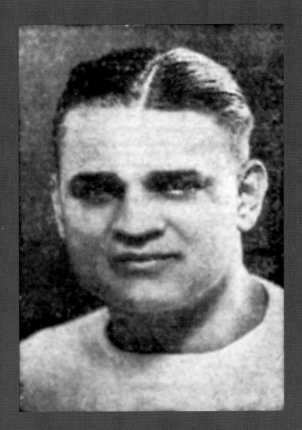

KIPKE DRILLS WOLVERINE MACHINE FOR FINAL GAME

Kipke not only led the Wolverines to two national championships as a coach in 1932 and 1933, but he also led the Yostmen to a national title in 1923 as a halfback and punter. He is one of several Michigan greats to ultimately land a head coaching job with the program.

Alumni Are Satisfied With Kipke

est. 1927

STADIUM APPROVED

Above is a view of Michigan's new 70,000 seat stadium, from the northeast as it will look upon completion. The stadium will be built as a rectangular bowl and will have approximately 70 rows of seats. Entrance to the stadium from the west, north, and south will be made "over the top" while the east entrance, the one shown in the illustration, will be made through portals or tunnels.

APR. 23, 1926

REGENTS AUTHORIZE BUILDING OF NEW FOOTBALL STRUCTURE; LEAVING DETAILS TO BOARD

70,000 Seats Will Meet Approval; New Athletic Body Will Handle Problem

Construction of a new University football stadium, with no definite limit on the seating capacity and all the details left to the Board in Control of Intercollegiate Athletics, was authorized by the Board of Regents last night. The report adopted declared that, in the opinion of the Regents, a stadium of 70,000 seats "would not be objectionable."

With the single provision that "stadium construction should be so handled as 'not to overdo it'", the entire problem was left to the present Board in Control of Athletics, headed by Coach Fielding H. Yost, and to its successor, a new board in control created last night, which will go into office on May 1. The new board is to consist of two students, three alumni and nine faculty representatives.

> " The hole that Yost dug, Crisler paid for, Canham carpeted, and Schembechler fills every week. "
> — Bob Ufer,
> *Michigan announcer*

SEPT. 20, 1969

All eyes on 'The Rug' in Vandy opener

By JOEL BLOCK
Sports Editor

When 22 men trot onto the field today to play what is called the Michigan - Vanderbilt football game, no one will be looking at them.

True, there will be 70,000 plus maniac football fans in Michigan Stadium surrounding them, but they won't be looking at the players. Nor the coaches. Nor the band. Nor the male cheerleaders.

They will be looking at the Rug.

The Rug is ½" high, 88,285 square feet in area and the most expensive wall-to-wall carpeting job ever designed in Michigan.

The Rug is the ingenious invention of some highly-paid chemist of the Minnesota Mining and Manufacturing Company and is called Tartan Turf. And it works.

The Michigan football team has conducted its entire fall practice on the Rug the equivalent of 12 full games of wear, and it looks like carpet-layers just finished the north end zone. It's that beautiful.

OCT. 7, 1956

STATE POWER SUBDUES 'M', 9-0

By DICK CRAMER
Associate Sports Editor

History repeated itself yesterday—but with a twist—as a generally outplayed Michigan State football squad capitalized on Michigan mistakes to pull out a tight 9-0 victory before a record crowd of 101,001 in Michigan Stadium.

The first game when the stadium held more than 100,000 people was a loss to Michigan State on Oct. 6, 1956.

'U' breaks ground for expansion of Big House

MICHIGAN SPORTS INFORMATION

The University added 5,000 seats to Michigan Stadium — bringing the capacity to 107,501 seats. The addition made the Big House the largest stadium in the country.

OCT. 20, 2006

'U' offers public first peek at Big House renovations

By Gabe Nelson
Daily Staff Reporter

If the University Board of Regents approves the Athletic Department's new stadium plans, the Big House could become the Brick House.

The Athletic Department released schematic designs yesterday for its divisive renovations to Michigan Stadium.

The drawings show club seats, suites and a new press box built into brick facades on the east and west sides of the stadium.

The brick structures would rise 85 feet above the ground outside the stadium, 10 feet higher than the scoreboards on both sides of the field.

The $226-million renovation plan also includes a number of amenities for fans, like more bathrooms and concession stands, wider bleacher seats, handrails in the aisles and handicapped-accessible seating.

To make room for these changes, a few thousand bleacher seats would be eliminated. The addition of 3,200 club seats and 83 suites above the seating bowl would make up the difference and keep the total number of seats at or above the current 107,501.

Courtesy of the University Athletic Department

JAN. 29, 2010

Michigan and MSU will meet in 'Big Chill at the Big House'

A fireworks celebration following Michigan's 5-0 win over Michigan State in the Big Chill at the Big House on Saturday. The game, which was the first outdoor hockey game in Michigan Stadium, drew a record-setting crowd of 113,411. (Dec. 13, 2010)

SAM WOLSON/Daily

1930 1931 **1932** 1933 **1934** 1935 **1936** 1937 **1938** 1939

FEB. 18, 1931

COMMITTEE CHAIRMAN SCORES TACTICS OF LOCAL OFFICIALS IN FRATERNITY LIQUOR RAIDS

Dissatisfaction with the manner employed by the Ann Arbor police in raiding the five University fraternities was expressed yesterday by Frank P. Darin, chairman of the University committee in the state House of Representatives, who, with his committee was in Ann Arbor to discuss appropriations for the University.

"I am not satisfied with the way the raid was conducted," he said. "It is outrageous to get almost a hundred college students out of bed at 3 o'clock in the morning when they are in the midst of examinations.

"I understand," he continued, 'that in one house only two quarts of liquor were found. Why that is hardly a teaspoonful to each member!"

Darin emphasized that something permanent should be done to satisfy the rumor that the warrants were illegal. "If the Ann Arbor police faked the warrants on which the search of the five houses was based the legislature ought to know about it, for after all the legislature is the court of last resort so far as checking the police is concerned," he stated.

"I understand," Darin continued, "that they were signed with a fictitious name, 'Johnny Walker'; and if this is true the warrants were illegal."

OCT. 28, 1932

Martha Cook To Sponsor First Of League Teas

To Feature Dancing And Fortune-Telling On Entertainment Program

---

NOV. 9, 1932

Roosevelt Wins In Democrat Landslide; Hoover's Telegram Concedes Victory

---

NOV. 2, 1933

Daily Founder Dies Suddenly At Ohio Home

One of the founders and the first business manager of The Michigan Daily, Dr. Matthew B. Hammond, '91, died suddenly Sept. 28, at his home in Columbus, according to word recently received by The Daily.

Dr. Hammond, who was largely responsible for the financial success of The Daily in its earlier years, was a distinguished professor of economics at Ohio State University at the time of his death.

It was at the beginning of that famous period in American social history known as the "Gay Nineties" that Dr. Hammond, as one of the outstanding independents on the University campus, together with Herbert B. Shoemaker, '91, was able to get the University Independent association to establish a weekly newspaper in competition with the Chronicle, controlled at that time by fraternity men.

AUG. 3, 1934

Hitler In Absolute Control Of Reich In Role Of Chancellor-President

---

SEPT. 20, 1938

Two Million Dollar Grad School To Foster Research Activities

JULY 3, 1937

Earhart Lost At Sea Near Small Island

Navy Searches For Flier Around Howland Island; Fuel Shortage Blamed

Shark Threat Feared For Flier, Navigator

NOV. 6

VARSITY DRILLS HARD AS AS CRIMSON CLASH NEARS

Wolverines Rush Way to Triumph in Final Quarter

Hudson Snares Newman's Toss to Cross Line, Overcoming Harvard's Lead During Final Period.

VARSITY STOPS TWO GOAL THREATS

By JOE RUSSELL
(Special to The Daily)

SOLDIER'S FIELD, CAMBRIDGE, Mass., Nov. 8.—Fired to a fighting pitch by Barry Wood's well-placed drop-kick which gave Harvard a three-point lead with the last quarter less than a minute old, Michigan came back this afternoon with everything it had, rushed the Crimson down the field and ended with Hudson racing across the goal line after snaring one of Newman's passes to give the Kipkemen a 6-3 victory.

The Harvard lead was extremely short-lived, Michigan scoring within five minutes after their opponents had had their moment of hope. Lajeunesse kicked off to Huguley after Wood's score, but then Michigan held and Harvard punted on the Maize and Blue 33-yard line. From that moment until the ball was behind the goal posts the Wolverines were a fighting band which could not be denied. On the sixth play Newman standing on Harvard's 40-yard line, passed to Hudson who took the ball on a dead run on the Crimson's 15-yard line and eluded two would-be tacklers on his way to the touchdown.

MICHIGAN PASS DOWNS CRIMSON, 6-3

ON THE SIDELINES

Radio Report of Game Heard by 800 at Union

More than 800 students listened to the play-by-play account of the Michigan-Harvard game yesterday as it was received by the five radios in the Union building. This is the largest crowd yet to make use of the facilities provided by the Union for listening to the broadcast accounts of the out-of-town football games.

1932

OCT. 9

Contest Marks Downfall Of Purple Halfback; His Debacle In Contrast With Rise Of Harry Newman

Michigan Linemen Outplay Opponents

Petoskey And Williamson Have Prominent Roles In Maize-And-Blue Win; Wildcats Fumble Often

By JOHN THOMAS

The Wolverine licked the Wildcat. It can. And it did. Before 55,000 spectators it proved stronger by nine points, the margin between the two teams in a game that saw Northwestern's championship hopes dwindle as Michigan won, 15 to 6.

A mighty Michigan team stopped "Pug" Rentner in his touchdown habits. Two great ends bottled him up on most of his tries from the line of scrimmage and good open-field tackling kept him from his usual long runs.

Courtesy of Bentley Historical Library

Harry Newman's Accurate Heaves Render Buckeyes Helpless; Michigan Line Is Invincible In Crises

By JOHN W. THOMAS

COLUMBUS, O., Oct. 15—Helpless against Harry Newman's accurate passing, Ohio State bowed to the mighty Wolverines, 14-0, here this afternoon before 40,000 spectators. Although the Buckeyes worked the ball from midfield to the 20-yard line on several long power drivves, Michigan's line kept them at bay when the goalposts were in sight.

Michigan showed little regard for Ohio's highly touted running attack and used a long list of reserves, some of whom played for an entire half. With the Wolverine regulars on the bench, the Scarlet and Gray team piled up first downs, but to most of the fans, the game was won at the end of the first half.

OCT. 30

Undefeated Michigan Eleven Rallies To Down Princeton, 14-7; Regeczi's Kicks Help

NOV. 6

Slashing Thrust In Third Period Gives Michigan Only Score Of Contest; Field Wet And Slippery

Pass Threat Makes Score A Possibility

Newman Fools Hoosier Defense; He Carries Ball Around End For Score; Indiana Threatens Often

1932	MICH		OPPONENT
OCT. 1	26	0	Michigan State
OCT. 8	15	6	Northwestern
OCT. 15	14	0	Ohio State
OCT. 22	32	0	Illinois
OCT. 29	14	7	Princeton
NOV. 5	7	0	Indiana
NOV. 12	12	0	Chicago
NOV. 19	3	0	Minnesota

NOV. 20

Newman's Field Goal Gives Michigan Conference Title; Students Will Greet Victors

Wolverine Football Eleven Hailed National Champions Under Dickinson System

Courtesy of Bentley Historical Library

How Dickinson Rates Top Elevens

Team	Won	Lost	Tied	Points
Michigan	8	0	0	28.47
S. Calif.	9	0	0	26.81
Pittsburgh	8	0	2	26.49
Purdue	7	0	1	26.33
Colgate	9	0	0	25.00
Ohio State	4	1	3	23.60
Notre Dame	7	2	0	20.44
Army	8	2	0	20.00

ON THE SIDELINES

Band Mascot Assists Riley As Drum-Major

Bed-Post Baton Serves Little Bobby Weir In Miniature Role

The Varsity Band had a new solo attraction at the game yesterday when Bobby Weir, seven-year-old son of Mr. and Mrs. Henry J. Weir, 800 South Main street, "strutted his stuff" as mascot drum-major between halves.

Bobby, clad in a miniature drum-major's uniform and equipped with an authentic baton fashioned from the end of a metal bed-post, twirled his baton and stuck his chin in the air as he marched in and out of the ranks of Varsity Band drummers who stood in the center of the field while the rest of the "Fighting Hundred" spelled out an "N-W."

Michigan Places Three Men On Big Ten Eleven

Conference Sport Editors Put Bernard, Newman, Williamson On Team

By CHARLES E. FLYNN

CHAMPAIGN, Ill., Nov. 21.—(Special)—The Big Ten football season of 1932 produced some of the greatest individual stars in the annals of Big Ten football. From this outstanding group of stars, the Sports Editors of all Big Ten papers have selected an All-Conference Team.

Six of the conference schools are represented by one or more of their favorite sons. Ohio State, Michigan, and Purdue each have three representatives with Illinois, Wisconsin, and Minnesota one. The task of selection was extremely hard because outstanding linemen were sadly lacking while there was a wealth of great backfield men.

Wins Greatest Prize Collection Ever Presented

All-American Stars From Past And Present Attend Season's Celebration

By JOHN THOMAS

The greatest collection of honors and awards ever given to any college gridiron team was presented to the University of Michigan football aggregation last night between halves of the Illinois-Michigan basketball game in the Yost Field House.

No team in the history of football can compete with the 1933 edition of Kipke's Miracles in the number and value of the awards earned and presented last night.

All-Americans paraded past the fans in the spectacle, some of this year and some of former years. They helped to present the formal rewards of a great season and they accepted them in the name of the University.

OCT. 11
Kipke Says Wolverines Overrated; Predicts Michigan Defeat

OCT. 8
Powerful Running Attack, Kicking, And Wet Field Aid Michigan In Beating State

OCT. 15
Michigan Smashes Its Way To 40-0 Win Over Cornell; Regeczi, Everhardus Star

Huge Revenge Score Is Stacked Up Through A Series Of Long Runs

Entire Wolverine Backfield Smooth

Vaunted Offense Of Big Red Team Is Checked By Heavy 'M' Line

By ALBERT H. NEWMAN
(Sports Editor)

Unleashing a powerful attack from scrimmage, passes and the broken field, Michigan's 11 big, bad Wolverines exacted a 40-0 revenge yesterday afternoon in Michigan Stadium for a series of disastrous defeats inflicted by Cornell in the early days of football.

HESTON   REGECZI   FAY   EVERHARDUS

ON THE SIDELINES

Game To Be Pictured By Grid Graph Board At Union

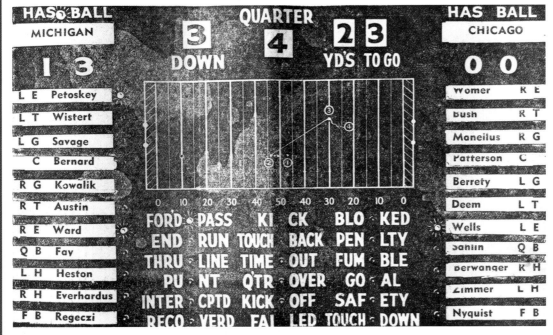

A small edition of the Grid Graph is shown recording a theoretical play in today's game. The lighted bulbs show that the ball is Michigan's on third down, 23 yds to go. The play is a forward pass, Petoskey to Ward, who was tackled by Wells, left end for Chicago.

The figures on the miniature gridiron indicate the successive positions of the ball on each part of the play. In the order shown here the ball was passed from center (1) to Petoskey who came around and passed it from the 45 yd. line (2) to Ward on the 30 yd. line (3) Ward then advanced the ball to the 22 yd. line where Wells downed him (4). The Grid Graph may be seen in the Union ballroom this afternoon, admission 25 cents.

Courtesy of Bentley Historical Library

FRANCIS 'WHITEY' WISTERT

NOV. 28

Michigan Smashes Way To Conference Championship In 13-0 Win Over Wildcats

By ALBERT H. NEWMAN
(Special to The Daily)

DYCHE STADIUM, Evanston, Ill., Nov. 25 —"Champions of the West!" Michigan's 1933 grid team clinched its claim to national honors as well as the Big Ten title here this afternoon as the powerful Wolverines outsmarted and outplayed the Northwestern Wildcats to win, 13 to 0. Two field goals and a touchdown with conversion accounted for the Michigan scores.

Wolverine Running Attack Is Featured In Season's Scoring

> **"** Play throughout was exceedingly bitter as the two elevens were keyed to the highest emotional pitch. Several fist fights broke out, both Petoskey and Ward coming close to personal combat with the Wildcats. **"**
>
> — Albert H. Newman, *The Michigan Daily*

MICHIGAN GETS NATIONAL TITLE

NOV. 28

Three Wolverines On All-Conference Team

Herman Everhardus, Chuck Bernard, and "Whitey" Wistert were named on the All-Conference football team released yesterday by the United Press. Ted Petoskey, the star Wolverine end, was named on the second team with Larson of Minnesota and Manske of Northwestern on the first team.

Michigan grid followers also hail the announcement of the Conference Championship on the basis of the Dickinson rating, which gives the championship to the Wolverines over Ohio State. Minnesota, four times tied, is rated third under the system.

Director of Athletics Fielding H. Yost and Harry G. Kipke, head of the University's football coaching staff, are shown above with the Knute K. Rockne National Intercollegiate Football Trophy which was presented to Michigan's championship football team last night for the second consecutive season.

1933	MICH	OPPONENT	
OCT. 7	20	6	Michigan State
OCT. 14	40	0	Cornell
OCT. 21	13	0	Ohio State
OCT. 28	28	0	Chicago
NOV. 4	7	6	Illinois
NOV. 11	10	6	Iowa
NOV. 18	0	0	Minnesota
NOV. 25	13	0	Northwestern

Campus Opinion

Willis Ward Summary . . .

It will be unfortunate if the Michigan coaching staff, as well as the coaching staffs of other northern universities, concludes that the manner to avoid situations of this type in the future is to refrain from coaching and playing promising Negro athletic material. That is certainly a possibility, and if it is one which the rabid pro-Ward group overlooked it is only another indication of the shortsightedness of that faction. But the easier and more decent way, both for the students who comprise the University and the people of the State who support that University, is not to schedule games with institutions below the Mason and Dixon line.

Michigan is democratic. Its history, its tradition, its honor is founded on a bed rock of education for all those who are capable of getting it, regardless of race, or color, or social and financial position. Those principles are incompatible with the South's position on racial differences. Let Michigan of the future play with those who are of her own eminently worthwhile type.

> **The Daily could have attempted a publication of news of what actually transpired even if it did not have the courage to condemn the treatment of Ward as a Negro rather than a Michigan Man.**
> — *Letter to The Michigan Daily*

> **That Georgia Tech game killed me. I frankly felt they would not let black athletes compete. Having gone through the Tech experience, it seemed an easy thing for them to say, 'Well, we just won't run 'em if Hitler insists.'**
> — Willis Ward, *Michigan right end*

OCT. 18

Secure 1,500 Signatures On Ward Petitions

United Front Committee Plans Mass Meeting For Tomorrow Night

Courtesy of Bentley Historical Library

Campus Opinion

Critique

To the Editor:

We charge that The Daily does not test ideas for merit. The source of the idea seems determinative of its reception, and the taboo of social discrimination as rigid as that of the caste system of India. Simply because a proposition springs from a group professedly radical is no reason to stigmatize it with the name "red," and avoid pressing it as deserving of the attention of intelligent people. Students are intelligent enough to figure out whether an idea is worthwhile regardless of who propounds it; and The Daily should be as intelligent in fighting for a principle regardless of its source. As Mr. Justice Holmes said: "But when men have realized that time has upset many fighting faiths, they come to believe even more than they believe the very foundation of their own conduct that the ultimate good desired is better reached by free trade of ideas — that the best test of truth is the power of the thought to get itself accepted in the competition of the market, and that truth is the only ground upon which their wishes safely can be carried out."

We hope for better things. We must content ourselves that the editor of The Daily cannot be both a Socrates and a Caliph of Bagdad, though he has cultivated an admirable country squire superciliousness. We want news on the news page and editorials on the editorial page. We do not want editorials in the news columns and doddering aphorisms and affectation in the editorial columns.

Cyril F. Hetsko, '36L.
Morris Weller, '35L.
Robert E. Acherburg, Jr., '35L.
Wm. Babcock, Jr., '35L.
A. D. Kennedy, Jr., '36L.

MICHIGAN FOOTBALL

OCT. 28 | MICHIGAN 6 / ILLINOIS 7

Illini Triumph Over Michigan

> " Metaphorically, Rome fell twice, once at Minneapolis and once at Columbus. It marks temporarily, at least, the end of a long tyranny over the Big Ten. "
>
> — Art Carstens,
> *The Michigan Daily*

NOV. 25 | MICHIGAN 6 / NORTHWESTERN 13

Michigan Concludes Its Most Disastrous Season With Seventh Loss, 13-6

Wolverines End In Cellar Position; Ward Makes Two Field Goals

Minnesota Wins Big Ten Championship

Northwestern Produces Powerful Running Attack In Second Half

By ARTHUR W. CARSTENS

Northwestern's Wildcats put an artistic finishing touch to Michigan's most disastrous football season here yesterday when they produced a powerful running attack in the second period to punch out a 13 to 6 victory after trailing, 3 to 0, at the half.

The defeat gave Michigan sole possession of the cellar position in the Big Ten. At the same time Minnesota was walloping Wisconsin, 34 to 0, to gain undisputed possession of first place when Indiana upset Purdue, 17 to 6.

Michigan took advantage of the breaks to keep Northwestern in its territory during the first half and to score three points on Willis Ward's place-kick from the 12-yard line.

Line Weakens Again

But in the second half Michigan's patched-up line weakened, especially after Jerry Ford had to leave the game, and the Wildcats marched 50 yards for their first touchdown and 35 for their second.

The same lack of scoring ability which marked Michigan's play all season was responsible for yesterday's defeat. Twice the Wolverines had the ball within Northwestern's five-yard line and couldn't carry it over, having to be content with two field goals kicked from placement by Ward.

Late in the second quarter, Michigan carried the ball deep into Wildcat territory but lost it when Ward's attempted place-kick from the 31 was wide. Wally Cruice fumbled on the next play, and Michigan again had the ball on Northwestern's 25. In four plays Chris Everhardus and Russ Oliver carried the ball to Northwestern's one-yard line. After two line plays lost three yards, Ward kicked his first field goal.

NOV. 27

★ STAR DUST ★ By Art Carstens

SOMEONE HAS SAID, facetiously, that Michigan lacked two things this Fall: an offense and a defense. That is undoubtedly true, but the defects can be narrowed down somewhat more than that.

It is a sport columnist's privilege to arrogate to himself all knowledge and pass that knowledge on as incontrovertable truth to his readers, but seldom does the columnist print what the man in the street thinks. Here are some opinions gathered hither and yon:

"The Alumni should yell about a losing team! It's all their fault! Kipke can't make a football team out of what he has on hand. He's got to have material to start with and it's up to the alumni to furnish it. With three good ball teams in the State we have to have players from outside if we want a championship team."

—An Alumnus

· · ·

"It's partly Kipke's fault. I can't say how much, but partly! He apparently assumed that he had a squad of veterans when practice started this fall, and started to give them plays right away, instead of working on fundamentals. No wonder that bunch of kids couldn't block and tackle all season and had to go back to drill on fundamentals before the last game of the season."

A Sideline Coach at Ferry Field

· · ·

"THE TEAM was too damn tame and well-mannered. I never saw a Michigan outfit with less spirit on or off the field. You can talk about your lily-white hard trainers, but give me boys like Pommerening and Allmendinger who trained on hard cider and straight liquor and some of last year's star who didn't turn down a drink or two in the middle of the week.

"The team has plenty of "do-or-die-for-Michigan" players but it hasn't a clown like John Kowalik who flipped wisecracks around the Michigan line like Beynon flips passes."

—A Student

· · ·

"Kipke gambled on Renner and lost. He put all his eggs in one basket in spring and early fall practice and Michigan learned to her sorrow that the punt and prayer are not enough when Renner cracked that bone in his ankle. I hate to see him come back next year for that reason."

—A Chicago Sport Writer

· · ·

"THE MICHIGAN system is fundamentally sound. The players Kipke has this year couldn't make any system look good. The modified punt formation from which Michigan plays are run is still one of the most deceptive in football, but, again, capable players are needed to make it effective."

—A Faculty Member Who Knows Football

· · ·

ON THE SIDELINES

Varsity Carries $810.15 Worth Of Equipment Into Each Game

By FRED DE LANO

According to Henry Hatch the 11 men that start for Michigan Saturday against Minnesota will be carrying, besides the good wishes of thousands of Wolverine grid fans, $810.15 worth of Michigan football equipment.

Henry Hatch, who for 15 years has taken care of the athletic equipment at the Field House is the man who outfits the squad with their uniforms, each of which is worth $73.65 at present prices. The shoes are the most expensive articles of a player's equipment, costing the Athletic Association $12.50 a pair.

The shoulder pads go for $12.00 and the helmets cost $10.50 apiece. Michigan's pants cost $9.50 a pair and the hip pads $9.00. Four dollars are paid out for each pair of knee pads and three more for each of the yellow and blue jerseys. Hose cost the department $1.25, undershirts, supporters, and ankle wraps fifty cents each with the sweat socks selling for forty cents.

Gerald Ford is one of the six Wolverine regulars who will end his football career this afternoon against Northwestern.

Playing his first season as a regular, Ford has started and played the greater part of each game, despite enough injuries to keep several less hardy men confined to bed. He suffered his most serious hurt, a bruised hip, in the Ohio State game last week, which forced him out of uniform earlier this week, but will start today.

Ford picked law over pigskin

By COURTNEY RATKOWIAK
Daily Sports Writer

Presidential aide Robert Hartmann once said that Gerald Ford was prouder of his athletic achievements than his political accomplishments. But 40 years before he became president, Ford turned down the opportunity for a professional football career in favor of law school.

After playing behind All-American center Chuck Bernard for his first two years, Ford became a starter for the Wolverines as a senior in 1934. Even though he was not selected as a captain — one of his primary athletic goals — Ford's teammates named him the Most Valuable Player of that 1-7 team.

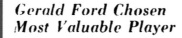
Gerald Ford Chosen Most Valuable Player

Ford Will Play With East In New Year's Tilt

Wolverine Center To Leave With 22 Man Squad On Dec. 19 For Coast

Gerald Ford, selected by his teammates as the most valuable man on Michigan's 1934 football team, has accepted an invitation to play with the eastern stars in the annual East-West charity game New Year's Day in San Francisco.

Ford, another of Michigan's mighty centers, received his offer from Dick Hanley Monday. Hanley and Andy Kerr, Northwestern and Colgate mentors, coach the eastern aggregation and each selects 11 players from his section of the country.

FORD

Three members of Minnesota's great team will play with the East. They are "Pug" Lund, All-American backfield star, Larson and Bengston, linemen. Veller, versatile Indiana quarterback, has also accepted Hanley's offer along with Monahan of Ohio State, Whalen of Northwestern and Purvis of Purdue.

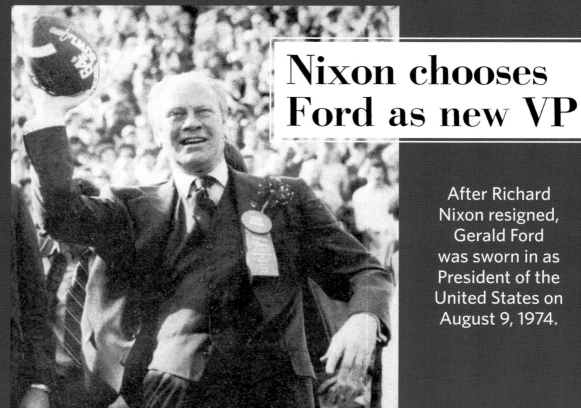
ALAN BILINSKY AND ANDY FREEBERG/Daily

Nixon chooses Ford as new VP

After Richard Nixon resigned, Gerald Ford was sworn in as President of the United States on August 9, 1974.

Frosh Football Star Whitewashed As Tulane Flaunts Athletic Probe With Bid For Harmon's Services

By IRVIN LISAGOR

(Copyright, 1937, By The Michigan Daily)

Openly flaunting investigations of Michigan's rumored subsidization of athletes, a representative of Tulane University has reiterated an "offer" made to Tom Harmon, brilliant freshman back enrolled here, according to a telegram released exclusively to The Michigan Daily last night.

The wire was signed by Bill Bevan, former All-American guard at Minnesota and present line coach at the southern school, and was evidently prompted by Michigan's athletic board's recent statement to the effect that certain freshman gridders were under suspicion of being subsidized by alumni groups.

Harmon, a graduate of the Horace Mann high school in Gary, Ind., was one of the freshmen which campus gossipers associated with the rumors. By virtue of his enviable record as a prep star, he was the recipient of bids from more than a score of universities located in every corner of the nation.

Labelling Michigan a "simon pure school," Bevan's wire suggested that Harmon may be completely exonerated of the charges leveled at him by covert whisperers. The Gary youth has been vehement in his denials of aid, pecuniary or otherwise, since the rumors received official cognizance by the athletic board Nov. 10. He admitted being encouraged to enter Michigan by his high school coach, Douglas Kerr, a former Wolverine athlete, and alumni in Gary whose only overtures consisted of a lecture on the educational advantages of the local institution.

Supporting Harmon, the Michigan alumni of Gary forwarded a prepared statement to the University's athletic board, which stated, as evidence, that they merely influenced the youth's action by extolling the school's virtues. Moreover, they asserted that his means were derived wholly from his parents.

In November 1937, the University conducted an athletic probe after it was reported that some of the football team's freshmen were receiving illegal athletic subsidies from alumni groups. The negative publicity ultimately played a role in the firing of Harry Kipke and it affected the status of freshman halfback Tom Harmon.

> **All of this placed Michigan football under a shroud of adverse speculation. And the boys themselves began to feel the effect, the 'sport,' at which they were supposed to have fun, they found conditions almost unbearable. The tension and general atmosphere was morgue-like. And naturally, they, too, began to feel doubts about the coaching.**
>
> — Irvin Lisagor, *The Michigan Daily*

Kipke 'Surprised' At His Ousting

Former Coach Says He Had No Chance To Present Own Side Of Story

Choice Of Leader To Depend On Yost

By IRVIN LISAGOR

Harry G. Kipke, whose dismissal as head football coach was announced yesterday afternoon, expressed complete surprise last night of the athletic board's action.

Contacted on the telephone by the Daily, the ousted mentor said, "The first I found out about it was when an Ann Arbor newspaperman phoned me this morning. Then I was called in at noon and notified."

Kipke added that he was bitter toward no one, although he remarked, "I think the Board should have given me a chance to present my side of the case."

It was reliably learned last night that the Wolverine coach appeared before a Board committee on Tuesday and was aware at that time of the action the Board might take. The same sources revealed he had "ample opportunity" to confer with Athletic Director Fielding H. Yost on Wednesday.

The decision to oust Kipke was made by a unanimous vote of the Board in Control at an adjourned meeting yesterday. The announcement said Kipke's contract would officialy terminate in June, 1938.

The Board also empowered its officers to interview possible successors to Kipke, coach here since 1929.

No action will be taken in regard to assistant coaches until a new coach has been appointed, the Board said.

The Board's action followed on the heels of a recent storm of publicity which surrounded the local athletic situation with charges and counter-charges of subsidization and coaching dissension.

CRISLER: CAREER OF CONQUERING

1938-1947

PRESS PASSES . . . . . THE BEST ELEVEN

. . . . By Bud Benjamin

THE MIST was settling on Ferry Field. A dark and dreary day was nearly at an end. Fritz Crisler, his deeply tanned face enveloped in thought, was slowly trudging off the gridiron surrounded by a corps of muddy, somewhat bloody, and definitely exhausted football players. Suddenly he stopped, approached the press mob, and said:

"Don't mention such and such a play until after the first game, eh boys."

The group nodded. Journalistic confidences are not uncommon at the outset of the season. And they're usually respected.

"Well what's new, Fritz?" ventured United Press Correspondent Pat Conger. "Invented any ends yet?"

Crisler smiled. "No inventing," he returned. "Give 'em all a chance you know. Shift 'em around, mix 'em up, and then put them back to-gether again and see how they look. Why? Simply because we're after the eleven best men no matter what position they play."

Yes, boys and girls, there's a lot new. Crisler has shown reticence in talking about it—the old press sessions have lost much of their former zest—and the players don't gab about it too freely. They're all playing a waiting game, waiting for the day when everyone can see what's new and different in the 1938 edition.

You'll find an attitude that's brand new. It's the kind of an attitude that can keep 50 odd men going six hours a day, seven days a week on a strict and rigorous football diet. It's the kind of an attitude that makes men talk, fight, and encourage with an ebullient enthusiasm so absent in former years.

You'll find a big, rugged team with plenty of new faces. It's a team that will be trained to a razor edged fineness after the most intense training season in many years. You will find backs that can move, linemen that can charge blockers that can clear a path. It's that or a seat on the 50 yard line for the candidates this season.

Over all hovers the shadow of Crisler. Apparently detached and disinterested, his keen eyes see all. He shouts a word to one of Munn's charges; walks over and assists Martineau; chastises a Dickson student. He presides over 50 with the effortless efficiency that he would instruct one. The boys know who's boss this year on Ferry Field.

Yes, the authority is new, the spirit is new, and some of the material is encouragingly new. And the outlook? Yes, if we must, "whither O whither Michigan?"

The clarion call resounds from every nook and corner of the campus. Football fever has hit sleepy old Ann Arbor, and the chant of the fanfare can again be heard.

CAPT. FRED JANKE   COACH FRITZ CRISLER

Crisler Selected for 1947 'Coach of the Year' Award

Herbert Orrin "Fritz" Crisler, suave master strategist of last years unbeaten untied Michigan football team, ended his coaching career in a blaze of glory as he received the Coach of the Year award for 1947.

The grey-thatched ex-coach, who piloted the Wolverines most point hungry grid machine since 1905, thus became the 13th winner of the New York World Telegram's annual Coach-of-the-Year, succeeding Earl "Red" Blaik as the top man in football.

> 66 **Crisler noted that the Stadium's seating capacity has been swelled to 101,001 because of the elevated structure of the box. 'And only one person knows where that one extra seat is,' said the beaming Crisler. 'That's me.'** 99
> — Steve Heilpern, *The Michigan Daily*

COACH OF A DECADE:

Crisler Establishes Impressive Record During Ten Coaching Years at Michigan

By POTSY RYAN

"Coach of the Year" Fritz Crisler, the man who makes the Wolverines growl, might easily be nominated for the honor of "coach of the decade" if the sportswriters had gone a little deeper into Crisler's history at Michigan.

For ten years, Crisler has been pulling the strings here in Ann Arbor, and over the span of those same ten years, he has compiled a record that is an awesome thing to behold.

Eighty-nine times he has sent the Wolverines to the post, and on seventy of those occasions he has welcomed them back into the winner's circle. Only sixteen opponents have been able to humble the Maize and Blue, while three enemies have escaped with ties.

Points have rolled out of the Michigan machine like autos roll off an assembly line. The lights on the scoreboard have flashed to the tune of 2200 markers during the past half score years, and in cold hard figures, that means that the Wolverines have averaged four touchdowns every time they have taken the field.

Crisler's teams have shown no partiality. It has been, "Come one, come all—and take your chances with the rest of them." From Columbus to New York, from Iowa City to New Haven, from Berkeley to Cambridge, the Michigan maulers have cruised. Only way down below the Mason-Dixon line have they escaped the claws of the Wolverines—and the schedule makers from the cotton-country don't appear overly anxious to tangle with the damnyankees from Ann Arbor.

CRISLER RETIRES AS COACH

THOMAS R. COPT/Daily

Happy Players Toss Crisler Into Shower

A delirious Rose Bowl-bound Michigan football squad tossed happy "Fritz" Crisler into the showers yesterday after crushing a hapless Buckeye eleven in a colorful climax to the 1947 gridiron season.

The dripping coach climbed laughingly out of his impromptu dunking, as thoroughly satisfied with his pigskin juggernaut as were the 86,000 fans who had braved the elements to view the final Ann Arbor appearance of the team.

RETIRING MICHIGAN ATHLETIC Director Fritz Crisler surveys an empty football stadium, that was twice expanded during his tenure to its present size of 101,001. Appointed Michigan head coach in the spring of 1938, Crisler coached the Wolverines for 10 seasons, his teams recording the exemplary record of 71 wins, 16 losses, and three ties.

| OCT. 2 | MICHIGAN | 14 |
| | MICHIGAN STATE | 0 |

Kromer Leads Wolverines To 14-0 Victory Over Spartans

Michigan coach Fritz Crisler introduced the winged helmet in his first year at the helm of the Wolverines.

Courtesy of Bentley Historical Library

Sophomore Star

Paul Kromer, sophomore halfback, yesterday scored 13 of Michigan's 14 points by ringing up two touchdowns and an extra point when he crossed State's goal line after recovering a blocked attempt for the point after touchdown. Kromer will receive the season pass offered by the Michigan theatre to any player scoring on State.

| NOV. 20 | No. 17 MICHIGAN | 18 |
| | OHIO STATE | 0 |

Wolverines End Four-Year Jinx By 18 To 0 Win Over Ohio

Wolverine Eleven Thwarts Ohio State's 'Five-Year-Plan'

SHEELINE/Daily

It was Michigan's sophomore "touchdown twins," Tom Harmon and Paul Kromer, who "stole the show."

Playing well over 100 minutes of yesterday's rout of the "Scarlet Scourge," these speed-merchants, the sensations of this year's Conference tussle, had the Buckeyes' ponderous forward wall talking to itself before the final gun signalled the fall of the Ohio goal posts.

It was especially Kromer, pictured here tossing a forward pass in the second quarter, who monopolized the spotlight. Running, kicking, passing, blocking, Paul played his finest game of the year. Esko Sarkkinen, fleet Ohio end, who was the best man on the field for Ohio, is shown rushing Kromer.

Chicago Maroons Are Smashed 85-0 By Michigan's Steamroller Before Meager Crowd Of 4,800

Educated Toe Boots Four Goals

WILLIAM MELZOW

Chicago Team Held To Center Of Field For Full Four Quarters; Wolverine Second And Third Teams Are Used

By MEL FINEBERG

CHICAGO, Oct. 21.—There was another Chicago massacre at historic Stagg Field yesterday afternoon while 4,800 fans watched, but there was no one to blame for it except the schedule makers and those who insist that a Simon Pure educational university can play big time football.

The game, which by the way was won by Michigan, 85 to 0, was more like the band drill. The first team, the second, the third, and part of the fourth marched up the field and down again and nothing stopped them but the goal line.

Every time, with the exception of three, that the Wolverines gained possession of the ball they scored. Twice they quick-kicked on the first down, and the other time they lost the ball on downs.

The parade started within two minutes after the game began, when Fullback Bob Zimmerman counted, and by the time the half rolled around, halfback Herc Renda, end Ed Czak, halfback Tom Harmon, quarterback Forest Evashevski, halfback Fred Trosko, fullback Bob Westfall, and halfback Dave Strong had tallied to bring the score to 55-0.

The third quarter was comparatively dull with the Wolverines tallying but one. However, the first team returned for six minutes in the final chapter and found time enough for Harmon to score one touchdown and kick a field goal, and to have Westfall burst through center for 23 yards and a score.

Called It A Day

Then Crisler called it a day for the first stringers and sent them to the showers. But the Wolverines kept plugging and added another touchdown before the game ended. The comptometers showed Michigan with 12 touchdowns, 10 conversions and one field goal. Shades of the point-a-minute teams.

The Maroons never had a chance. They were both hapless and hopeless. The closest they ever got to the Wolverine goal line was the 30-yard line in the second quarter where the Wolverines took the ball on downs.

Crisler started his second team but that didn't delay the massacre a bit. Bill Melzow, guard, kicked off to Miller on the Chicago 20-yard line, and end Harlin Fraumann pulled him down on the 25. Co-captain Johnny Davenport's third down kick was blocked by tackles Bill Smith and Bob Ostroot, the other Wolverine tackler recovered on the five yard line. Zimmerman ripped off left guard on the first play for a touchdown, and Melzow converted the kick for the extra point.

ON THE SIDELINES

Subs Go To Showers; Cheer-Leaders Remain

As the end of the game neared, Fritz Crisler sent his men directly to the showers as they came off the field.

"What will he do if someone is injured?" someone inquired.

A Michigan supporter, face lined with disgust, explained, "That's why he didn't send the cheer-leaders to the showers, dope."

> **Sure we're outclassed. But so what. The Chicago players like to play football. What does it matter if they miss a tackle or have a pass intercepted. Some people think losing a football game is a national disaster. We don't. We play for the fun of it.**
>
> — Clark Shaughnessy, *Chicago football coach*

DEC. 8, 1941

WAR! JAP ATTACKS TAKE 'HEAVY' U.S. TOLL

AUG. 14, 1945

EXTRA **The Michigan Daily** EXTRA

ANN ARBOR, MICHIGAN, TUESDAY, AUGUST 14, 1945

PEACE!
TOKYO ACCEPTS TERMS

Long-Awaited News Finally Here; Nips' Reply Follows Three Days Of Stalling; Nation Hears Truman

WASHINGTON, Aug. 14-AP—President Truman announced at 7:00 p. m. tonight Japanese acceptance of the Potsdam declaration which specifies the unconditional surrender of Japan.

They will be accepted by General Douglas MacArthur when arrangements can be completed.

Mr. Truman read the formal message relayed from Emperor Hirohito through the Swiss government in reply to the message forwarded to that government by the Secretary of State on August 11.

"I deem this reply a full acceptance of the Potsdam declaration which specifies the unconditional surrender of Japan.

In this reply there is no qualification.

"Arrangements are now being made for the formal signing of surrender terms by Japan."

"General Douglas MacArthur has been appointed the supreme Allied commander to receive the Japanese surrender.

"Great Britain, Russia and China will be represented by high ranking officers.

"Meantime, the Allied armed forces have been ordered to suspend offensive action.

"The proclamation of V-J Day must wait upon the formal signing of the surrender terms by Japan."

Events Preceding News

"U" To Suspend All Activities Tomorrow

ATOM RESEARCH CENTER TO BE 'U' WAR MEMORIAL

Phoenix Plan To Benefit Man
Huge Program Will Probe Peaceful Application of Atom

MAY 17, 1948

MARCH 21, 1948

Wolverines Capture National Hockey Title

AUG. 25, 1944

Michigan Takes Eight Of Nine Big Ten Crowns

Won Big Ten championships in all sports except basketball and hockey. No Big Ten competition in hockey.

DEC. 1, 1948

From the GRANTSTAND
By MURRAY GRANT ... *Daily Sports Editor*

WITH EVERY KIND of "All" team except an "All-Lefthanded Grandfathers" coming out at about this time it was with a great deal of satisfaction that we noticed a progressive step being taken.

The International News Service (INS) has done something that should have started long ago. They've named not one team, but two elevens having equal strength. This may sound like merely a continuation of the long list of All-Anythings—but it isn't.

The INS has taken cognizance of the two-team system, started here at Michigan and now spreading throughout the country. They've come up with both a DEFENSIVE All-American as well as an OFFENSIVE team. And it's about time.

The game of football is no longer the sixty-minute, do-or-drop struggle of the '20's and '30's. Like everything else it has become a specialized field where certain men are delegated certain tasks and they work at those tasks until they become highly proficient.

It all started with the place-kicking specialist. A few years back one man would trot on the field after every touchdown and calmly boot the hapless pigskin squarely between the goal posts. Then the pro outfits began to go to work on this specialization business. And it paid off. The Chicago Bears, one of the first to use specialists, were invincible for a while until the other teams began to catch on.

DICK RIFENBURG
• • •

THIS "NEW ERA" came to college football in a grand manner with the Michigan "two-team system" devised by Fritz Crisler. It was carried on by freshman mentor Bennie Oosterbaan this year and it spread to such schools as Army with "Red" Blaik's two-platoons.

Other top teams have developed variations on this theme by Crisler and instead of "eleven iron men" of yore we now have 15 or 18 or even 22 men who have special tasks and who make the football field often like a shuttle bus system.

OCT. 27 | No. 3 MICHIGAN 14 | No. 8 PENNSYLVANIA 0

Wolverines Humble Pennsylvania, 14-0 As Harmon And Westfall Lead Offensive

WILL SAPP/Daily

The highly-touted Francis Reagan was caught just over the line of scrimmage by Center Bob Ingalls. The dancing Wolverine to the left (63) is Guard Ralph Fritz.

Double Attack Slices Quaker Line Defense

By DON WIRTCHAFTER

Michigan poured its mighty gridiron potion over a challenging Pennsylvania menace in the Stadium yesterday and smashed all doubts of its greatness before 59,913 howling spectators.

Capitalizing on an early break and applying the wizardy of all-American Tommy Harmon thereafter, the undefeated Wolverines staggered George Munger's pride of the East with a thundering 14-0 triumph.

It was Michigan's double-barreled attack that knocked Penn's vaunted forward wall into a state of dizziness yesterday. When Harmon wasn't slicing off tackle or skirting the ends, fullback Bob Westfall was bolting through the center. If one didn't gain yardage, the other did.

All told, Tornado Tom streaked 19 yards for Michigan's first score, rifled a brilliant pass to Ed Frutig in the end zone for the second, and successfully converted on both occasions to add eight more points to his season's total which now has swelled to 87.

A Band Of Battering Rams

With Michigan's powerful front line, from end to end, charging like a band of battering rams, Harmon's publicized duel with Francis Reagan never materialized. Terrible Tom completely stole the spotlight from Penn's heralded ace.

He out-ran, out-passed, out-punted and out-classed Reagan from beginning to end. Carrying the ball 28 times, Harmon rolled 142 yards from scrimmage, while the Quaker halfback gained but 10 yards in 12 attempts.

NOV. 17 | No. 6 MICHIGAN 20 | No. 10 NORTHWESTERN 13

76,749 Fans See Inspired Squad Make Comeback

Michigan Staves Off Northwestern Drive In Closing Minutes As Westfall Halts Hahnenstein At Line On Crucial Plays Harmon Scores Thirtieth Touchdown

Hell hath no fury like a Michigan football team on the comeback trail.

Building up a two touchdown lead in the first half, the whirling Wolverines staved off a determined Northwestern drive in the dying minutes of yesterday's Stadium battle to score their sixth triumph of the year by a 20-13 score. The season's record crowd, 76,749 shivering spectators, saw a weary but gallant Michigan team halt the Wildcats' desperate final 72-yard march on the six yard line.

It was the bulleting bomber, fullback Bob Westfall, who charged in from his position in the Wolverine secondary to ground Ollie Hahnenstein's fourth down smash on the scrimmage line when only a yard of the brisk Stadium turf was needed to give Northwestern a first down deep in the shadows of the Michigan goal.

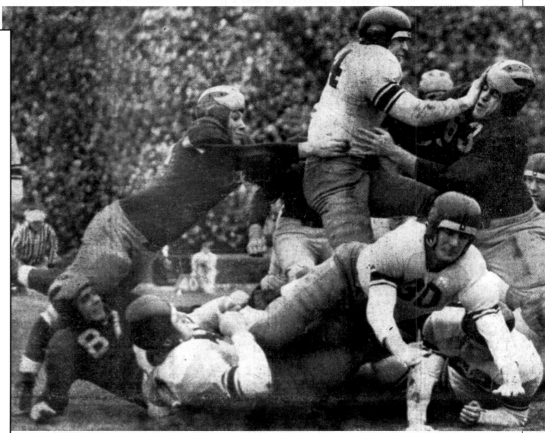

Wolverine guard Fritz tames Wildcat Chambers . . . but he's still playful.

1940

Coast Experts Rate Harmon Finest Player Seen In West

Hard Blocking Wolverines Vanquish Golden Bears In Season's First Game; Sub Backs Promising

Game With Spartans To Provide Real Test

(Special To The Daily)

By DON WIRTCHAFTER

ENROUTE TO ANN ARBOR, Sept. 30.—The Golden West will never forget Michigan's sensational Tom Harmon.

Newspaper reporters, grid experts, coaches and the like from one end of the Pacific Coast to the other came to an agreement after Tommy's amazing birthday party in Berkeley last Saturday that California has never seen a more brilliant football player.

From the opening kickoff, when Harmon tucked the ball under his arm and carried it 94 yards for a touchdown until 42,000 disappointed but thrilled rooters rose to their feet to pay tribute to the mighty Wolverine as he left the game, it was the most phenomenal and history-making party since a group of Bostonians dumped some tea into the Atlantic Ocean.

WILL SAPP/Daily

Tom Harmon Drives Viciously Behind Scythe-Like Interference
Dave Nelson, (23) and Guard Ralph Fritz, (63) lead the way for charging Tom Harmon (98) as he cuts across midfield for a sizeable gain in the second quarter of yesterday's game.

Powerful Wolverines Wallop Ohio State, 40-0, Climaxing Great Season With Scoring Rampage As Tom Harmon Shatters Red Grange's Record

By DON WIRTCHAFTER
(Special To The Daily)

COLUMBUS, OHIO, Nov. 23.—Michigan's thundering football forces roared all over the Ohio Stadium today before winding up one of the greatest years in Wolverine gridiron history.

With brilliant Tom Harmon leading the way, Michigan battered a completely demoralized Buckeye squad, 40-0, to carry off its seventh triumph of the campaign.

In his final collegiate appearance, the Hoosier Hurricane treated a sellout crowd of 73,648 spectators to a dazzling display of football, if there ever was one.

All in all, he drove over the Ohio goal three times to smash Red Grange's former Western Conference three-year touchdown record of 31, passed to teammates for two of the other Wolverine tallies, place-kicked four points after touchdowns, and maintained a punting average of 50 yards per kick.

Talented in three departments is sophomore Tom Harmon, the publicized halfback candidate, who hails from Gary, Ind. He'll be used chiefly in a running and blocking capacity. (Sept. 20, 1938)

FILE PHOTO/Daily

Harmon put on a tremendous display in his final game of the 1940 campaign. He threw two touchdown passes, rushed for three touchdowns, kicked four extra points, intercepted three passes and punted three times for an average of 50 yards. At the end of the game, the Ohio State faithful gave him a standing ovation.

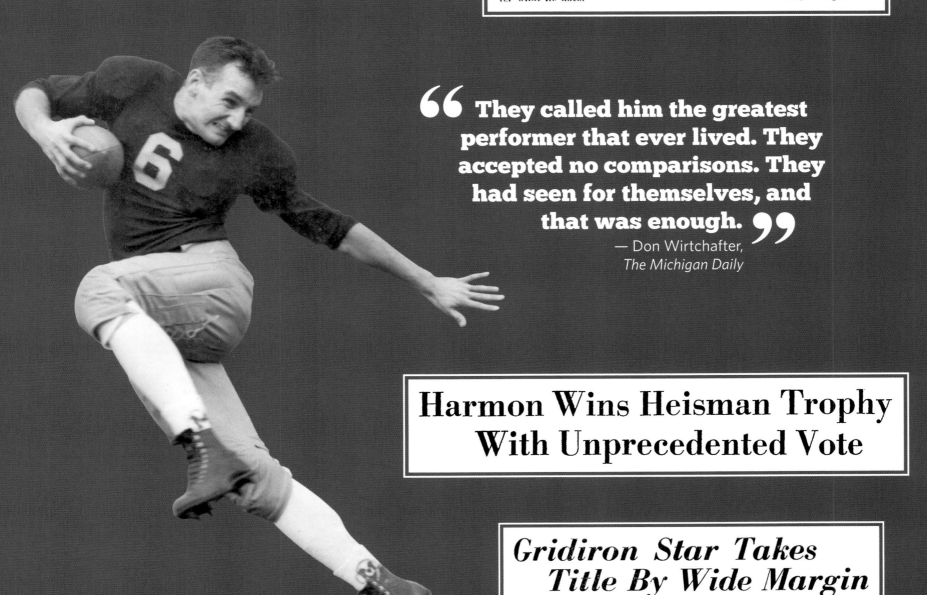

Harmon Scores All Wolverine Points In 21-14 Victory

Harmon Repeats On Associated Press All-America Team

Harmon Finds No Private Life As An All-American Halfback

By WOODY BLOCK

"Glory—but no peace."

That's the life of Michigan's All-American, Tom Harmon. No one in these parts has ever tucked a football under his arm, set two muscular legs in motion and scampered off with the headlines as Coach Crisler's durable halfback.

Ever since the season opened, and even before that, the name of Harmon was flashed from coast to coast. And now that the popular Wolverine has worn a path down the middle of every turf he's stepped on, that name and his number '98' is news no matter what he does.

Fans Love Winner

"I guess they make all this fuss because everybody loves a winner," Tom explained. "Fans have been sending me from 10 to 15 letters every day requesting pictures, and autographs, and right now I'm about 100 behind."

"The prize of the whole bunch came the other day," Harmon went on. "It was from some agent who was ready to guarantee me $75,000 in my first three years under his management."

Besides the fan mail he gets, which is probably the least troublesome of his requests, Tom has to pose for newspaper photographers and newsreel men from morning to night.

> **"They called him the greatest performer that ever lived. They accepted no comparisons. They had seen for themselves, and that was enough."**
>
> — Don Wirtchafter,
> *The Michigan Daily*

Harmon Wins Heisman Trophy With Unprecedented Vote

Gridiron Star Takes Title By Wide Margin

Courtesy of Bentley Historical Library

Wolverines Gridders Cop First Conference Title Since 1933

1943

Bucks Fall Before Fast Ground Attack

By ED ZALENSKI

Coach Fritz Crisler's tenth edition of the Michigan grid machine ended a 10-year title drought yesterday afternoon with a pulverizing 45-7 triumph over Ohio State, tying Purdue for the 1943 Conference championship.

It was the eighth victory in nine games for the Wolverines and the second largest point total in the series with the Buckeyes since 1897. The Crisler machine completely routed the hapless Buckeye civilian eleven by piling up 426 yards and 23 first downs to 68 yards and two first downs for the losers.

Wiese Scores Twice

In writing a grand finals to the 1943 season the Maize and Blue gridders were sparked by hard-driving Bob Wiese, pony back Wally Dreyer, stocky Earl Maves and reserve back Don Lund.

Wiese whose spinner plays bewildered the Buckeye line constantly, led the seven-touchdown parade by scoring twice on short plunges.

TAKING IT EASY
By ED ZALENSKI
Daily Sports Editor

NO ONE WAS SURPRISED yesterday when the Wolverine gridders dedicated their 45-7 victory over Ohio State to their coach, Fritz Crisler during the post-game celebration in the locker room. It was his first title in 10 years at Ann Arbor even though he did have to share it with Purdue. The human interest angle was tossed in about 10 minutes after the final gun.

Shortly after the game ended the Wolverine gridders raised Crisler, Backfield Coach Earl Martineau and Line Coach Biggie Munn on their shoulders and marched off the field to climax their most successful season since 1933. But where was the fourth coach, Bennie Oosterbaan, who had worked with the ends all these years?

High above the battle-scarred field in the Michigan press box sat a happy man with a pair of binoculars. It was Bennie taking a last look at the boys. He had missed the triumphal parade off the field. We mentioned to Bennie that it was too bad he couldn't share this victory feeling with the boys. Bennie swallowed. "Yes," he said, "it is too bad." It was obvious that Bennie would have enjoyed sharing the triumph with Crisler, Marty and Biggie.

About 10 minutes later a dozen Wolverines dashed across the field from the dressing room, some minus blue jerseys and shoulder pads flapping. They clambered up the steep stands into the press box. They grabbed the surprised but happy Bennie, raised him to their shoulders and bore him back to the dressing room—an added climax to their first triumphant exit . . .

NOV. 18

Will Lead Wolverines Against Buckeyes

BOB WIESE

. . . named acting captain for Saturday's game. Wiese, now playing fullback after starting the season at quarter, ranks third among Michigan ground gainers with a total of 203 yards on 47 attempts.

Wiese, Lund Set Pace As OSU Line Crumbles

Michigan Routs OSU But Misses Crown

Wolverines Miss Title Train To Wind Up Second

Runnerup Jinx Plagues Crisler 3rd Year In Row

MAN OF THE HOUR—Michigan's record busting Bob Chappuis who had an aerial field day against Ohio State yesterday to smash two Big Nine passing marks.

Chappuis Tosses Three Touchdowns, Scores One, Breaks Two Records

By CLARK BAKER
Special To The Daily

COLUMBUS, Ohio, Nov. 23 — Rolling up eight touchdowns and a field goal, Michigan's revived Wolverines wound up their 1946 season with a bang by completely outclassing Ohio State, 58-6, before 78,634 stunned fans here this afternoon.

But the Wolverines' huge final explosion wasn't enough to rocket them into the Western Conference championship as Illinois, needing only a win over Northwestern today to take the crown, did just that by grinding out a 20-0 triumph over the Wildcats. Michigan's win gave it undisputed second place to the Illini.

The Maize and Blue just could not do anything wrong this afternoon. Their corps of fast-charging linemen ripped wide holes in the Buckeye line while checking the Ohioans on the ground with a net rushing yardage of 77 yards. And the Michigan backfield, operating with beautiful deception, opened the air lanes with a spectacular exhibition of passing.

The Wolverines just could not be denied. Their 16 completed passes in 29 attempts amassed 300 yards while the ground attack, playing second fiddle today, ground out another 209 yards.

If there was any individual hero it was Bob Chappuis. Needing only 95 yards to surpass Otto Graham's Big Nine total offense mark, the Wolverine tailback polished off that mark in the first period and spent the rest of the game raising the new record a little higher.

NOV. 26

CLIMBING UP:
Michigan Takes Sixth Rung On Nation's Football Ladder

ON THE SIDELINES

OCT. 1, 1946

'Tie-In Sales' At Game Protested

Student's Letter ...

To the Editor:

The first game of the Michigan schedule has been played, and the upperclassmen are still not sitting in the choice seats. But strangely enough, this is not the subject of my Letter-To-the-Editor.

During the intense heat of the football game, many of the fans wanted to enjoy a "coke" or some other non-intoxicating beverage. But most of us learned that if we wanted "pop" it was also necessary for us to purchase a very unappetizing looking frankfurter at the exhorbitant rate of fifteen cents. Another favorite racket of the shyster concessionaires working at the University, of Michigan Stadium was to sell the unsuspecting student a warm soda, and a minute later charge him or her ten cents for ice to cool the soda.

What is this University coming to when it allows such illegal practices to take place on their premises? Not only is it illegal from the professional standpoint, but look at it from the moral point of view. If we students are to go out into the world and benefit society, then we here at this institution of higher education would surely learn better business practices than those used by the petty crooks operating in our football stadium.

There is a great possibility that the University officials have no inkling of these practices, as this was the first game of the season. But, if these unscrupulous acts are tried again, then I urge the University officials, to throw (bodily or otherwise) the owners and workers of these concessions off of the university grounds, and at the same time bring suit against them for this "tie-in" sale racket they are perpetuating on our campus.

Preston R. Tisch

SEPT. 28

Spartans Prove Easy Meat For Hungry Wolverines

1947	MICHIGAN		OPPONENT
SEPT. 27	55	0	Michigan State
OCT. 4	49	13	Stanford
OCT. 11	69 (No. 2)	0	Pittsburgh
OCT. 18	49 (No. 1)	21	Northwestern
OCT. 25	13 (No. 1)	6	Minnesota
NOV. 1	14 (No. 2)	7	No. 11 Illinois
NOV. 8	35 (No. 2)	0	Indiana
NOV. 15	40 (No. 2)	6	Wisconsin
NOV. 22	21 (No. 1)	0	Ohio State
JAN. 1	49 (No. 2)	0	No. 8 U.S.C. (Rose Bowl)

ON THE SIDELINES

Michigan Band Stages New Stunts in Bowl

'Crisler Coached' Says Sports Writer

Michigan's colorful marching band, composed of 128 precision drilled members, staged a brilliant array of high stepping antics during the pre-game and halftime ceremonies that never before have been seen in either the Rose Bowl or Michigan Stadiums.

One sportswriter remarked that "The band's maneuvers are so well executed, it looks like they were drilled by Coach Crisler." This is fine tribute to Conductor William D. Revelli, who rejuvenated the marching style with some high-kicking, about-face swivel steps that made the fans sit up and take notice.

Led by flashy drum major, Noah Knepper, the Wolverine music makers struck up several varsity songs before the initial period of play. During halftime ceremonies, they saluted SC with 'Hi Neighbor' and then quickly started forming the different seasons of the year.

First of the drills was a tribute to March as a large shamrock was formed with all the members dancing a jib. Next stunt changed the formation into an umbrella for April showers, then into a bell signifying June weddings.

An exploding firecracker was followed by a large fish while the band played "Three Little Fishes" as its concluding number.

> **" Michigan probably had the greatest aggregation of football players ever assembled on one college campus. "**
>
> — Dick Anderson, *Evansville Ind. Press* writer quoted in *The Michigan Daily*

OCT. 5

Michigan Blitzkrieg Routs Stanford, 49-13

Bob Chappuis tossed three touchdown passes and picked up 77 yards on the ground to run his total offensive record to 1,088 yards in eight games. (Nov. 16)

Michigan Whips Wisconsin, 40-6, To Grab Crown

Chappuis, Derricotte, Yerges Pace Wolverine Attack on Sloppy Field

By BOB LENT
(Special to The Daily)

MADISON, Wis., Nov. 15—Billed as the 1947 Big Nine "dream game," the Michigan-Wisconsin grid battle in Camp Randall Stadium today turned into a Badger nightmare as the Wolverines romped to a 40-6 triumph for their first undisputed Conference title since 1933, thus gaining a date in the Rose Bowl New Year's Day.

Playing their best game of the year before a sellout throng of 45,000, the Maize and Blue lived up to all advance notices of being a great ball club. Their highly touted backfield was all it was supposed to be and more, and their line held the hitherto explosive Wisconsin offensive to a pitiful six first downs.

Chappuis Shows Mettle

Bob Chappuis added to his All-American stature by piling up a 156-yard offensive total, while Bump Elliott was close behind with 141 yards. Jack Weisenburger added 81 yards to his Conference rushing leadership.

'ALL BY MYSELF' . . . No one was near Howie Yerges as he drifted out into the flat from his quarter-back position to snag this Chappuis pass then raced to the one foot line before being tackled by a Trojan line backer.

'M' MAGICIANS AMAZE USC

JAN. 6

> **They were just plain Michigan at 2 p.m. on New Years Day ... but a scant two hours and 49 points later the Maize and Blue had become the 'Mad Magicians of Michigan.'**
>
> — Dick Kraus, *The Michigan Daily*

JAN. 6

Michigan Victory Brings Irish Fans To Crisler 'Fold'

California's Sports Writers Praise Maize and Blue; Scorn Southern Cal

By DICK KRAUS
Daily Sports Editor

They were just plain Michigan at 2 p.m. on New Years Day, a fast tricky outfit that looked like a two touchdown winner over Southern California, but a scant two hours and 49 points later the Maize and Blue had become the "Mad Magicians of Michigan," the Merlins of Michigan," and "maybe the greatest team ever to appear in the Rose Bowl."

From coast to coast dyed in the wool Notre Dame supporters, like Gene Kessler of the Chicago Sun and Times, were hopping off the Irish onto the Michigan band wagon.

The once highly partisan California observers were equally loud in praise of Michigan and condemnation of Southern California and the brand of football played on the coast.

Duplicate 1902 Score

The dpulication of Michigan's 1902 Rose Bowl feat, a 49-0 victory, was the worst beating ever absorbed by a Trojan eleven in 60 years of football. Still worse the sentimental attachment Michigan has for the 49-0 count made it look like the Wolverines could call their shots, and they very nearly could.

Whether the Wolverines played their best game of the year or not is an argument with as little chance for a solution as the "who's better Michigan or Notre Dame" squabble, but best or not the Maize and Blue were a great football team.

Michigan Tops Irish in Free Press Sports Poll

In a private poll conducted by Lyell Smith, Sports Editor of the Detroit Free Press 72% of the nation's top sports editors and experts selected Michigan over Notre Dame as the country's top gridiron powerhouse.

In an attempt to settle one of the most-heated arguments in modern football history the Free Press sent ballots to experts in every one of the 48 states and the District of Columbia with the exception of Michigan.

The home state editors were not included in order to insure impartiality.

The results of a similar poll conducted by the Associated Press will be revealed tomorrow.

Typical comments supporting Michigan's claim to superiority over the Irish follow:

R. G. LYNCH, MILWAUKEE JOURNAL—"I saw Michigan play Minnesota and Illinois and also saw Notre Dame defeat Army. If Michigan played Notre Dame I would take the Wolverines. I have never seen a better all-around attack except among the pros."

RAYMOND JOHNSON, NASHVILLEE TENNESSEEAN—"Michigan with plenty to spare."

BUS HAM, WASHINGTON (D.C.) POST—"Michigan for me. All season we rate teams on comparative scores. Michigan-USC and Notre Dame-USC provided a direct comparison."

Captain Plays Excellent Game

OCT. 15, 1927

Capt. Benny Oosterbaan

Whose stellar work at the end of the Michigan line was one of the features of yesterday's game with the Badgers. Time after time the fleet Wisconsin backs were stopped at his end and his playing on offense constituted a constant threat that Michigan would unleash a passing attack.

To Remain at 'U'; Oosterbaan Gets Head Grid Duties

AUG. 15, 1948

NEW HEAD FOOTBALL COACH—Filling an awfully big pair of shoes will be the job of Michigan's new head football coach, Bennie Oosterbaan. A former Wolverine All-American end, Oosterbaan served as end coach for many years under the man he succeeded, 'Fritz' Crisler. Last year he very ably directed the Michigan backfield and upon Crisler's retirement at the beginning of this year, he became head coach. Previously he also served as Wolverine basketball coach, retiring from that Ozzie to make way to Cowles.

FRITZ CRISLER and BENNIE OOSTERBAAN
". . . the best assistant I've ever had"

ASSOCIATED PRESS

66 **Michigan needs the coach that Oosterbaan is. It needs a man with a philosophy of football which can allow him to adapt to the pressures put on him by the academic side of the University and still produce a winning football team.** 99

— Jim Baad, *The Michigan Daily*

Coach Bennie Oosterbaan Finishes His First Season Unbeaten, Untied

A Philosophy

(EDITOR'S NOTE: The following excerpts are reprinted from the final column written by Jim Baad, last year's Daily Sports Editor, now a freshman in Dental School.)

By JIM BAAD

I HAVE BEEN down to talk with Bennie Oosterbaan many times in the course of my duties, and on one occasion he gave me a long yellow sheet of names. It was a list of the men who had played on the undefeated team of 1948 and it described what each was doing ten years after graduation.

It's no use going over the list — every man on it was a success — but the list itself is symbolic of the man who gave it to me. The man who runs Michigan's football team is most interested in what his players have accomplished off the field.

Always when I have come out of his office, I have learned a little of what happens on the gridiron, and a whole lot concerning the academic and post-graduation success of the players. Is this the way for a football coach to act, showing such an interest in a field other than football?

• • •

AT MICHIGAN it's most certainly the way for a football coach to act. Because Oosterbaan hates recruiting and is satisfied completely with the basis of need aid plan which takes the bidding out of the job, because he completely adheres to the recommendation of the admissions committee and is unwilling to take a chance on a boy's flunking out just because he's a good football player, because he is interested in the educational opportunity he can offer to athletes, and because he is most interested in seeing his players graduate and become successful after graduation, he is the right man in the right job in the right place.

MICHIGAN NEEDS the coach that Oosterbaan is. It needs a man with a philosophy of football which can allow him to adapt to the pressures put on him by the academic side of the University and still produce a winning football team. This is the important thing. In the face of stiff entrance requirements and study schedules, Oosterbaan has established a Conference record second only to Woody Hayes and his Ohio State Buckeyes.

Because of my relationship with Oosterbaan, knowing that he hates recruiting and the high pressure football that is the college sport today, and knowing that he is interested in his players as students, I can't held but feel that a man like this couldn't hold a job in a college not interested in bringing athletes into perspective.

• • •

HE SAYS the saddest part of his job is turning away the boys whose grades don't merit entrance to the University. It's just as sad to him if the boy's a highly-rated All-Stater or a not-so-highly-rated All-Stater. He wouldn't take a chance on anyone flunking out when the admissions committee assures him that the chances are high. For his reason he can feel proud of the 99 per cent graduation average that his lettermen since 1952 have established.

Because he loses so many players in this way he is severely criticized for sloppy recruiting. Also, because he excuses athletes occasionally who are way behind in their work or who have an unavoidable class, he is criticized for holding a sloppy practice.

I don't think he cares about this criticism, however. He is trying in the ways he can to approach a situation that is ideal. True, fooball is far from deemphasis, but it is more casual here than other places, and for this Oosterbaan can be proud, especially proud since he's won three titles, and never had a season below .500 in 10 years of Big Ten play.

OOSTERBAAN IS COACH OF YEAR

WORDS OF WISDOM—Coach Bennie Oosterbaan briefs his squad on what is needed today to spill Northwestern from the ranks of the unbeaten. Michigan meets the Wildcats in Dyche Stadium at 1:30 p.m. in an effort to gain its first Big Ten win after a 12-12 tie with Michigan State. The Wolverines are a slight favorite. (Oct. 18, 1958)

DAVID GILTROW/Ensian

OCT. 17

Defense Sparkles In Crucial Victory

Dworsky, Kempthorn Outstanding; Teninga's Punts Keep NU in Hole

By MURRAY GRANT
(Daily Sports Editor)

Michigan still reigns supreme over Big Nine football.

The Wolverines demonstrated their supremacy before 85,938 fans yesterday as they rolled over previously unbeaten Northwestern, 28-0 at Michigan Stadium, to notch their 18th straight victory.

SHOWING AMAZING defensive play and capitalizing on almost every break, the Maize and Blue changed the game from a breathtaking struggle into a near rout in the space of five minutes.

For three full quarters it was anyone's game. But then the roof fell in on the Wildcats. On the last play of the third quarter Wally Teninga smacked a jump pass into the arms of Leo Koceski for the second Michigan score.

Forty seconds later the Wolverines had the bag tightly sewn up and tucked away. Harry Allis recovered Art Murakowski's fumble of Michigan's kickoff and Chuck Ortmann tossed to Koceski for the touchdown.

To make sure, the Wolverines added another as Irv Wisniewski intercepted a pass, and Bob Erben recovered Koceski's fumble in the Northwestern end zone.

ALEX LMANIAN/Daily

HIGH POINT MAN — Wolverine sophomore, Leo Koceski, as he is off on one of his frequent gains of yesterday afternoon. Koceski rattled off three touchdowns for Michigan and was closely connected with the scoring of the Maize and Blue's last tally.

SEPT. 26

Wolverines Squeeze Past Spartans, 13-7

Winning Margin Comes in Fourth

By BUD WEIDENTHAL
Associate Sports Editor

The roses looked a little wilted, the blue ribbons a little tattered, but when it was all over Michigan's Wolverines emerged a 13-7 victor over a vengeful Michigan State eleven yesterday at East Lansing's new Macklin Field.

A spirited Spartan aggregation kept the crowd of 50,011 on its feet through much of the spine-tingling thriller as it constantly thwarted Wolverine scoring attempts and flashed a speedy, deceptive offense of its own.

ALEX LMANIAN/Daily

END OF THE LINE—Wolverine tacklers evidently won't shake off a Duck's back as easily as the proverbial water. Guard Quent Sickels and Halfback Bob Van Summern administer the old one-two punch to Webfoot halfback Johnny McKay.

OCT. 27

Ortmann Rated Top Offensive Threat in Big Nine Competition

Bucks Fall, 13-3; Wolverines Cop 23 Straight Wins

Coach Bennie Oosterbaan Finishes His First Season Unbeaten, Untied

By MURRAY GRANT
(Special to The Daily)

COLUMBUS, O.—Michigan wrote finis to one of the most glorious pages in football annals today as they vanquished a stubborn and, at times, brilliant Ohio State eleven, 13-3 at the Ohio Stadium to capture their second straight Big Nine title.

Playing before 82,754 fans, the second largest crowd ever to see a football game in Columbus, the Wolverines struck with characteristic suddenness for two scores in the second and fourth periods to overcome a 3-0 lead the Buckeyes had built up.

· · · ·

INSTEAD OF CHUCK ORTMANN, it was Wally Teninga, who stepped into the limelight with his kicking, passing and running. He almost single-handedly paced the Wolverines to the game-clinching marker late in the final period.

Teninga's punting was often phenomenal as he kept the Buckeyes bottled up deep in their own territory. He averaged 42 yards per boot with two of them going over 60 yards each. And it was these long punts that kept Michigan in the ball game.

They met an inspired Ohio State team that would settle for nothing less than the upset of the year.

They struck savagely over the ground in the first period, but their attack bogged down on the Michigan 29, when Jim Clark fumbled and Wolverine end Ozzie Clark pounced on it.

'M' CRUSHES INDIANA, 54-0

1948	MICHIGAN		OPPONENT
SEPT. 25	13	7	Michigan State
OCT. 2	14	0	Oregon
OCT. 9	40 (No. 7)	0	No. 15 Purdue
OCT. 16	28 (No. 4)	0	No. 3 Northwestern
OCT. 23	27 (No. 1)	14	No. 13 Minnesota
OCT. 30	28 (No. 1)	20	Illinois
NOV. 6	35 (No. 2)	0	Navy
NOV. 13	54 (No. 1)	0	Indiana
NOV. 20	13 (No. 1)	3	No. 18 Ohio State

ALEX LMANIAN/Daily

I'M GONNA DO IT — Dick Kempthorn (38) Wolverine fullback shows his tongue to a white-shirted Hoosier defender who cannot get to him in time to stop the husky Wolverine from plunging over for one of Michigan's eight touchdowns. Dick Rifenburg (89) detains another Indianan while a third seems to be more interested in rolling on the soft turf than in stopping the hard-hitting Kempthorn.

It's Final: 'M' First in Nation

'M' RETAINS BIG NINE TITLE

JUNE 7, 1950

FLAMES GUT HAVEN HALL; DAMAGE HITS $3,000,000

MAY 21, 1951

HARLAN HATCHER NAMED AS RUTHVEN SUCCESSOR

Board Picks OSU Veep As Eighth 'U' President

MAY 11, 1954

'U' Witnesses Cite Fifth Amendment in Hearings

THREE ON FACULTY SUSPENDED

No Action Taken On Two Students

By JIM DYGERT

University President Harlan H. Hatcher ordered late yesterday the immediate suspension of the three faculty members who appeared before the House un-American activities subcommittee yesterday in Lansing.

No statement was issued in regard to University action concerning the two graduate students, Ed Shaffer and Myron Sharpe, who also appeared before the committee.

SEPT. 17, 1952

New Campus Now Under Construction

Huron River Site Of 'U' Expansion

Gigantic plans for a multi-million dollar "overflow" campus in the hills beyond the Huron River will go into effect this year now that the initial surveying and ground-breaking has been completed.

IT PROVIDES for immediate construction of a "research campus" of four buildings and a long-range development of perhaps 20 or more buildings, including housing, dining and recreational facilities.

Also in the project are a fine arts center, including an outdoor amphitheatre and television station, and a veritable mecca of research facilities.

A 267 acre tract directly north of the new Veteran's Administration Hospital has been purchased over the past two years by the University from eight major owners at an average cost of about $1,000 per acre.

APRIL 12, 1955

SALK POLIO VACCINE EFFECTIVE

By LEE MARKS

Salk vaccine works.

After months of anticipation, an anxious world today heard Dr. Thomas Francis, Jr. report that the vaccine is between 80 and 90 per cent effective.

It is absolutely safe.

Speaking at a meeting of more than 500 scientists and physicians, Dr. Francis claimed the vaccine had produced "an extremely successful effect" among bulbar patients in areas where vaccine and a harmless substitute had been used interchangeably.

There is now no doubt that the fight against polio is nearing an end. Children can definitely be inoculated successfully against the crippling effects of paralytic polio, Dr. Francis' report proved.

NOV. 5, 1952

EISENHOWER LANDSLIDE SWEEPS ENTIRE NATION

AS OF 1950...

410-112-23
MICHIGAN FOOTBALL PROGRAM RECORD

30-12-4
VS. OHIO STATE

33-6-3
VS. MICHIGAN STATE

9-2
VS. NOTRE DAME

24-13-2
VS. MINNESOTA

19,487
ENROLLMENT

$150
IN-STATE TUITION

$400
OUT-OF-STATE TUITION

$19,983,069
ENDOWMENT

Bennie Oosterbaan
FOOTBALL COACH

Alexander Grant Ruthven
UNIVERSITY PRESIDENT

NOTABLE GRADUATES

1952 Dr. Jack Kevorkian, euthanasia activist

1959 Edward Higgins White, first American to walk in space

One Half Too Many:

ARMY UPSURGE WHIPS 'M', 27-6

Special to The Daily
By BOB SANDELL
Associate Sports Editor

NEW YORK—A brilliant second half rally and a couple of reserve halfbacks gave mighty Army its 23rd straight triumph yesterday and fourth win without loss over Michigan's Wolverines.

The two backs, Al Bollard and Vic Pollock, sparked third and fourth period drives that brought the Cadets a smashing 27-6 victory before 67,076 fans in Yankee Stadium.

• • • •

THE WOLVERINES, led by Charlie Ortmann, put on a tremendous first half show for the huge crowd, and narrowly missed running the Cadets right off the field before intermission.

But beginning late in the third quarter the Cadets could do no wrong, and they took advantage of the breaks to score three quick touchdowns and doom the Michiganders to their second setback in three starts.

Michigan lost the services of their right halfback, Leo Koceski, early in the second quarter and the Wolverines sorely missed his running and kicking.

• • •

THE INVADING Maize and Blue scored with little more than eight minutes gone in the first period, and narrowly missed tallying several other times before the Cadets tied the count just before the half ended.

Fullback Don Dufek plunged for the lone Wolverine score while Pollock scored twice and Pollard and Jack Martin once each for the Cadets.

Michigan received the kickoff and on the third play nearly lost the ball to Army deep in their own territory. Pete Kinyon finally recovered Ortmann's fumble on the 13 yard line.

ED KOZMA/Daily
TOO LITTLE AND TOO LATE—Ralph Straffon (32) is caught from behind after going 20 yards with a pass from Chuck Ortmann in the waning minutes of the game after the Cadets with their great second half drives had safely tucked the game away.

ED KOZMA/Daily
SOMETHING MISSING—Lowell Perry (85) star sophomore end for the Wolverines just fails to grab potential touchdown pass from Ortmann in the early part of the first quarter before Michigan took a temporary lead in the initial half.

Cadets Roar Back In Second Half To Extend Skein

Pollard and Pollock Star for Army As Ortmann's Arm Sparks Michigan

In horrendous weather conditions, Michigan came out on top in what was later dubbed the Snow Bowl.

California Here We Come:

'M' UPSETS BUCKEYES 9-3 TO GAIN BIG TEN CROWN

Blocked Kicks, Ortmann's Punting Give Wolverines Victory in Snow

By BILL CONNOLLY
Daily Sports Editor

COLUMBUS—Michigan's relentless Wolverines saved the space for another chapter in the rags-to-riches tale that records the activities of the 1950 Maize and Blue gridiron squad, by beating Ohio State's Buckeyes in a blizzard here yesterday.

> "**The din of the locker room was broken every now and then by a shout of somebody that apparently had just awakened to the fact that he was actually going to Pasadena.**"
> — Bob Sandell, *The Michigan Daily*

ED KOZMA/Daily

Don Dufek tackles All-American Vic Janowicz after short gain on a snowy OSU gridiron.

Pandemonium Prevails in Lockers

By BOB SANDELL
Associate Sports Editor

COLUMBUS—From a blinding, swirling snowstorm in Ohio's huge stadium to visions of beautiful sunny California on January first. The joyous Wolverines could still hardly believe it, long after the final gun had ended one of the weirdest days of Big Ten football in history.

• • •

YOU COULD hardly blame them. Captain Al Wahl summed it up nicely like this, "from rags to riches in one afternoon."

It had been a season where nothing had gone right. Injuries and inclement weather had hampered and harrassed the Wolverines to the point where they were apparently headed for their worst season in 13 years.

Then in the space of about two and a half hours they had once again soared to gridiron heights by taking the conference glory and gravy.

ROGER REINKE/Daily

Michigan's football victory combines with the offerings of local taverns to give celebrating students that rosy feeling.

PASADENA ROSES BLOOM FOR MIGHTY MICH-AGAIN

112 TO 6!

Michigan Makes It Three for Three

By JIM PARKER

Three Rose Bowl games—Michigan 112, opponents 6!

It's an impressive record that the Wolverines have posted in the annual New Year's Day classic, a record that now includes a victory in the first game of the Rose Bowl series, a spectacular triumph in the most recent Pasadena extravaganza, with another great win in 1948 sandwiched in between.

Back in 1902 Fielding H. Yost, in his first year as coach at Michigan, took a Maize and Blue team —an iron-man crew twelve strong —to the innaugural game of what is now the Rose Bowl post season classic series.

Joe Wardlaw, California guard, drops Michigan's Don Dufek on the Bear thirty-yard stripe.

JACK BERGSTROM/Daily

> " Contrary to its expectations, a nerve-shattered crowd of over 100,000 saw the Golden Bears pounded into submission by the Wolverine defenders' vicious tackling. "
>
> — Bill Connolly,
> *The Michigan Daily*

Sportswriters, Fans Invade Michigan Dressing Rooms

By BOB SANDELL
Associate Sports Editor

PASADENA, Cal. — Even the wildest New Year's celebration wouldn't compare with the din of the Michigan dressing room just after the Wolverines had staged one of the most amazing comebacks of all times in the 37th annual Rose Bowl classic.

Hordes of reporters, photographers, and well-wishers jammed the tiny room to congratulate Bennie Oosterbaan and his courageous Blue-shirted gridders. The bedlam after the Ohio State game was nothing compared to this.

OOSTERBAAN was herded off into a separate room to meet the newspapermen. As after the Ohio game, however, Bennie appeared calm and would merely say that he was "as happy as a man could be and was proud of his boys."

The greatest thrill of his life? "No," was his answer, "I have had quite a few of them in my day."

He said Don Dufek had played as good a game as he has ever seen a fullback play, and that the team turned in its best game of the season.

THE REPORTERS wanted to know what happened at half time, and what had caused the Wolverines to explode in the final 30 minutes. Bennie replied by saying that the "boys fired themselves. Several of them talked a little, including Al Wahl."

He praised the California team as a hard-driving, well-coached outfit and had a lot of praise for the trio of California backs that made things miserable for the visitors in the first half.

WOLVERINE DEFENSE TRIPS BUCKEYES, 7-0

Sun Shines On Spirited 'M' Rooters

By RON WATTS
Daily Associate Editor

PROBABLY the biggest single factor in Saturday's festivities was spirit. It caused the usually objective Voice on the public address system to change the standard "Perry intercepted" to "Perry picked that one out of the air."

And in the press box, a miniature battle of cheers and catcalls were exchanged between Ohio and Michigan sports writers. Many students left the stadium with the happy comment that "beating Ohio State makes it a successful season."

ROGER REINKE/Daily

WHOA, BOY!—Ted Topor vaults over an Ohio State defender after snaring a Bill Putich pass during the second quarter touchdown drive.

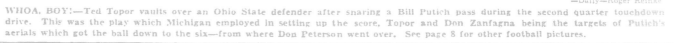

WHOA, BOY:—Ted Topor vaults over an Ohio State defender after snaring a Bill Putich pass during the second quarter touchdown drive. This was the play which Michigan employed in setting up the score, Topor and Don Zanfagna being the targets of Putich's aerials which got the ball down to the six—from where Don Peterson went over. See page 8 for other football pictures.

Even though the Wolverines entered the Ohio State game with a 3-2 record, the win over the Buckeyes was considered a big upset. The win salvaged Michigan's otherwise disappointing season.

ROGER REINKE/Daily

UP IN THE AIR— Ted Topor sails to the turf after getting his feet knocked from under him by an unidentified OSU defender. Topor had gone back to pass but was forced to run with the ball when all of his receivers were covered.

> "We're not making any alibis about the game. Michigan played a great game. The Wolverines had the more determined spirit and that was the difference."
> — Woody Hayes, *Ohio State football coach*

MICHIGAN FOOTBALL

MARCHING BAND --- 146 STRONG:

NOV. 15, 1953

Bandsmen Display Perfection In Musical Ability, Marching

Twenty-five thousand miles, or a distance greater than the circumference of the globe, is traversed each season by the University of Michigan Marching Band without leaving its practice field in Ann Arbor.

The Band steps this distance in preparation for approximately 45 minutes on the field at halftime. But all this work shows up in flawless performances that have earned the group a reputation as the finest college marching band in the country.

PRECISION FORMATIONS range from the traditional Block "M" to dance stunts that are so complex they have never been attempted by any other band.

• • • •

THE MARCHING BAND dates back to 1895 when the official band was organized by order of the Regents to play at football games, socials and other events. It has been growing ever since and today 146 take the field at halftime led by drum major Floyd Zarbock, '54 A&D.

It is the Band's unusual balance between music quality and marching which gains the attention of both the layman and the professional. An instrumentation is employed with a balance between woodwinds and brasses that is generaly absent from college bands. Instruments are spread throughout the band instead of in separate sections so that the quality sounds equally good from all sides. It is really four bands in one, Prof. Revelli explained.

Entering the field at a snappy 210 steps per minute, the band maintains a cadence ranging from a slow 100 steps per minute to 176 during formations, depending on the music. However, Prof. Revelli maintains that the cadence which dazzles spectators takes second place to unity, precision and coordination which is what really makes a band stand out.

MICHIGAN'S CHEERLEADERS DEMONSTRATE PERFECT PRECISION AS THEY LINE UP FOR A SPIRITED 'YEA MICH!'

NOV. 21, 1951

Pep Leaders At 'U' Practice Long Hours

It may look glamorous and easy, but behind every colorful precision formation executed by Michigan's cheerleaders stand many months of hard work.

Would-be cheerleaders begin their training in May each year when the current squad d rects sessions on the fundamentals of jumping and yelling for those men who plan to try out for the team.

* * *

THESE SESSIONS a n d all cheerleaders' activities are limited of course to men by a traditional taboo against the feminine sex that has never been broken.

CAPT. ED BUCHANAN FLIPS OFF TRAMPOLETTE

NOV. 15, 1953

IMMEDIATELY before the game, the controversial trophy, Paul Bunyan, standing regally on a map of Michigan, was unveiled at midfield as flashbulbs exploded. The trophy was then taken out the north entrance and promptly forgotten by the crowd.

In 1953, Michigan Governor G. Mennen Williams presented an eight-foot tall statue — now known as the Paul Bunyan Trophy — to the winner of the Michigan/MSU game.

CHEERLEADERS 'PRAY TO ALLAH' FOR POINT AFTER TOUCHDOWN

Photos by Malcolm Schatz and Jim Easley

Story by Alan Luckoff

ANN ARBOR, MICHIGAN, SUNDAY, OCTOBER 9, 1955

'M' BREAKS ARMY JINX, 26-2

Everything Goes Wrong For Cadets

Michigan Elated, Army Deflated

By JIM DYGERT
Daily City Editor

It was a black day for the Black Knights.

Army saw its invincibility, usually established merely by putting in an appearance, dismantled before some 98,000 screaming fans yesterday afternoon.

The 26-2 score, someone remarked after the game, seemed somehow even more humiliating than a shut-out.

Nothing Right for Military

From the time the train carrying 600 senior cadets into Ann Arbor arrived an hour late until the final gun punctuated Michigan's first victory over the cadets in history, nothing went right for the military.

Even half-time offered no respite, as Secretary of the Army Wilber M. Brucker and top military brass, while attempting to cross the field, found themselves tangling with the University's Marching Band.

Though there were no casualties, Army dignity had been ruffled, and even Michigan fans were grumbling about the band's audacity. As it was learned later, the military contingent had been expected to go via the end zone and the band was supposed to wait for it to complete the trip.

Revelli Not Informed

Prof. William D. Revelli, director of University Bands, said afterwards he had not been informed of the trip across the field.

During the game, Army couldn't even penetrate Michigan territory until the final period. Until then, fans tensed forward every time the cadets neared the mid-field stripe, and sat back when they fumbled or were pushed back.

That was when they weren't standing. There was plenty to stand for. Wolverine halfbacks scampered down the field with the pigskin and ends hugged in passes, even if only to have the play called back on account of a penalty.

They Had to Stand

The cadets were standing, too. But they were standing because they had to stand, out of deference to tradition. So they stood, and watched their team unable to gain even on an official's error

that would have given Army six yards less to go for a first down if Ron Kramer hadn't noticed the mistake and thwarted the cadets on that one, too.

Though Army's misery was Michigan's joy, the shouting and cheering, especially after Terry Barr's second touchdown on an 82-yard punt return, was suspended a bit by the one event that blackened Michigan's afternoon and possibly its 1955 future.

Kramer was hurt. After clearing two Black Knights from Barr's run for a touchdown, Kramer didn't get up, and the stadium, almost as a unit, groaned.

'Don't Give Up Now'

But losing the big left end didn't stop Michigan's Wolverines, who went right on grinding Army's prestige into the turf to chants from the stands of, "Don't give up now, Army, the worst is yet to come."

First blood— Michigan tailback Terry Barr plunges over from the one-yard line to give the Wolverines an early 6-0 lead.

CHUCK KELSEY/Daily

"Nothing went right for the military."
— Jim Dygert, *The Michigan Daily*

MICHIGAN FOOTBALL

| Illinois . . . . 16 | Ohio State . . . 7 | Purdue . . . 29 | Army . . . . . 14 | Indiana . . . . 12 | Oklahoma . . 40 | S. Methodist . 20 | Geneva (Pa.) 41 |
| Mich. State . . 0 | Wisconsin . . . 7 | Notre Dame . 22 | Pittsburgh . . 14 | Miami (O.) . . 7 | Kansas State . 6 | Ga. Tech . . . 6 | Slippery Rock 20 |

CONQUESTS IN
SPACE RACE
See Page 4

The Michigan Daily

Sixty-Eight Years of Editorial Freedom

RAIN, COOLER

VOL. LXIX, No. 35   ANN ARBOR, MICHIGAN, SUNDAY, OCTOBER 26, 1958   FIVE CENTS   EIGHT PAGES

Michigan Keeps 'Brown Jug' with 20-19 Victory

Missed Extra Point Saves Wolverines

By CARL RISEMAN
Daily Sports Editor

Michigan claimed its second victory of the season yesterday, as it edged Minnesota, once again by the margin of an extra point.

The Wolverines built up a third period 20-7 lead over the Gophers, but had to stave off two late tallies to claim a 20-19 win, and to retain the Little Brown Jug. The score was identical with the first victory of the season over Southern California. Both teams were hungry for a victory. Minnesota had failed to win in four previous starts this year and Michigan was still smoldering over the 55-24 loss to Northwestern last week.

Lose Eight Straight

Minnesota managed to outgain the Wolverines in almost every offensive department but lost because of its defensive mistakes. The hapless Gophers thus suffered their eighth straight defeat and 10th in their last 12 starts.

For the Wolverines this was a "must" game. After falling completely apart in the Northwestern debacle, a victory, any type of victory, would mean nothing less than a tremendous comeback.

Michigan Scores Early

The Homecoming crowd of 72,981 saw Michigan strike early in the first period. Fullback Tony Rio recovered a fumble by Minnesota's Tom Robbins on the Minnesota 42-yard line. Bob Ptacek then completed two passes to Gary Prahst, which brought Michigan down to the Minnesota 12-yard line.

The Wolverines held off a fourth-quarter surge from Minnesota in Bennie Oosterbaan's final win as Michigan's coach. Wins were few and far between at the end of Oosterbaan's tenure.

PETER ANDERSON/Daily

TOP: OFF AND RUNNING—Wolverine Darrell Harper springs loose on his 58-yard touchdown gallop in the third period of yesterday's Minnesota game. **BOTTOM:** PTACEK SCORES—Michigan quarterback Bob Ptacek scores his and Michigan's second touchdown from the one-yard line with less Minnesota game.

1959-1968

'U' Regents Name Elliott Head Coach

Mentor Completes Home Career Today With Indiana Game

By AL JONES
Daily Sports Editor

The Regents officially appointed Chalmers "Bump" Elliott to replace Bennie Oosterbaan as Michigan's head football coach yesterday.

In their monthly meeting the Regents approved Oosterbaan's request to retire from the position and approved the resolution of the Board in Control of Intercollegiate Athletics naming Elliott as the successor, both effective January 1, 1959.

At that time Oosterbaan will step into a new position with the Athletic Department as an assistant to the Athletic Director.

Chappuis, Elliott Make Coaches' All-American

ALEX LMAMIAN/Daily

TOUCHDOWN EXPRESS—Bump Elliott, flashy Wolverine wingback, high-balls his way through a maze of Illinois players and heads for touchdown territory after taking a punt from Eddelman of the Illini. (Nov. 6, 1947)

Elliott had just five winning seasons in his 10 years as head coach, but his impact on the program was evident when Bo Schembechler took over. Elliott earned the game ball after the team's win over Ohio State in 1969. Schembechler recognized that Elliott's players had pulled off the historic upset.

the vandal . . . howard kohn

BUMP ELLIOTT'S dreams were made of mended knees and shorter crossbars.

Elliott coached football when other coaches manipulated, analyzed and stampeded their players through the mechanics of winning games. Elliott won but he didn't have the guts or the insensitivity to win as much as he could have.

He's gone now, coveyed aside for a winner. He's the new associate director of athletics, which is much like being a second-string stud at a cattle farm. "I gave up coaching because I didn't know if this job would be offered again," Elliott said. What he meant of course was that he didn't know if his coaching job would be offered again — once he returned to losing as he inevitably would have.

ELLIOTT'S FIRST five years at Michigan were equivocating years filled with fifth-place finishes and criticism tempered by the caution he needed time to build a Yostian dynasty. But when he won it all in 1964 with a heavily sophomoric team Elliott placed himself in double jeopardy.

He was expected to continue to win. And he expected to continue to win.

Elliott Offers No Excuse For Wolverines' Defeat

RIDING CREST OF VICTORY—His face sporting a well-earned grin, Michigan head coach Chalmers "Bump" Elliott is hoisted upon the shoulders of appreciative team members and admiring fans at the triumphal conclusion of yesterday's game. Wolverine followers swarmed onto the playing field at the final gun, roaring approval to the victory their yearling coach gave them over favored Ohio State. (Nov. 22, 1959)

FRED SHIPPEY/Daily

462-148-26
MICHIGAN FOOTBALL
PROGRAM RECORD

35-17-4
VS. OHIO STATE

35-13-4
VS. MICHIGAN STATE

9-2
VS. NOTRE DAME

31-15-3
VS. MINNESOTA

23,541
ENROLLMENT

$280
IN-STATE TUITION

$750
OUT-OF-STATE TUITION

$46,746,283
ENDOWMENT

**Chalmers
"Bump" Elliott**
FOOTBALL COACH

Harlan Hatcher
UNIVERSITY PRESIDENT

**NOTABLE
GRADUATES**

1962 Red Berenson,
Michigan hockey coach

1962 Stephen Ross, Ross
School of Business
namesake

1967 Ted Kaczynski,
"Unabomber"

OCT. 14, 1960

Kennedy Arrives for Campaign Foray
Crowd Welcomes Senator at Union

JAMES WARNEKA/Daily
DEMOCRATIC NOMINEE — Sen. John F. Kennedy was greeted by
approximately 10,000 cheering students as he arrived in front of the
Union early this morning.

MARCH 10, 1965

King Defies Court Order, President; Leads Marchers

NOV. 22, 1963

JFK KILLED
JOHNSON TO TAKE OFFICE

MARCH 21, 1965

'M' STUNNED BY UCLA FOR NCAA TITLE, 91-80

MAY 26, 1966

U.S., Russia Locked in Tight Race to the Moon

MAY 26, 1966

Viet Nam: It's Time Now To Pack It In

STUDENTS CLOSE IN on the Regents
meeting yesterday to protest the board's
most recent decision to move forward
with a proposal for an administration-run
University book store.

Regents split 5-2 on plans for 'U'-operated bookstore

SEPT. 20, 1969

400 STUDENTS INTERRUPT REGENTS MEETING TO PROTEST NEW DECISION ON BOOKSTORE

ERIC PERGEAUX/Daily

the 1960s

1965

HOW THE WEST WAS WON:

Wolverines Cop Roses, Clobber Beavers, 34-7

'M' Gridders Post Perfect Record In Four Rose Bowl Appearances

By BILL BULLARD
Sports Editor
Special To The Daily

PASADENA—Michigan's Big Ten Champions rolled through an outmanned Oregon State defense with a crushing 332-yard rushing attack for a 34-7 victory here New Year's Day in a Rose Bowl contest critics immediately termed a mismatch.

Criticism of Oregon State's selection as the West Coast representative to face Michigan reached new heights after the Wolverines dominated the game in almost every possible way. Michigan had been heavily favored to win but the decisiveness of the one-sided triumph left the Beavers stunned.

RAMBLING FULLBACK Mel Anthony is off and away for Michigan's first touchdown in the Rose Bowl, 84 yards to a new game record.

ED LANGS/Daily

VOTED MVP:

Anthony: Nobody Touched Me

By TOM ROWLAND
Associate Sports Editor
Special To The Daily

PASADENA—Mel Anthony looked a little bit overwhelmed by the entire situation.

He stood perched on a table in the midst of Michigan's post-game bedlam under the Rose Bowl stands, one hand clasping tight onto the silver Helms Trophy for the Most Valuable Player in the 34-7 walloping of Oregon State, the other arm around a grinning Carl Ward.

The flashbulbs popped, cameras whirred, and somewhere in the turmoil of hand-shaking, back-slapping and general roar of congratulations came the cries of reporters and photographers. Anthony put a smile on his face—not hard to do after scoring three touchdowns in the Rose Bowl — and blinked into the barrage of flashbulbs and questions:

"No, I wasn't aware I tied a Rose Bowl record (for most points in a game).

"Yes, I played high school football in Cincinnati.

"Well, all I know is that I could see daylight after Carl Ward and John Henderson sprung me on that pitchout. Nobody ever touched me." He added that he wasn't aware that he had set a record for the longest run from scrimmage with that 84-yard gallop for the Wolverines' first touchdown either.

Michigan topped Oregon State in the only season Bump Elliott won a Big Ten title as head coach.

> " The Beavers were hapless, unimpressive, flattened, helpless, engulfed, disembodied, bombed, barbecued, terrible and poor schnooks. "
>
> — *Los Angeles Times writer quoted in The Michigan Daily*

Flash! Johnson 34, Wisconsin 9

The future Pro Bowler Ron Johnson rushed for 347 yards and five touchdowns — the single-game rushing mark remains a Michigan record.

> ❝ **Johnson gave the greatest one-man performance I have ever seen. He should definitely be rated an All-American football player.** ❞
>
> — Bump Elliott, *Michigan football coach*

By DAVID WEIR
Sports Editor

Ron Johnson shattered ten rushing records to single-handedly demolish Wisconsin 34-9 in a downpour yesterday and set up a "Dream Game" showdown with Big Ten co-leader Ohio State in Columbus next Saturday.

Johnson racked up five touchdowns and gathered 347 yards in 31 attempts to turn a two-point first-half deficit into a one-man runaway in the third quarter.

It was Michigan's eighth straight win, and combined with Ohio State's 33-27 squeaker over Iowa, sets the stage for next week's titanic struggle which will determine the Big Ten championship and a trip to the 1969 Rose Bowl in Pasadena, California.

Johnson's touchdowns came on explosive spurts of 35, 67, one, 60, and 50 yards as he raked Wisconsin's defense for the highest rushing and scoring totals in Big Ten football history. He was taken out of the game early in the fourth quarter.

Michigan Head Coach Bump Elliott said "Johnson gave the greatest one-man performance I have ever seen. He should definitely be rated an All-American football player."

All in all, Johnson managed to eclipse three Big Ten single game marks, three Michigan single game records, three Michigan season totals and one team career record.

Johnson's new Michigan and Big Ten single game marks:
- Most Points . . . 30
- Most Touchdowns . . . 5
- Most Yards Rushing . . . 347

Johnson's new Michigan season records:
- Rushing Attempts . . . 234
- Most Yards Rushing . . . 1300
- Most Touchdowns . . . 17

Johnson's new Michigan career record:
- Most Yards Rushing . . . 2349

(Johnson broke the career mark for rushing attempts last week against Illinois. He now has 466.)

JAY CASSIDY/Daily

RON JOHNSON, greatest Michigan halfback since Tom Harmon, breaks the last tackle on the way to his fifth touchdown of yesterday afternoon. The score broke the modern Big Ten single game record, one of the many marks shattered by the big halfback.

DAN HABIB/Daily

The 1985 season provided several pleasant surprises for the Fiesta Bowl bound Wolverines. Bo Schembechler regained his tall reputation while guiding his team to a 9-1-1 record.

Welcome to the hot seat, Bo

JAN. 9, 1969

In the early '60's when the Detroit Lions had a respectable football team, one of America's most forgettable comedians was lamenting the death of appropriate names for sports heroes.

He said, "Years ago, there were MEN like Red Grange, the Galloping Ghost, Bronko Nagurski and Johnny Blood lugging the pigskin.

"Now, who is that great leading Detroit against Green Bay? — Milton Plum, that's who."

So where does this leave Bo Schembechler? The name may be hilarious but the role he has to perform isn't much of a joke. Sooner or later he has to produce a highly successful football team.

Schembechler does have one thing going for him. He joins the great non-Michigan tradition of Wolverine coaches. Coming from the University of Miami, Ohio, the starting point of many great mentors, Schembechler, along with basketball coach John Orr, has succeeded in breaking the old system of having Michigan alumni named to coach Michigan teams.

That habit did seem rather silly in view of the fact that the outstanding records of non-alumni like Fielding Yost and Fritz Crisler easily surpassed the more mild success of Wolverine All-Americans Harry Kipke, Benny Osterbaan and Bump Elliott, when they became coaches.

Bo vs. Woody . . .
. . . that's where it's at

Bo takes on 'M' tradition

By ROBIN WRIGHT
Associate Sports Editor

There's been Fielding, Fritz, Bennie, Bump . . .

. . . And now there's Bo. Glenn Edward Schembechler — who compensates for his last name with the nickname Bo — has succeeded Chalmers 'Bump' Elliott as Michigan's head football coach.

Schembechler described his coaching personality as "semi-conservative. I don't like the odds on risk plays. I like to rely on what I know is successful.

"And I'm a tough and unyielding coach if I think I'm right," he added.

Despite his tough guy attitude towards coaching, Schembechler feels he is equally devoted to the players as to the game.

He explained, "I like a close association with the players. I don't want to know them just between four and six each day at practice.

"My players take precedent over anything if they have a problem and need my counsel. I'll be available at all times.

"I don't want them to feel all I give a damn about is their knocking around the football."

Schembechler practices what he preaches.

Devoted to the game twelve months a year, Michigan's new coach "feels guilty if I don't do something about my job every day — Sundays too.

Although he is a fan of most sports, especially baseball, Schembechler has no hobbies, except playing handball at noon to keep in shape.

He explained that "since I don't smoke, and I don't have any hobbies, I eat when I'm nervous. After a game I eat and go to bed to work off nervous energy. I sleep until ten the next day and then go over to see the game films. I like to get at it right away."

Young and personable, Schembechler appears to be much like Elliott — only with a stronger desire for his own way.

Asked if his name was derived from some connection with football or athletics — as did the nicknames of Fielding "Hurry-up" Yost and Chalmers "Bump" Elliott — Schembechler explained "When I was about a year old my sister started calling me "Bo-Bo" probably because she couldn't pronounce brother.

"It stuck with me all the way through school. In fact, I think some of my friends don't even know my real first name."

Bo stays
Loyalty tops A&M money

JAN. 16, 1982

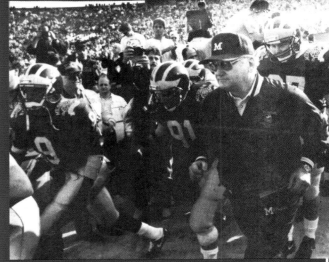

DAVID LUBLINER/Daily
Coach Bo Schembechler runs onto the field with his team for the last time.

By MARK MIHANOVIC

"Money talks" suffered a setback last night.

Bo Schembechler announced to a roomful of surprised reporters and Athletic Department officials that he had rejected a multi-million dollar deal to become coach and athletic director of Texas A&M University to remain head football coach at Michigan.

AT 9:00 p.m. a misty-eyed Schembechler ended the speculation of the previous 36 hours by apologizing to those present for delaying his decision — which many had been expecting as early as 11:00 a.m. — and then expressing his intention.

"There are things that are more important than money, and one of them is Michigan. I'm staying were I belong," he said, prompting a spontaneous round of applause.

"I'd never been much of a guy who looked forward to economic security and opportunities of that nature," the 52-year-old mentor said. "It was more than your normal job offer. I felt that, in the best interests of my family and myself, I had to seriously consider it.

"BUT MICHIGAN is Michigan. There's a special spirit here. I feel good about the decision. It's been a long day — and a long night."

Indeed it had been. The lure of the long-term contract, reportedly in the neighborhood of $2.25 million to $3 million spread over 10 years, caused Schembechler to measure his options carefully, as he conferred with his family, his coaching staff, Michigan Athletic Director Don Canham, and University President Harold Shapiro.

Talk of Schembechler's departure became more intense after an early-evening report from WXYZ-TV Detroit said current Texas A&M coach Tom Wilson, with one year remaining on his contract, had submitted his resignation.

Among those most satisfied with Schembechler's choice was Canham, who agreed to increase Schembechler's salary of $60,030 to an undisclosed amount should the coach stay.

"You can't fight Texas oil money," Canham shrugged. "It certainly wasn't a bidding war. We did what we could, within the limitations of the University's (salary) schedule. He didn't make the decision because of anything I said. Michigan is what made the decision."

Courtesy of Bentley Historical Library
Bo Schembechler and Gerald Ford at football practice.

Bo's philosophy produces winners—on and off the field

DAVID LUBLINER/Daily
Showcasing his vintage on-the-field demeanor, Bo Schembechler yells. He continued to yell, mostly at the referees, until Michigan's losing Rose Bowl performance and his illustrious coaching career came to an end.

> ❝ You don't win championships in football by yourself. Many things help and I am convinced one of our biggest assets at Michigan is the support of our students. ❞
> — Bo Schembechler, *Michigan football coach*

WE'RE NUMBER ONE!!
'M' BLASTS BUCKS, 24-12

All-American Tom Curtis rambles with a Buckeye pass.

JIM DIEHL/Daily

Wolverines bust Woody

By JIM FORRESTER
Associate Sports Editor

"Nobody has a better defense — unless maybe its the Minnesota Vikings." So said Purdue's Jack Mollenkopf last week after his team was raped by Ohio State.

Well, somebody else has a better defense and it's the Michigan Wolverines. Michigan blasted the Buckeye offense, holding them scoreless in the second half, as the Wolverines outplayed Ohio State, 24-12.

The Defense told Woody "Fat Boy" Hayes it was going to be a long day when they stopped the hapless Bucks on their first drive holding them on fourth and one on the Michigan 10 yard line. Jim Otis smacked the middle of the big Blue line for the last y a r d but met Henry Hill, professionally known as the great Pumpkin, on the way and fell inches short. In all Hill made 13 tackles, including eight solos, the game high for both squads.

But the big man on defense, all 178 pounds of him, was defensive back Barry Pierson. Pierson was peerless, intercepting three passes, making five tackles and returning a punt 60 yards to set up the Wolverines' insurance touchdown.

Coach Bo Schembechler sum-med up the incredible Michigan victory.

"We wouldn't have wanted to go to the Rose Bowl," said the Wolverine mentor after the game, "if we lost, and they wouldn't have wanted us. Now we're going as co-champions of the Big Ten and don't you forget it."

But Schembechler couldn't say enough about the defensive game. "Great plays on defense saved us in the second half," he said. But the coach was quick to mention who they were aiming at in the Buckeye attack. "The strategy was to contain Rex Kern because we knew Otis would get his yards but Kern wouldn't." The prediction was solid as Fat Boy went to his second string quarterback Ron Maciejowski in the f o u r t h quarter.

NOV. 21

Jim Mandich speaks on Ohio State

(EDITOR'S NOTE: The following article gives some of Captain Jim Mandich's thoughts about Saturday's game with Ohio State and the season in general. They are taken from an interview by Daily reporter Robin Wright).

By JIM MANDICH
as told to Robin Wright

I feel sort of meloncholy about it, my last game at Michigan. The greatest part of my life has been here and I hate to think it's finally coming to an end.

There was one time I thought it could go on forever, and I'm sad in a way, but I'm looking forward to new things. I've exhausted almost everything there is to do in college and I'm looking forward to stepping out in the real world.

I lump both these last t w o years together as being the most exciting period of my football career. Winning in itself is exciting. As far as personal performance, I would say that this year has been my most satisfying year.

THIS YEAR'S GAME against Ohio State is so much the same as last year's; I'm very thankful that we have this second chance to face them. I can't say any more. We're just fortunate enough to be back where we are — in a position to knock them off.

I would be the last to deny that the Rose Bowl hasn't been on our minds.

I don't like to think of going to the Rose Bowl having lost to Ohio State.

After Ohio State beat Michigan 50-14 in 1968, the Wolverines entered the 1969 game as major underdogs against the undefeated and defending national-champion Buckeyes.

One observer of the game was President Nixon who brought a TV set along to a medical appointment in order not to miss any of the action.
— Bill Alterman, *The Michigan Daily*

GOODBYE, COLUMBUS

Victory, Oh, Sweet Victory

Suck it up, Fat Boy

No longer do Fat Boy's comments on the best team going to the Bowl matter. Michigan has proved to be the best club and no one can ever take that away. Bo Schembechler will go to Pasadena in his first year as a head coach and Fielding Yost is the only other man who has done so. "It's unbelievable, really," commented Schembechler, and most people are inclined to agree with him.

Michigan is in euphoria and everything else besides the game is disjointed. Ann Arbor started on a drunk last night and it may not be over yet. The contents of this story probably prove that, but, who gives a damn? I don't. All I'm going to do is grab another beer and enjoy the hell out of myself.

Good-by Woody, it was fun while it lasted.

— Bill Cusumano

ON THE SIDELINES

Liberating the field

Daily photographer Sara Krulwich poses for television cameras during the Washington game Sept. 27 as the first University woman ever to set foot on Michigan's football field. Previously, the only women on the field were visiting cheerleaders. (Oct. 11, 1969)

— joel block —

No upset . . . . . . for the Buckeyes

Yes, fans, it's all true. The Champions of the West proved just that yesterday, as they showed the "Fat Boy", Woody Hayes that press clippings don't win football games.

"It may sound funny, but we knew before we went out there that we were going to win," safety Tom Curtis said yesterday afternoon in the Michigan lockerroom. It was this confidence that dethroned the allegedly number one team in the nation.

"Anyone can be ordinary, all you have to do is breath. But WE'RE NUMBER 1, WE'RE NUMBER 1," Wolverine halfback Bill Taylor said so aptly yesterday.

THE MICHIGAN locker room yesterday was right out of a Tex Maule novel. University President Robben Fleming greeted the players and then bear-hugged athletic director Don Canham.

Coach Bo Schembechler professed, "It was a great win. Now all the sour sportswriters on the coast will have to look me in the eye." Schembechler was referring to all the pre-game talk about how the West coast wanted the Pacific Eight champion to meet a "truly representative team" from the Big Ten.

Now the world knows the only "representative" squad from the Big Ten is the victorious eleven from Ann Arbor.

THE STATISTICS for the game are deceiving. The first down totals were remarkable even. But the interesting item is that first-string quarterback completed 10 passes; six of them were to Buckeyes and four were to Wolverines. Likewise, second-stringer Ron Maciejowski completed three of ten passes to his own receivers and two to Michigan defensive backs.

The plain truth is that the Wolverines stopped the Ohio State running attack and when Kern and his back-up tried to pass they fell prey to the best defensive secondary in the world.

I sat in the press box next to Roger Stanton, editor of the Football News. If you've read this week's edition, you'd know about his article how sad it is that Ohio State can't go to the Rose Bowl this year. Stanton unfortunately wrote it before yesterday's trial of strength. During the game all of the Michigan partisans in the press box kidded Stanton about his erroneous editorializing.

I must confess that this column is being written when this writer is in a state of drunkeness. I am drunk with the notion that Michigan is the greatest team in the country. I am drunk with the idea that USC will suffer the humiliation of the century next January 1st.

JIM MANDICH told me in the locker room that Friday night the Michigan team saw a Paul Newman flick called "The Prize." Whoever scheduled that movie must have had the unpredictable premonition that Michigan would earn the most-coveted trophy of the century, the "unwinnable" win over the Buckeyes.

Henry Hill revealed to me the basis for the Wolverines' success: "We knew all week we could bean 'em. How can you compare any college team to a pro team (Minnesota)?"

The unanimous consensus of Hill, wolfman Tommie Darden, and defensive tackle Pete Newell (who, by the way, played his best game) was that Michigan's win was due in a large measure to its being an "emotional" game.

1970
1971
1972
1973
1974
1975
1976
1977
1978
1979

the 1970s

MARCH 8, 1971

JOE FRAZIER FIGHTS MEAN, TAKES ALI IN 15

AUG. 31, 1971

'U' men land on moon

SEPT. 9, 1971

Drinking age cut by state to 18

Michigan's 18 to 20-year-olds will be able to order alcoholic refreshments starting next January.

Through legislation passed in July, the state's more than 500,-000 18-to 21-year-olds will also be able to enter into legal contracts, sue and be sued, and share other rights previously reserved to those over 21.

The measure, in effect lowers the states age of majority to 18.

SEPT. 6, 1979

Shapiro to assume 'U' presidency Jan. 1

APRIL 2, 1972

A happy toker and Lt. Staudenmeir   JIM WALLACE/Daily

Cops stand by as kids get high

By CHARLES STEIN

Who is it that neither rain, nor sleet nor snow can stop? The mailman, you say. Well perhaps, but from now on you'll have to include your friendly Ann Arbor dope-smoker in that once exclusive category.

For despite freezing temperatures, intermittent snow showers and the possibility of arrest, some 500 hardy souls ventured out to the diag, yesterday for the First Annual Hash Festival.

The Festival coincided with the effec-tive date of the state's new marijuana law. The law lowers the penalty for possession to the level of a misdemeanor punishable by a maximum jail sentence of ninety days plus a $1000 fine.

The threat of punishment seemed far away yesterday, however, as people got into the holiday spirit by openly puffing away on "the evil weed." No attempt was made by participants to disguise their activity, and several even flaunted Ann Arbor Hash Festival T-shirts.

JAN. 23, 1973

NATIONWIDE ABORTION MADE LEGAL IN SURPRISE SUPREME COURT RULING

AUG. 10, 1974

Nixon resigns! Ford to take oath of office at noon today

TOM GOTTLIEB/Daily
Vice President Ford addresses graduating seniors at Crisler Arena Saturday. (May 8, 1974)

The agony that was Columbus

Ohio State methodically ruins Wolverines' unblemished record

OSU's Hayden (22) finds a hole.
MORT NOVECK/Daily

— on this and that —
Nine and one is no disgrace

eric siegel

COLUMBUS

THE MICHIGAN players walked slowly down the entranceway to the visiting locker room at Ohio Stadium here yesterday, unbuttoning their chin straps, removing their helmets, bearing the jeers and the catcalls that the Ohio State fans poured down on them.

No one was crying over the 20-9 loss to the Buckeyes—not then, anyway—but it was obvious they were trying to hold back their tears.

Later, in the Michigan locker room, there was some evidence that there might have been some tears. Coach Bo Schembechler, who had led his team to a 9-1 season and compiled a 17-4 record in two seasons as head coach of the Wolverines, was backed against some lockers, surrounded by a group of reporters, and his eyes were red and his voice was low.

"I don't want anyone talking to the kids," Schembechler said, almost choking on the words. "You can ask me anything you want—but I don't want anyone talking to the kids."

The kids were, of course, the Michigan players—Don Moorhead, Billy Taylor, Glenn Doughty, Fritz Seyferth, Henry Hill, Jim Betts, Tom Darden and on through the four dozen players who made the Michigan traveling roster, and who had just gotten beaten in a game that would have given them the Big Ten championship and a possible shot at a number one ranking in the wire service polls.

They did not play all that poorly yesterday; their defense did almost everything one could expect of it.

But they did commit three costly fumbles, two of which wound up in the hands of the Buckeyes; Moorhead threw an interception that led to a score; and they were penalized a costly 48 yards, yards that contributed to stalled drives on some occasions and caused a loss of good field position on another.

It was not a perfect game and it was not, by Michigan standards, even a good game, but Schembechler would not find fault with his players.

"I'm not the least bit disappointed in Michigan," he said, in his most forceful voice of his 10-minute press conference. "We were high but we weren't nervous, we played with good enthusiasm. You have to give credit to OSU."

Bucks trample Wolverines

By ERIC SIEGEL
Special To The Daily

COLUMBUS — Ohio State pulled a dark curtain down over Michigan's finest season since 1964 here yesterday, downing the Wolverines 20-9 and winning the Big Ten football championship.

The Buckeyes, spearheaded by a rugged defense and helped along by three Wolverine turnovers and a costly Michigan penalty, pulled to a 10-3 halftime lead and added 10 points in the final quarter to salt away their second victory in three years over the Wolverines.

The Wolverines, who had been averaging over 30 points and 400 yards per game, were held to just 155 total yards, a second period field goal and a third quarter touchdown.

"We didn't move the ball on the ground and that hurt," said Michigan coach Bo Schembechler, whose team totaled just 37 yards on the ground in 30 rushing attempts. "We felt their defense would have

to crack somewhere if we were going to win — but it didn't.

"Our defense was good," Schembechler added, "but we just couldn't move the ball and we helped them make points with our mistakes."

Ohio State's Coach Woody Hayes, winning his second outright conference title in three years, also praised the Buckeye defense. "I said last week our defense was great, but it was even better today," Hayes said.

"I tell you right now if there has to be a coach of the year it should be our defensive coach," Hayes added. "The defense was unbelievable — just absolutely amazing."

That Buckeye defense, which yielded a meager 10 first downs, held the Wolverines in check throughout the second half after Michigan had narrowed the Bucks' lead to 10-9 at the beginning of the third quarter.

Blue surge busts Bucks

OH WHAT A LOVELY DAY!

Michigan secured its first undefeated regular season since 1948 with 11 wins, but the Wolverines eventually fell to Stanford in the Rose Bowl.

TOM GOTTLIEB/Daily

TOM DARDEN (35) picks off a Buckeye pass intended for Dick Wakefield (91) to stave off a last minute OSU drive. Ohio State head coach Woody Hayes claimed pass interference on the play and stormed out onto the field to protest.

Fans explode with joy

By CHIP, EGGSUCKER, BULL and TOR

Pandemonium.

The goalposts, raised like a chicken leg and waving like a willow in the wind. Borne out of Michigan Stadium by thousands of adrenalin, crazed young fans, to come to rest splintered in a thousand sorority rooms and student garrets.

Michigan had beaten Ohio State and the fans exploded out of the stands like so many race horses straining at the bit. Most of the cops smiled, intimidated by a crowd that totaled 104,-016, more than any football crowd yet. One Ohio State player, aiming for an over-exuberant fan, clipped a sorority girl in the jaw. The violence of the moment was reduced to a bitter memory, to be recollected and hashed over at a more silent moment.

A thousand kazoos, distributed in the stands before the game, took their place in the wailing, roaring mass which spewed out over the field. "We won" or "We're number one" or "I'm drunk" or some other happy obscenity shrilled out in the crowd.

Perhaps the crowd and the cops were taking a hint from the addled behavior of Mister Woody Hayes, who had thrown a few tantrums on the field as the gridiron action turned against his Buckeyes.

from tolstoy to tinkerbell

Tough luck

Woody Hayes

jim kevra

THE MICHIGAN WOLVERINES slipped by a rampaging Ohio State Buckeye squad yesterday afternoon before an All-Time World Record football crowd, but it was the **delightful gnome from Columbus** who stole the show.

Woodrow "Woody" Hayes, the indefatigable mentor of the Buckeyes, stormed the field twice during the fourth period after the referees failed to rule pass interference on a Tom Darden interception.

Woody's one-man show took place during the waning moments of the contest as the Buckeyes were launching a last-minute drive to upset the Wolverines. With third and 16 on the OSU 49-yard line, Don Lamka's pass to Dick Wakefield was snatched by Tom Darden, the Wolverine safetyman.

After making the interception, Darden tumbled into Wakefield before setting off upfield. At least that's the way the referees ruled it as they called the pass interception legal.

But Woody saw things differently.

According to Hayes, the contact between receiver and defender was made **before** the interception, which would mean that Darden was guilty of interference.

When the referees failed to concur Hayes started to stomp out on the field, thought better of it and turned around to walk off, changed his mind again, and ambled out to midfield to engage in a little friendly chatter with the referees, no doubt about the weather.

The referees, being cold and wet decided to call a 15-yard penalty on Hayes for a little known rule which states, that coaches shall not amble onto the field to discuss the weather during a football game.

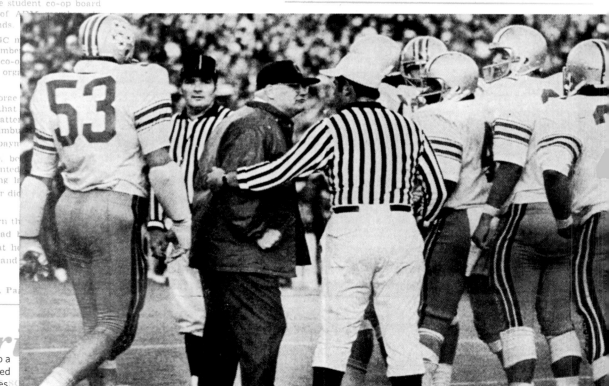

WOODY HAYES, coach of the Ohio State Buckeyes, racks up a penalty for his team in this argument with a referee after a disputed call yesterday. Hayes' players finally got him to the sidelines.

SARA KRULWICH/Daily

MICHIGAN FOOTBALL

Michigan ground game smothers Bruins

Courtesy of Bentley Historical Library

By JOHN PAPANEK
Special To The Daily

LOS ANGELES—It was just like old times last night, as Michigan handed a crushing 26-9 defeat to sixth-ranked UCLA before 57,129 spectators at the Los Angeles Coliseum.

While it may be a little too early to order your Rose Bowl tickets, you can rest assured that the Wolverines are not the pushovers that many cynics said they would be.

"It was a key game for us," Coach Bo Schembechler said after the game. "We had to prove we could move the football and we did. We are going to get better and our players will get better."

In walloping the Bruins, Michigan officially ended its mysterious "Southern California Jinx." The Wolverines were upset in their last two visits here, by Southern Cal and Stanford in the 1970 and 1972 Rose Bowls.

Two-point underdogs against UCLA, the Wolverines ground out 381 yards on the ground and spiced their attack with four key pass completions, all thrown by sophomore quarterback Dennis Franklin.

Powerhouse fullback Ed Shuttlesworth was the big workhorse of the game, carrying 24 times for 115 yards and two touchdowns. He was named offensive player of the game.

ON THE SIDELINES

SEPT. 13, 1970

Whiskey, a fox terrier, was snuck into the Big House for half-time performances.

by BETSY MAHON

Half-time shows have traditionally been dominated by marching bands and stars of a bygone era, but for the past year and a half fans at Michigan Stadium have been treated to a different type of performer.

This new scene stealer is Whiskey, a five-year-old wirehaired fox terrier belonging to grad student Dave Rodgers and his wife Trudy.

When the Rodgers came to Ann Arbor, Dave and some of his friends decided that it would be "a nice prank to put her out on the football field and see what she would do."

Whiskey, wrapped in a blanket, was smuggled into the stadium before the 1968 Michigan-Michigan State game. During half-time fans and attendants watched as she pushed a green and white ball around the field, symbolizing the way the Wolverines were shoving the Spartans about. The fans loved the display but a Flint newspaper and many of the spectators misinterpreted Whiskey's antics and thought she was cheering for State.

Trudy then made her a maize and blue jacket and painted the ball to match as the Rodgers continued to sneak her into the games. The gate attendants were not as impressed with Whiskey as the fans were and while the dog could be easily hidden, disguising the ball became a problem. They finally persuaded friends to carry the ball through the gates so that even if a curious attendant decided to search them he would not discover the dog.

Whiskey achieved national fame during the Rose Bowl when a picture of her barking at an umpire was run in several papers. Besides the trip to Pasadena, Whiskey has also accompanied the team to Columbus and to East Lansing.

The Rodgers have received letters about Whiskey from alumni and others but one of their favorites comes from Dean Shaw, who after a dinner engagement wrote, "I am now a hero with my own kids because I know the dog that runs across the field."

'WE NEVER PROMISED YOU A ROSE GARDEN'

Everything's coming up weeds!

The Buckeyes earned a controversial Rose Bowl bid after a 10-10 tie.

BOB JORDAN/Daily
AN ANGRY BO SCHEMBECHLER strikes a pose yesterday to tell it all.

> " For 24 hours, 100 Michigan football players and all Maize and Blue partisans bathed in euphoria of a Rose Bowl trip ... But at 2:01 P.M. Ann Arbor time last Sunday, the sledgehammer fell and crushed the rosy dreams of the Wolverines. "
>
> — Chuck Bloom, *The Michigan Daily*

Bo lashes out at Big Ten decision

By DAN BORUS and CHARLES STEIN

In the wake of the Big Ten Athletic Directors' shocking 6-4 vote to send Ohio State to the 1974 Rose Bowl, a visibly shaken Michigan coach Bo Schembechler yesterday lashed out at the directors, charging that their decision "was based on ignorance, petty jealousies and the exaggerated issue of Franklin's injury."

Speaking before the weekly gathering of the 'M' Quarterback Club, the five year Michigan mentor further charged that Big Ten Commissioner Wayne Duke unfairly influenced the vote by his handling of information related to Wolverine quarterback Dennis Franklin's injury.

DUKE PROMPTLY LABELED Schembechler's charges "totally absurd.'" Similarly, the athletic directors contacted by The Daily denied that personal vendettas played any role in their final decision.

The directors' comments notwithstanding, the Wolverine field marshall urged the Rose Bowl committee to take the selection decision out of the hands of the directors. He described them as "incapable of making an impartial judgement."

Obviously stunned by the weekend balloting, Schembechler went on to praise his squad in the most glowing of terms. "They did everything I ever asked of them," he recounted. "They outplayed Ohio State.

"THEY EARNED the right to go to the Rose Bowl and to a man every one of them wanted to go. It's no secret that this isn't always the case."

"With this decision," Schembechler added, his voice growing crisp and taut, "the Big Ten has shown that they put prestige above the players."

The coach's claim that petty jealousies rather than gridiron performance swayed the vote has aroused the most bitter exchanges in this generally bitter affair.

IT IS NO SECRET among members of the Michigan sports establishment that Don Canham has made enemies in his tenure as athletic director.

One official referring to this situation said, "Let's face it, Canham is one of the most aggressive and influential directors in the whole conference, and a lot of people resent it. This vote was the perfect chance for them to get back at him."

According to these same sources Canham is resented at Northwestern for his part in a decision prohibiting the Chicago Bears from playing their schedule at the school's Dyche Stadium.

Decision stuns 'M' players

By BOB HEUER

It was a win, then a tie, then a loss.

As Larry Gustafson knelt at the 34-yard line waiting for Mike Lantry's strong left foot to finish off Ohio State's desperate Buckeyes, victory seemed imminent.

But as Lantry's field goal attempt went a few feet wide to the right, an anticlimactic, immensely satisfying, yet agonizingly frustrating 10-10 verdict flickered in the scoreboard lights.

Then came the shocker.

Disregarding the edict of all who witnessed Saturday's titanic struggle, the Big Ten athletic directors voted to send Ohio State, not Michigan to the Rose Bowl on New Year's Day.

Sunday's decision came as a cold slap in the face to the Wolverines, not to mention the howling Michigan partisans (an NCAA record 105,233) who watched their team come from the brink of disaster to within inches of a win over the nation's number one ranked football team.

But how six prestige-minded politicos voted Sunday in no way diminishes the fact that one helluva football game unfolded beneath the threatening skies over Michigan Stadium on November 24, 1973.

JOHN UPTON/Daily

BUCKEYE TAILBACK ARCHIE GRIFFIN (45) scoots between Michigan defenders Dave Brown (6) and Walt Williamson (91) and over fallen giant John Hicks (74) during the much ballyhooed 'showdown' last Saturday. Griffin, Brown and Hicks are A.P. Big Ten first-team performers, while Williamson made the second squad.

> ❝ **It's nothing but goddamn politics! The athletic directors were playing with us and we really got screwed in the end. I hope Southern Cal beats the shit out of Ohio State. I've got nothing against Ohio. I won't be rooting against them, but against the Big Ten.** ❞
>
> — Don Coleman, *Michigan defensive end*

City Council praises Wolverines' season, rips Rose Bowl decision

By JACK KROST

The widening uproar over the decision by the Big Ten athletic directors to send Ohio State to the Rose Bowl, has now extended to the hallowed halls of Ann Arbor's City Council.

In a special session last night, Council unanimously passed a resolution chastising the athletic directors for their decision and complimenting Bo Schembechler and the Michigan football team on an otherwise successful season.

THE RESOLUTION maintains, that "Michigan clearly demonstrated its superiority over Ohio State" in the game last Saturday, and that "the people of the city of Ann Arbor oppose their (the athletic officials) decision."

It concludes with the statement, "We know that Michigan deserves to be in the Rose Bowl."

Buckeyes shatter Michigan dream

KEN FINK/Daily

GORDON BELL (5) picks up some of his 108 yards rushing on this play, as Buckeye Arnie Jones (42) sprawls frustrated on the ground and Ken Thompson (9) sets for the tackle. But Bell's efforts were not enough, as Ohio State won 12-10.

Climactic battle . . .
. . . just a kicking contest

Klaban's four FG's pace 12-10 triumph

By MARC FELDMAN
Special To The Daily

COLUMBUS — Michigan placekicker Mike Lantry narrowly missed a 33-yard field goal with 18 seconds left, and Tom Klaban booted four Ohio State three-pointers, lifting the Buckeyes to a 12-10 win and a share of the Big Ten title for the third straight year.

Lantry, who gave Michigan a 10-0 edge with a first quarter 37-yard field goal, was just wide to the left on the boot that would have given Michigan an undisputed Big Ten Championship, an unbeaten season, and a sure trip to the Rose Bowl.

A CZECHOSLOVAKIAN import, Klaban kicked three field goals in the first half and another in the third period, giving the Buckeyes the nationally televised victory.

Stopping an Ohio State team without a touchdown for the first time in seven years, the Wolverine defense held the Bucks to 253 total yards and kept them bottled up for much of the afternoon.

In a pressure-packed final two minutes, the Wolverines did nearly everything right, but still came up short.

> **Bo said this game would be decided on the kicking game and he was right. I heard that and decided we would work hard all week on kicking and punting—and we did work hard on it. Sometimes you can learn something from another coach.**
> — Woody Hayes, *Ohio State football coach*

MICHIGAN FOOTBALL

Orange Bowl: The Sooners the better

The 1976 Orange Bowl berth began Michigan's streak of 33 consecutive bowl game appearances, which ended in 2008 as the second-longest streak in NCAA football history.

By LEBA HERTZ

STRAIGHT from the Florida sunshine tree, strutting down Biscayne Boulevard, leading a battalion of flag bearing band members, America's own Anita Bryant heralded the opening of the King Orange Jamboree Parade with her rendition of I'm a Yankee Doodle Dandy and It's a Grand Old Flag. And the crowd loved it.

In the 42nd annual Orange Bowl parade, over 600,000 spectators watched as 32 floats and 25 bands glittered and shone in what was to be a prelude to the showdown between Oklahoma and Michigan and the National Championship.

With such showstoppers as McDonald's Boston Tea Party, Burger King's Architects of Freedom, and Michigan and Oklahoma's marching bands, the crowds showed their approval with thunderous applause.

WHISTLES and hoots greeted Copperstone's float of smiling bathing beauties as it passed the obviously excited crowd.

When Michigan's band passed the grandstand, partisan fans waved homemade "Go Blue" banners and their choruses of "Hail to the Victors" drowned out the other bands.

Oklahoma fans were no less quiet. Boomer Sooner rang through the bleachers and the entrance of Big Red, super fan, riding in his vintage crimson car, sent the crowd into a fever pitch.

Just as the parade was its usual sparkling pool of indulgence, the Orange Bowl game also lived up to its hype. The momentum accelerated immediately prior to kickoff, when Sooner and Wolverine fans realized that mighty Ohio State was about to be upset by the UCLA Bruins. Suddenly, the Orange Bowl became a battle for the coveted National Championship.

AS PREDICTED by sports analysts, the game became a defensive struggle. Quarterback Rick Leach and running back Gordon Bell were stifled by the strong and quick Oklahoma defense. At the same time, Michigan's highly touted defense was impressively containing the Sooner's premier runner, Joe Washington.

But a few big plays, highlight-ed by a stunning 39 yard touchdown run by Oklahoma's unheralded Billy Brooks, pushed the momentum over to the Sooners. When the game was over, and the confetti had floated to the ground, there was no question as to who was the best team in the nation.

The parade's glittering patriotism and commercialism was revived and intensified during the half-time show. Continuing the Odyssey to Freedom and Bicentennial theme, the Orange Bowl Committee staged a half-time affair which could put the Rockettes to shame.

Beneath a cloud of American flags waving in the cool Miami air tutu clad dancers, baton twirlers, spruced up bands, fancy floats, and Uncle Sam converged on the playing turf in one cymbal-crashing, cannon-blasting tribute to America's 200th anniversary.

AND SO IT was—another parade, another game, another year, and another heartbreaking defeat for a Michigan team which season after season just can't seem to clinch the big one to ice the cake.

KEN FINK AND PAULINE LUBENS/Daily

BLUE ROSES!

> **This is the biggest thing in my college career. This right here is the climax of everything.**
>
> — Greg Morton, *Michigan defensive tackle*

PAULINE LUBENS/Daily

EUPHORIC MICHIGAN PLAYERS carry their coach Bo Schembechler off the field on their shoulders, while raising their index fingers high to accompany their chants of "We're number one."

> **You've heard the theories. Michigan couldn't win in Columbus. The Wolverines were 'jinxed.' According to the theories, the Wolverines outplay the Buckeyes statistically, but when the big or key play is needed, they aren't able to come up with it. ... Michigan buried all "jinx" theories here yesterday.**
>
> — Rich Lerner, *The Michigan Daily*

'M' blanks OSU 22-0

By BILL STIEG
Special To The Daily

COLUMBUS, Ohio — At long last, sweet victory.

There were no missed field goals to agonize over no goal line stands to painfully recall, and no intercepted passes to moan about Not this year.

MICHIGAN IS going to the Rose Bowl.

The talented and confident Wolverines winless against Ohio State since 1971 made up for the years of frustration yesterday with a masterfully executed and thoroughly convincing 22-0 clubbing of the Buckeyes.

With their satisfying win, the 10-1 Wolverines gain a share of the Big Ten championship and, at last, a berth in the Rose Bowl opposite Pacific Eight champion Southern California Jan. 1 in Pasadena, Calif.

THE 8-2-1 Buckeyes will play the Big Eight champion in Miami's Orange Bowl.

A record Ohio Stadium crowd of 87,250 and a national-television audience watched Michigan score three second-half touchdowns to avenge three losses and an infamous tie over the last four years. And the players loved it.

"This victory takes care of all four of those games," said senior co-captain Rob Lytle. The Wolverines' star running back once again led all rushers, this time with 165 yards in 29 carries.

BRAD BENJAMIN/Daily

Defeat won't change Bo

By BILL STIEG

Some things never change — especially Michigan football and coach Bo Schembechler.

Once again, the Wolverines failed to win the last game of the season, and once again, Schembechler sees nothing seriously wrong with his team.

THIS TIME the season-ending sour note was a 14-6 loss to the University of Southern California (USC) in last Saturday's Rose Bowl. The year before ended with a 14-6 Orange Bowl loss. In his eight years at Michigan, Schembechler's teams have compiled an 0-7-1 record in season-ending games.

But Schembechler isn't worried. Despite criticism from fans and the media concerning Michigan's poor passing and pass defense, he's not going to change anything.

"This is the winningest program in the country — we're not going to make any big changes," he said yesterday. "We're always one of the best teams in the country and I think we'll continue that."

MICHIGAN quarterback Rick Leach completed only four of 12 passes in the Rose Bowl, while USC's Vince Evans hit 14 of 20, including several third down completions that kept the Trojans moving all afternoon.

Many pinned the blame for Michigan's loss on the Wolverines' poor passing and pass defense. Similar complaints were lodged after each of Michigan's losses over the past eight years. But Schembechler predictably discounted the importance of the pass.

"I don't care about the fans," he said. "We didn't throw very well, but it wasn't the passing that beat us. It was our failure to possess the football in the second half. Our defense had to play too much and we got tired. (USC) is a strong, capable team that moved the ball."

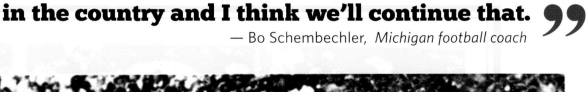
A pass fails, a runner stumbles...Roses wilt

> **This is the winningest program in the country – we're not going to make any big changes. We're always one of the best teams in the country and I think we'll continue that.**
>
> — Bo Schembechler, *Michigan football coach*

> **Once again the Wolverines had missed that elusive national title they seemed destined to win at last. They had taken the big one from the guy in Columbus and Pasadena had at last become a reality. But they never quite made it all the way.**
>
> — Pauline Lubens, *The Michigan Daily*

SCOTT ECCKER AND PAULINE LUBENS/Daily

Blue crunches Badgers, 56-0

By SCOTT LEWIS

A showdown battle at Michigan Stadium yesterday, turned into no more than a confirmation that "Big Two and Little Eight" aptly portrays the Big Ten in 1977.

Previously undefeated and 14th-ranked Wisconsin, perched atop the conference standings, was forced to face reality by a devastating Michigan team, and became the victim of a 56-0 thrashing.

THE SCORE definitely indicated the relative strengths of the two teams yesterday. Michigan continually pounded away at the relatively powerless Badgers with a balanced offensive attack, and a stingy defense. Wisconsin's highly-touted offense did not get into Wolverine territory until but 2:43 remained in the game.

"They'd been leading the Big Ten in a lot of categories, and we just wanted to show them the type of football that we could play," said Michigan quarterback Rick Leach, who has been disproving his critics week-by-week.

For the second time in three weeks,

Michigan's passing game, counteracting a defense geared toward the run, helped by converting many key third downs and blew the game wide open.

LEACH AND his mates converted 16 of 21 third down situations into either first downs or touchdowns with a mixture of pin-point passes and straight-ahead running plays.

"We played the option well and we forced them to throw," said Wisconsin coach John Jardine. "But they tore us up on third down with the pass and the draw. They took the steam out of us.

"We played a great football team today. They embarrassed us. We got beat by a hell of a team," he added.

THE SWEETNESS of the victory was further enhanced by the play of backup tailback Roosevelt Smith. Starting in place of Harlan Huckleby, who sat the game out with a pulled leg muscle, Smith tallied 157 yards on 25 carries, and grabbed two third-down passes on Michigan's first drive of the game.

"Rose did a good job in his first

start," prased Schembechler. "He came in here and got hurt as a freshman last year and didn't play, but he's done a great job. He started fourth team this year and worked his way up. It's great to see a young guy like that come through when the pressure is on."

The Wolverines virtually put the game away in the first half. The 21-0 locker room lead, though impressive, still did not reflect the Wolverines' total dominance over the Badgers in the first half.

ALTHOUGH THE Michigan offense marched within Wisconsin's 30-yard line on each of its six possessions of the half, only three of those resulted in scores.

After taking the opening kickoff, Michigan took less than six minutes in marching to the game's winning touchdown.

The offense seemed in control the whole drive, but it took a desperation fling into the end zone by a scrambling Leach to get the points.

Making a leaping catch, over the outstretched hands of the Wisconsin defender, in the end zone was sophomore tight end Doug Marsh.

Battle of unbeatens just a laugher as Blue romps

> ❝ **You saw a great performance by a great little quarterback. He picked them to pieces.** ❞
>
> — Bo Schembechler,
> *Michigan football coach*

BO SCHEMBECHLER and his quarterback Rick Leach proved something to the world yesterday. Wisconsin has no doubts about it and I hope some skeptical Wolverine fans can now believe it.

They proved that the Wolverines know what the forward pass is and they can use it effectively.

The Wisconsin Badgers came into yesterday's contest undefeated with visions of Pasadena dancing in their heads. Their defense had allowed a mere 34 points in five games including an impressive shutout of Illinois the previous weekend while their offense had rolled up 111 points.

But yesterday the Badgers had their high hopes dashed as Michigan unceremoniously dumped them on their ears.

The game was never close. Michigan blew it open early with the pass and then hung around to pick up the pieces on the ground.

— *BY JOHN NIEMEYER*

ALAN BILINSKY/Daily

Tight end Gene Johnson tiptoes through the Badgers for an early score.

The Bucks stopped here!

ANDY FREEBERG/Daily

Dynamite defense destroys OSU; bring on the West Coast kids!

Michigan handled the Buckeyes, but it eventually suffered its third-straight Rose Bowl loss.

Tom Cousineau (36) has an eye for Wolverine quarterback Rick Leach (7) and all his muscles have been activated, but the Michigan lefty has turned his thoughts and body to the goal-line—the stripe he crossed at the conclusion of this play.

DELAYED REACTION

—By Scott Lewis—

Take this Buckeyes . . .

. . . in yo' face

OL' WOODY HAYES might be a good coach, but he can never win the big ones.

It wasn't too long ago that there was talk about an Ohio State jinx around Ann Arbor but that seems ever so far away right now. There's no doubt about it—the Wolverines now control the Michigan-OSU rivalry and all I can say is: it's about time.

Those tortuous years of the early seventies have given way to utter delight in the present. Year after year Michigan would outplay Ohio State on paper, only to be denied by those little things that deny victories.

But it's a different story now. Without a doubt, the Buckeye offense out-dueled Michigan's. It ran more effectively, passed better and controlled the ball for most of the game. Had the Ohio State runners not fumbled so often, the Buckeyes could very well have won this one.

But who cares?

It's so nice to have the breaks go Michigan's way for a change. It gives you faith in the old adage that the breaks will even out in the long run.

Now it's the Buckeye fans who must mutter about their team's ugly misfortunes. They'll be the ones to remember that although Ohio State marched into Wolverine territory five times in the second half, only three points appeared on the scoreboard.

John Anderson, Mel Owens and Curtis Greer   ALAN BILINSKY/Daily

Good-bye Woody

Woody 'large person' Hayes seen here in pre-game action underneath the M Go Blue banner. Sorry Woody, we never promised you a Rose Bowl. Hope you enjoy New Orleans.

Blue Pasadena Express rips Buckeyes

MICHIGAN LINEBACKER Ben Needham (83) latches on to Buckeye quarterback Art Schlichter (10) during Saturday's 14-3 whipping of Ohio State.

ALAN BILINSKY/Daily

> **What was out of the ordinary was hearing Bo explain how important it would be for his team to have a good time on the coast. Suddenly, Schembechler was complaining about the lack (you heard correctly) of entertainment in the proximity of Michigan's hotel (in Pasadena).**
> — Bob Miller, *The Michigan Daily*

Underdog Blue . . .
. . . Bo likes role

WHO WOULD HAVE believed it? For one of the few times since Bo Schembechler became coach at Michigan, his team would be an underdog in a game . . . and Bo was happy about it. He wasn't exactly doing cartwheels, but he didn't look like a man whose team was expected to lose.

Actually, there is more to the story than that. Last Saturday Bo's boys beat Woody without giving up a touchdown and earned the right to go to the Rose Bowl for the third straight year.

"We're happy we won. We can attribute this victory to the tenacity of the Michigan team. Because of the problems we had preparing for and playing this game, I think this win means as much to me as any," beamed Bo.

So, the Wolverines will head west to Pasadena for the third straight year and the fifth time in the 10-year tenure of Schembechler in Ann Arbor. But for the first time, Michigan will most likely be getting points on the Las Vegas betting boards.

That being the case, Bo is determined to take as much pressure off the players as possible. "Let them (USC) worry about being the favorites," he quipped.

Last year Bo tinkered with the prospect of practicing out in Arizona before moving on to Los Angeles, but the idea didn't prove feasible. "I thought about that, I thought about a lot of different things. I want to make some changes, but I don't know what. I am going to talk to some of the players who have been there before and get their reactions," Schembechler said.

— Bob Miller

ALAN BILINSKY/Daily

Third time the charm? Blue hopes so
Michigan eyes Roses after belting Bucks

PHOTOS BY BRAD BENJAMIN AND MAUREEN O'MALLEY/Daily

Same old story— wilted roses

By BOB MILLER

If Michigan had to lose the 1979 Rose Bowl, it might as well have been to the number one team in the country. But the questions after the game were, did Michigan really lose and is Southern Cal really No. 1?

In the spirit of diplomacy, the answers are yes and no on both counts.

AS FAR AS THE final score, the records, and the results are concerned, it will forever stand at USC 17, Michigan 10. Still, there will be people who contend that Charles White fumbled at the goal line and that this cost Michigan the game.

Bo Schembechler is one of those people. He said, after viewing the replay of the fumble-non-fumble touchdown, that his game plan changed to try to get the Wolverines back in the contest.

At that point the score was 14-3. Rick Leach opened up the offense by passing and was intercepted. A patented Frank Jordan last second field goal ballooned the Trojan lead to 17-3 at the half

THE 10 POINTS USC scored as a result of the celebrated fumble/touchdown were more than enough to give Southern Cal the victory.

What might escape the memory of those who saw the game was that Leach threw an interception just four minutes

into the game which led to USC's first TD. The Trojans scored all of their points by way of gifts from the Wolverines and the referees.

But Michigan was not able to do anyting spectacular themselves on offense. Leach threw for 137 yards, but one-third of that yardage came on the Wolverines' only touchdown of the afternoon, a 44 yard aerial bomb from Leach to Roosevelt Smith. However, that was the only scoring in the second half.

DESPITE THE WHITE fiasco, despite a roughing the kicker penalty (which should be nominated for best acting job of the young year). Michigan was not going to win the Rose Bowl, not the way they played

"Our defense played well enough to win, our offense didn't," lamented Schembechler.

USC coach John Robinson felt the same way. "It was like the game two years ago. It was a very physical game. You've got to give the defense credit, they played exceptionally."

THE IRONIC POINT is that Michigan's defense was supposed to be suspect all season long and the offense was purportedly in a class by itself. But when the 1978 season is reviewed, it will be the defense from after the Michigan State game until the end of the season that really held the team together.

> **A bouquet of Roses and a Bowl of Blues.**
>
> *The Michigan Daily*

A² gets a piece of the Rock

Michigan welcomed the Slippery Rock University football team to the Big House in 1979 during one of the Wolverines' away games. Michigan fans had been cheering for the Rocks since 1959 when an announcer accidentally read the score of Slippery Rock's game during a Michigan halftime. Students went wild, and reading the score became a tradition. Even today, fans cheer as Slippery Rock's scores are announced during halftime.

PAUL ENGSTROM/Daily

YOU MAY NOTICE the Slippery Rock runner has on some shades, but for he and his mates the result of yesterday's game just wasn't too cool.

Slippery Rock press guide

Here & there

Rock loses roll, 45-14

By DAN PERRIN

The day of The Rock was not to be. Going into yesterday's Pennsylvania Conference battle with Shippensburg State at Michigan Stadium, Slippery Rock had everything going for it. They had been labeled the home team, they had the majority of the 61,143 Band Day fans rooting for them and they had all the pre-game hoopla pointed their way. In other words they had it made.

But the hot and humid day instead belonged strictly to the Shippensburg State Red Raiders, who spit in the eye of adversity and rolled to an easy 45-14 victory over the Rockets.

Blue cages Cal, 14-10

By BILLY SAHN
Special to The Daily

BERKELEY, Calif. — In spite of their faltering kicking game, the Michigan Wolverines maintained their composure as they defeated the California Golden Bears 14-10 at Memorial Stadium before a crowd of 57,000.

Michigan quarterback John Wangler, who started the game over B. J. Dickey, played brilliantly as he led his offensive unit down the field time and time again. However, the offense only scored twice, both touchdowns coming in the second half.

That pass! Blue tops Hoosiers
Wolverines grab win, 27-21, in final seconds

A miracle in A²

By BILLY SAHN

Pity those who had their backs turned.

Pity those, who, convinced of a 21-21 tie, did not witness a miracle as they filed out of Michigan Stadium yesterday.

They missed perhaps one of the most exciting moments in 100 years of Michigan football when John Wangler connected with Anthony Carter for a 45-yard touchdown pass as time ran out, securing a 27-21 victory for the Wolverines over Indiana.

The Hoosiers, determined to play the Wolverines to the hilt, put their best foot forward as they battled Michigan to a 21-21 tie late in the fourth quarter, sending the Homecoming crowd of 104,832 into a frenzy.

DOWN 14-7 AT halftime, the Wolverines quickly regained their composure in the third quarter, as they scored two unanswered touchdowns against the strong Hoosier defense.

But for all their effort, the Wolverines just could not put Indiana away as the opposing defense foiled two touchdown drives, forcing head coach Bo Schembechler to send in placekicker Bryan Virgil to attempt two three-point conversions. But neither one sailed through the uprights, enabling Indiana to retain a glimmer of hope.

The Hoosiers smartly capitalized on Michigan's field goal misfortunes, notching the tying touchdown late in the fourth quarter.

HOOSIER QUARTERBACK Tim Clifford, who performed brilliantly all afternoon, racking up 232 yards net-passing, let loose a series of passes on their final drive, the last one resulting in six-points.

Moving the ball from their 21-yard line 20 yards, Clifford released a 54-yard bomb to Nate Lundy, who was pushed out-of-bounds by Mike Jolly on the Michigan two yard line.

After a recovered fumble, Clifford scored the Hoosier's third touchdown of the day as he passed to Dave Harangody, preceded by the one-point conversion.

WITH ONLY 55 seconds showing on the clock, it appeared as if Indiana had put the Wolverines on ice, settling for a tie. But it was not to be, as Schembechler pulled all stops.

With only a mere six seconds remaining, Michigan quarterback John Wangler, who substituted for second quarter-injured B. J. Dickey, laced a pass up the middle to his receiver Carter waiting at the 25-yard line of Indiana.

Carter eluded two defenders, one when he caught the ball and the other grabbing at his leg at the two-yard line to scamper into the end zone for the ultimate score.

IT WAS A miraculous play for the seemingly ill-fated Wolverines. The fact that the ball got into Carter's hands would have satisfied many a coach, but it did not satisfy the young freshman. He was determined to score.

"If I'd been tackled," said the jubilant Carter in the post-game press conference, "the game would have been over. One guy hit me, and the next grabbed me by the leg on the two-yard line.

"I thought I'd have no chance, but I managed to get by him," he added.

DAVID HARRIS/Daily

A JUBILANT ANTHONY CARTER holds the game ball high above his head just an instant before he is swarmed by fellow Wolverines and fans in yesterday's homecoming game. The Wolverines pulled off a miraculous 27-21 victory with a John Wangler to Carter 45-yard pass play as time expired.

ON THE SIDELINES

Isaacson is 'ham' with apples at half-time

By BILLY NEFF

He started out with the rocks and bottles lying on the beach when he was a lifeguard. Sometimes these days he switches to peaches, tomatoes, or tennis balls.

But to the audience of 105,000 that's his every home football game, Jim Isaacson is the blond kid who makes apples fly, the extrovert out in front of sections 30 and 31 who juggles red orbs like nobody's business.

"ONE GAME I did peaches," says the junior biology major from New Jersey. "They didn't have apples in the store. It was real juicy. I have in the past done tomatoes and squished them on my head."

Apples, it turns out, are just right for biting in mid-flight, Isaacson's specialty.

Isaacson has run his one-man half-time show for three years with a difference — juggle or fumble, it's all for fun.

"PEOPLE WILL boo when I drop them and I like that. I almost like it as much when they boo . . . I really enjoy it. I'm a ham. I like the attention. It's fun, it's something to do that's different," he says.

Half the pleasure of juggling is in the celebrity status it brings. "You meet a lot of people who come up to you and say, 'You're the juggler, aren't you?' " he says. "Some people will come up and tell me that it was a good job."

Isaacson's act is expanding. He says he met a couple hockey players at Dooley's last year who asked him to juggle at their games. He was more than willing, he says, to add to his audience.

1980
1981
1982
1983
1984
1985
1986
1987
1988
1989

AUG. 12, 1981

New law library to open

Three underground levels provide much needed space

SUNLIGHT STREAMS onto construction workers as they put the finishing touches on the University's new law library, even though the library's three levels are completely underground.

KIM HILL/Daily

MAY 17, 1984

No surprise: Berenson will return to coach 'M' icers

SEPT. 4, 1986

'U' hospital gets off to a healthy start

By ELLEN FIEDELHOLTZ

In a time when competition for hospital patients is high, the University's new 586 bed hospital is flourishing.

After four years of planning, the University Hospital and the A. Alfred Taubman Health Care Center was officially dedicated in June. The hospital cost $365 million to build and is the most expensive hospital in the state's history.

JAN. 29, 1986

Shuttle explodes; 7 die
U.S. shocked by Challenger catastrophe

MAR. 25, 1987

'U' Regent commits suicide
Sarah Power falls from bell tower

SEPT. 8, 1988

Dude, a new prez
Provost takes over top 'U' post

OCT. 24, 1988

Regents divest holdings

BY STEVE KNOPPER

The University will divest the rest of its holdings with companies operating in South Africa within the next few weeks, Vice President and Chief Financial Officer Farris Womack said Friday.

After years of debate, protest, and a legal suit against the State of Michigan, the University's Board of Regents voted Friday, 5-0 with two abstentions, to divest its remaining $500,000 in South Africa-involved companies.

APR. 4, 1989

We are National Champions!

Rumeal's clutch free throws with :03 give 'M' NCAA title

Michigan forward Glen Rice scored 31 points as the Wolverines beat Seton Hall in the NCAA championship game by the score of 80-79. Rice broke Bill Bradley's 24-year old NCAA tournament scoring record with a total of 184 points and was named the NCAA tournament MVP.

ROBIN LOZNAK/Daily

NOV. 1, 1989

Leaders react as Berlin Wall comes tumbling down

PASADENA BOUND!

> **"At a time people thought we were dead, we vowed to come back. And we did."**
>
> — Bo Schembechler,
> *Michigan football coach*

NOV. 22

THE WOLVES ARE HUNGRY!

HEY ART, DO YOU HEAR FOOTSTEPS?

PASADENA

EARLE BRUCE

> **"It was orgasmic, it was better than sex."**
>
> — Matt Gluckman, *Michigan student*

NOV. 25

Schembechler
. . . relied on the defense

Relaxed Bo discusses team's Cinderella football season

By MARK MIHANOVIC

Michigan coach Bo Schembechler, perhaps more relaxed and jovial than he has ever been during a football season, reflected on his team's Cinderella year during the last press luncheon of the year yesterday at Webers' Inn.

Following a campaign during which his team won eight straight games and the Big Ten championship despite a 1-2 start, Schembechler opted to discuss the Wolverines' accomplishments rather than look ahead to New Year's Day and the Rose Bowl against the Washington Huskies.

"IT'S FUNNY how the season changed from where I had no confidence in the defense to where I relied totally on the defense to win it," Schembechler said of the unit which yielded a mere three points during the last 18 periods of play.

"They (the players) did exactly what they had to do to win," he continued. "They won, and they improved as they did. At the very outset of the season and through those two losses, we knew that we were going to have an effective offense. The remarkable improvement of the defense, particularly in the secondary and the defensive line, was the key."

It was a defense that had improved itself enough to pressure Ohio State quarterback Art Schlichter into an eight-for-26 performance in Saturday's 9-3 victory over the Buckeyes.

TOP: MICHIGAN FULLBACK Lawrence Ricks is brought down by a Buckeye defender. (JOHN HAGEN/Daily)
BOTTOM: FANS PACK THE street yesterday in front of the Michigan Union, celebrating the Wolverines' 9-3 victory over the Ohio State Buckeyes. (BRIAN MASCK/Daily)

Wolverines savor bowl victory— 'We wanted to give Bo a win'

By MARK MIHANOVIC

New Year's Day was a day of retribution for the Michigan Wolverines—the consummation of a long struggle to win a bowl game for Coach Bo Schembechler.

"We wanted to go out there and give Bo a win in the Rose Bowl," said center and co-captain George Lilja. "We went out there knowing it would mean a lot to him if we won. You could tell after the game it really did."

SENIOR DEFENSIVE TACKLE Mike Trgovac also testified to Schembechler's personal jubilance at his first bowl victory after seven such defeats.

"He came in and grabbed me, and I've never heard him sing 'Hail to the Victors' so loud. It was tremendous," Trgovac said.

Schembechler's glee wasn't easily hidden. When mammoth offensive tackles Ed Muransky and Bubba Paris hoisted their coach onto their broad shoulders after the game, they could have turned off the lights in the grand old stadium. Bo's beaming face could have lit the place up all by itself.

IT WAS A MOMENT not soon to be forgotten by those who witnessed it, either those present or those watching on television sets across the nation. As the coach thrust his fists into the California air and gleefully banged on the maize and blue helmets around him, viewers could see the relief on his face.

The Wolverines avenged a 1978 Rose Bowl loss to Washington to garner their first bowl win since 1965.

DEC. 12, 1980

'M' seeks revenge in rematch

PAUL ENGSTROM/Daily
MICHIGAN TAILBACK Butch Woolfolk churns up yardage in the Wolverines' 23-6 Rose Bowl triumph over Washington.

Blue gives Bo 1st bowl win

1981

Washington defenders finally catch up with tailback Butch Woolfolk (24).

PAUL ENGSTROM/Daily

> **The bottom line is that the 1980 Michigan Wolverines will be remembered as the unit which gave Bo Schembechler his first bowl victory after seven defeats. And for many of the players, that alone was enough.**
>
> — Mark Mihanovic,
> *The Michigan Daily*

> **Bo's beaming face could have lit the place up all by itself.**
>
> — Mark Mihanovic,
> *The Michigan Daily*

JOHN HAGEN/Daily

JOYOUS WOLVERINE FANS celebrate Michigan's 23-6 win over the Washington Huskies at the 67th Rose Bowl in Pasadena last week.

SEPT. 13	No. 1 MICHIGAN	14
	WISCONSIN	21

Michigan jolted

Despite a preseason No. 1 ranking, the Wolverines dropped their season opener — the first time in 100 years Michigan lost its opener on the road.

" **Our problems were simple: our offense wasn't any good, our defense wasn't any good, and our kicking game wasn't any good, and our coaching was poor. When you put together these four things going against you, it's a miracle we were only beaten by seven points.** *"*

— Bo Schembechler, *Michigan football coach*

Badger 'D' devours Wolverines, 21-14

By MARK MIHANOVIC
Special to the Daily

MADISON — The 1981 football season may long be remembered as one in which Michigan's pre season number one ranking was a mirage as the Wolverines were humbled by Wisconsin yesterday, 21-14.

In front of 68,733 rabid Badger fans, Michigan coach Bo Schembechler suffered his first-ever opening game defeat. It was also the first time in 100 years that the Wolverines have lost a season opener on the road.

Unilke most other Michigan setbacks, the Wolverines were outplayed by the Badgers from the opening kickoff to the final gun.

Unquestionably the most embarassing statistic of the Wolverines, was that, quarterback Steve Smith, in his first start, completed as many passes (three) to Badger free safety Matt Vanden Boom as he did to his own receivers in 18 attempts. Anthony Carter caught only one pass for 11 yards.

Schembechler was discouraged by the offense's performance, but he indicated no plans to play "musical quarterbacks." "Offensively, we probably should have taken it to them more we probably should have run at them," he said.

"WE DIDN'T execute well, and we didn't throw well. However, I am definitely going to keep going with Smith. He's our quarterback."

SEPT. 20	No. 11 MICHIGAN	25
	No. 1 NOTRE DAME	7

Blue maims Notre Dame, 25-7

Irish run out of luck

By GREG DeGULIS

A swarming defense and the birth of the Steve Smith to Anthony Carter combination led the Wolverines to a domination of the Fighting Irish of Notre Dame, 25-7, in front of a crowd of 105,888 in Michigan Stadium and a national television audience yesterday afternoon.

The convincing victory evens Michigan's record at 1-1, while Notre Dame relinquished its short-lived number one ranking and undefeated season record.

The sold out contest showcased a myriad of talented Wolverines and provided an opportunity for revenge of last season's breathtaking loss in South Bend.

THE MOST TALENTED Wolverine of all, junior All-American Carter, caught three passes from Smith, including touchdowns of 71 and 15 yards. The 71-yard touchdown pass was the fourth longest in Wolverine history and was only the second pass caught by Carter this season.

The 71-yard strike to Carter came with 12:08 left in the second quarter and broke open a scoreless contest, providing the Wolverines with the momentum necessary to finally defeat the Irish.

"We really beat them the last two years. They just got more points," senior tackle and on-field cheerleader Ed Muransky commented after the game. "We know how lucky they are, so we had to blow them out."

Muransky spoke the truth as a fired up Michigan offensive line provided gaping holes for its talented trio of running backs, including senior Butch Woolfolk, who chalked up 139 yards on 23 carries for an outstanding 6.0 average. Woolfolk enjoys the spotlight of national television, as he has rushed for 161, 182 and 139 yards in the last three televised games.

Woolfolk passed Russel Davis and Harlan Huckleby for fourth place on the all-time Michigan rushing ladder.

BRIAN MASCK/Daily

MICHIGAN QUARTERBACK Steve Smith (16) charges through a hole created by key blocks from Wolverine guard Kurt Becker (65) and fullback Stan Edwards (32). Blocking proved to be a deciding factor to Michigan's 25-7 victory over top-ranked Notre Dame yesterday.

COURTESY OF THE MICHIGANENSIAN
BOB UFER does the play-by-play for a Michigan game. The Wolverines' number one fan announced 362 consecutive Michigan football games before his illness forced him to miss this year's Wisconsin contest. (Oct. 26, 1981)

> **66** He went down that mod sod like a penguin with a hot herring in his cummerbund. **99**
> — Bob Ufer,
> *Michigan announcer*

Ufer hopes to ignite *Wolverines*

> **66** Football Saturday's just aren't the same without Ufer's familiar 'Meechigan' cry blasting out of radios.
> — Carol Charltron,
> *The Michigan Daily* **99**

JAN. 16, 1982

Meechigan's Ufer dies

By GREG DEGULIS

Veteran Michigan football broadcaster Bob Ufer lost his bout with cancer yesterday morning.

Ufer died at Detroit's Henry Ford Hospital at 11:30 a.m. yesterday, three days after undergoing surgery to remove a blood clot in his brain. He was 61.

The broadcaster's death concludes an unparalleled support of the rich Michigan tradition, including 37 consecutive years of broadcasting 'Meechigan' football.

Ufer's 362-game streak of announcing Wolverine football was finally broken this fall after ill health forced the broadcaster to cease his play-by-play coverage. For the first four games this fall, Ufer could only participate in the opening and closing segments for WJR's Michigan football coverage.

After receiving his doctor's approval, Ufer returned to do the play-by-play for the intrastate clash between Michigan and Michigan State in East Lansing on October 10.

"I'll keep doing it (play-by-play) as long as my body holds together," Ufer said before the MSU contest. "The doctors said if I'm still anxious to do Michigan football, then go ahead and do it."

THE ENTHUSIASTIC Ufer went ahead and broadcast the play-by-play for the game in East Lansing, and even received some well-deserved recognition in Ann Arbor's rival town.

"Even the people at Michigan State respected him," Michigan coach Bo Schembechler said yesterday. "The tribute they gave him up there in East Lansing when he returned to the booth really pleased him."

Ufer continued play-by-play duties for the Michigan-Iowa game in Ann Arbor on October 17. A halftime tribute to the broadcaster was part of the festivities for that contest, the last game Ufer would announce. The tribute included a revision of the M Club banner, which read "Bob Ufer M Club Supports You" and a halftime opportunity for the broadcaster to address the crowd.

"God bless everyone of your cotton pickin' maize and blue hearts", boomed Ufer from the press box amidst the cheers of the crowd. He then asked the fans "What University has the finest football tradition in the country?" An enthusiastic "Michigan" followed, creating an emotional rapport between Wolverine supporters and the voice of Michigan football.

Ufer had planned to broadcast Saturday's Northwestern football game in Ann Arbor, but was admitted to the hospital for tests on Tuesday of last week. On Thursday, the broadcaster underwent surgery for an intracranial blood clot, a complication of the colon cancer from which he had suffered for three years.

Ufer's pro-Michigan rhetoric was missed at the Homecoming activities this weekend, and at Friday's pep rally coach Schembechler asked the crowd to keep Ufer in their prayers.

Ufer's illustrious career at Michigan was not limited to broadcasting football. A 1943 graduate of the University, Ufer established himself as one of the all-time greats in Michigan track in the early 1940's. In 1940, Ufer set eight different freshman track records. Two years later, at the Big Ten track meet in Chicago, Ufer set the world record for the indoor 440 (48.1), a mark which stood as the school record for 32 years.

Upon graduation from the University, Ufer was forced to forget any hopes of competing in the 1944 Olympic games. "Of course," Ufer once commented. "Hitler took care of that. There were no games in '44."

IN TYPICAL UFER style, the broadcaster did not limit his activities at Michigan to running track. He was an active member of Phi Delta Theta fraternity and was a member of Michigamua, the secret senior honorary society. Ufer remained active in these groups after graduation and was always willing to give advice or support when needed.

In addition to his involvement in the campus community, Ufer established an insurance agency in Ann Arbor in 1947. Ufer Insurance blossomed over the years and eventually made him a millionnaire.

Sweet Game for Defense

Auburn sours Michigan's Sugar Bowl in final minute, 9-7

> " **Bend but don't break ... It was a battle cry trumpetted throughout the New Orleans Superdome by the Wolverine defenders.** "
>
> — Ron Pollack, *The Michigan Daily*

BRIAN MASCK/Daily

TOP: Auburn quarterback Randy Campbell evades would-be Michigan tackler Al Sincich during Monday night's Sugar Bowl. **LEFT:** Doc Paul's band brings a bit of the Mardi Gras to Bourbon Street during a short New Year's Day parade.

Defense can't do it all; Blue falls, 9-7

By RON POLLACK
Special to the Daily

NEW ORLEANS — Bend but don't break.

That's been the battle cry of a Michigan defense beset by injuries all season. It was a battle cry trumpetted throughout the New Orleans Superdome by the Wolverine defenders on January 2 in the Sugar Bowl against Auburn.

AGAINST THE Tigers potent wishbone offense the Michigan defense never broke. In fact, it barely bent as it gave up points ever-so grudgingly. Unfortunately, for Michigan fans, the defense bent more than it could afford to in a last-second 9-7 loss to Auburn.

The Tigers won the game by methodically marching 60 yards in 7:21 to set up an Al Del Greco 19-yard field goal with 23 ticks left on the clock. "I sort of waited a long time at Auburn to do something like that," Del Greco said. "Everybody expected me to make it because it was short, and I should have."

While Tiger fans, coaches and players erupted into a fit of delirium, Michigan players sat solemnly on the Superdome turf wondering how they could lose despite keeping Auburn out of the endzone.

Party in New Orleans

Wolverine, Tiger fans celebrate on Bourbon Street

1984

Wolverines maul Miami, 22-14

By PAUL HELGREN

The hurricane that had been blowing across the nation to the top of the college football polls came to a sudden halt in Ann Arbor yesterday afternoon.

And Bernie Kosar, the quarterback who was riding that wind toward a possible Heisman trophy season, fell flatly on his rump, the victim of six Wolverine interceptions that strangled the vaunted Miami passing attack and paved the way for a 22-14 Michigan victory.

THE LOSS snapped a 13-game winning streak for last year's national champions, who beat Auburn two weeks ago in the Kickoff Classic in New Jersey and Florida last week in Tampa. While those two games ended in dramatic Hurricane flurries, the 105,403 Michigan Stadium fans would witness no last-second heroics from Miami yesterday. The Michigan defense saw to that.

"In a game like this," said a jubilant Bo Schembechler, "you remember the big plays on defense."

The biggest plays came courtesy of outside linebacker Rodney "Red" Lyles, who snagged two Kosar spirals in the fourth quarter and three on the day. His last pick-off came with 30 seconds to play, snuffing a last-gasp Miami drive.

DAN HABIB/Daily

TOP: Linebacker Rodney Lyles bowls over several Miami defenders as he returns the second of his three interceptions during the Wolverines' 22-14 triumph yesterday. **LEFT:** Miami's Alvin Ward tries his hand at a chokehold on Michigan's Joe Gray (92). In his eagerness to assert his point, Ward loses his helmet.

ON THE SIDELINES

JUNE 12, 1984

Motor City stuntman sets stadium record

By CHARLIE SEWELL

Ninety-six hours and twelve minutes after he began, Jim Purol sat in the last of 101,701 seats in the Michigan Football Stadium in June.

"Monotony was the most difficult thing about it," said Purol shortly after completing the stunt. The sitting marathon raised nearly $3,500 for the American Lung Association, according to Purol's press agent. Purol has now performed a total of 10 stunts to benefit a variety of charities.

IN HIS four days in the stadium, Purol slept only five and a half hours. During the day he had to be coated with suntan lotion and sprayed with water periodically.

Despite the lack of sleep and a little stiffness in his legs and shoulders, Purol said he felt good. To help him perform the stunt he stuffed a pad into the seat of his pants and used specially designed hand-held tools to protect his hands from blistering as he moved along the stadium benches. "I've been working out for about eight months. I haven't got the biggest arms, but I had enough to make it," he said.

As he drove out of the stadium parking lot at 2:45 p.m., Purol was on his way to a 4 p.m. appearance on television's "Good Afternoon Detroit". "I'm running on adrenalin right now," he said. "Tonight I'll sleep."

But Purol has little time for rest. He performs a nightly comedy musical act at a Detroit nightclub where he is known as Jim Mouth, a name he earned by performing such feats as smoking 140 cigarettes for five minutes and puffing on 40 cigars for a similar period of time.

Mouth hopes the Guiness Book of World Records will publish his newest record and create a new category he calls "stadium sitting." Presently he holds five Guiness records and five unpublished records which the publishers of the record book say are too ridiculous to be published.

Mouth cited several unusual records which do appear in the book, making the publishers' use of the term ridiculous seem contradictory. "I told (the publishers) I was the self-proclaimed world's record holder of the most world records and they told me I couldn't do that. Who do they think they are?" Purol joked during his marathon.

DOUG MCMAHON/Daily

Jim "Mouth" Purol takes a seat in Michigan Stadium in June during his attempt to sit in all of the 101,701 seats.

> " This is a great win because I don't have too many of these. I have to relish them. "
>
> — Bo Schembechler,
> *Michigan football coach*

Bob Perryman (left) and Pat Moons (right) lead Bo Schembechler's victory ride at Sun Devil Stadium in Tempe, Ariz. after Michigan defeated Nebraska, 27-23, in the Fiesta Bowl on New Year's Day.

'M' shreds Huskers in Fiesta

By BRAD MORGAN
Special to the Daily

TEMPE, Ariz. — Could it have ended any other way?

In a fitting finish to a surprising season, Michigan's defense once again rose to the occasion as it had done all year, stifling the Nebraska Cornhuskers in the second half to lead the Wolverines to a 27-23 victory in the Fiesta Bowl on New Year's Day.

THIS WAS a team that was supposed to go nowhere this year, to finish in the middle of the pack in the Big Ten. Instead, the win over Nebraska capped one of Bo Schembechler's best seasons at Michigan. The 10-1-1 record is the best since 1980, and the final No. 2 ranking in both the AP and UPI polls is the best ever.

"At the beginning of the season, we were a long shot team," said a jubilant Schembechler after the game. "My only disappointment was not winning the (Big Ten) championship. Even at that, I've enjoyed this team tremendously. This team has given me the most satisfaction I've ever had."

The tenth win came harder than any of the previous nine. Michigan took the early lead on 42-yard Pat Moons field goal, but Nebraska's potent running attack then took over and raced for two Cornhusker touchdowns and a 14-3 halftime lead. In the process, Nebraska managed to do what no team had done all year — push Michigan's defense all over the field and run its offense almost at will, scoring of 63 and 74-yard drives.

"THEY MOVED the ball better than any team we played this year," said Schebechler. "Our defense's confidence was a little shot when they moved the ball so well."

Mark Messner, who earned Defensive Player of the Game honors for his play on the defensive line, agreed with Schembechler.

"We weren't shocked, but we were upset and mad that we let something like that happen," said the sophomore standout who finished with nine tackles. "Their offensive linemen weren't firing off the ball like we thought they would. They were more of a reading, pushing team. They were opening holes that were just big enough, and we weren't closing them fast enough."

WHILE THE defense was struggling, the offense wasn't able to pick up the slack as it had the last three games. Jamie Morris rushed for 69 of his game-high 156 yards, but quarterback Jim Harbaugh was only five for twelve for 64 yards and was having trouble directing the offense. After the early field goal, Michigan could get no further than the Nebraska 42 in the first half.

"In the beginning, we were trying to balance it out between running and passing to do what it takes to win," said Harbaugh, "but they shut off our passing game very well. I give them a lot of credit for that."

It was obvious at halftime that Michigan would have to make some changes if they were going to win the game, but nobody was ready for what happened in the third quarter. On successive drives, Nebraska fumbled, had a punt blocked, fumbled again, and shanked a punt. With the Cor-

nhuskers apparently suffering from heat stroke in the Arizona sun, the Wolverines turned the miscues into 24 points and a 27-14 lead. It was a dramatic a turn around as seen all year, and once again, it was the hard-hitting defense that deserved the credit.

"AT THE half, we said 'We're a better team than them,'" said defensive back Garland Rivers. "We talked about it and then went out and played like we could play."

It was that idea — play like Michigan — that Schembechler stressed in the locker room and that the players remembered.

"We just made some adjustments," said Schembechler. "I didn't yell at them. I didn't give a speech — I'm no Knute Rockne," he growled in mock indignation.

"He said get out and move the ball," said Morris, who broke several key long runs in the second half to earn offensive player of the game honors. "He told us to go out and play like Michigan.

RIGHT: Paul Jokisch (84) and Gerald White (22) smother Eric Kattus (top right) in celebrating White's third-quarter touchdown run in Michigan's 27-23 Fiesta Bowl victory.
BOTTOM: Tailback Gerald White sails over a Mike Husar block to knock the six points off the Cornhuskers' 11-point halftime lead.

> ❝ **It was that idea – play like Michigan – that Schembechler stressed in the locker room and that the players remembered. 'We made some adjustments,' said Schembechler. 'I didn't yell at them. I didn't give a speech – I'm not Knute Rockne.'** ❞
>
> — Brad Morgan, *The Michigan Daily*

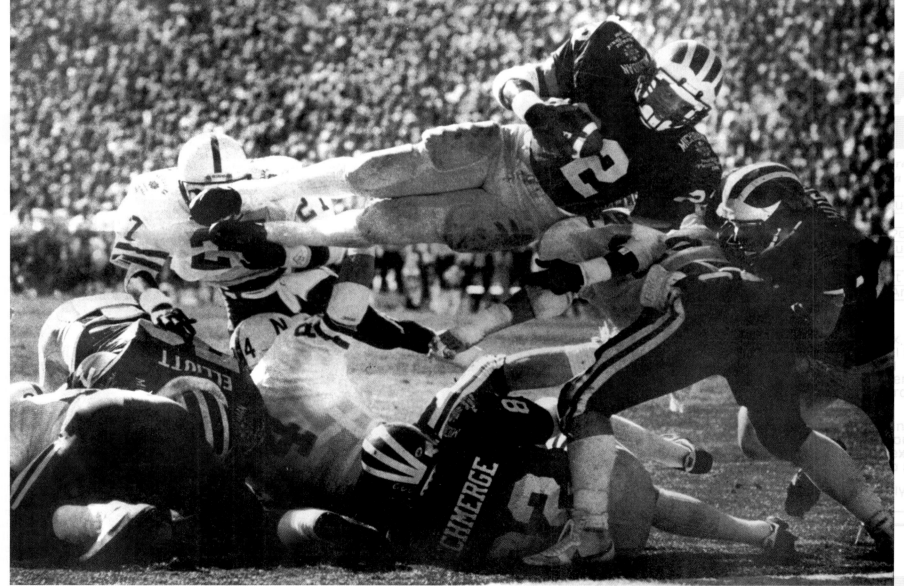

PHOTOS BY DAN HABIB/Daily

The Michigan Daily — SPORTS EXTRA

Bo-quet of Blue roses

Wolverines hold off Buckeyes, 26-24

By PHIL NUSSEL
Special to the Daily

COLUMBUS — Ohio State kicker Matt Frantz may have missed the game-winning field goal with a minute left yesterday, but to the Big Ten champion Michigan Wolverines, the kick was good, very good.

It gave Bo Schembechler and his boys a clutch 26-24 victory over the vaunted Buckeyes and a trip to the Rose Bowl in Pasadena, Calif. to meet Arizona State.

"IT WAS a heck of a game and I'm pleased that we won it," said a grinning Schembechler, who became the winningest coach in Michigan football history with 166 wins. "And I am particularly happy because it will be the first time for any of these players to go to the Rose Bowl.

"This is one of the finest squads I've ever had."

Buckeye head coach Earle Bruce will now take his team (7-1, 9-3) to the Cotton Bowl. It will be OSU's first appearance there. "We're pleased to play in a New Year's Day game," he said. "But when you are Big Ten co-champs, and have the championship game in your grasp, it's a letdown when you don't win It's going to take a while to get over this one."

MICHIGAN (7-1 Big Ten, 10-1 overall) had the game under control with 5:26 left, moving the ball to OSU's 44, but with 3:30 left, Thomas Wilcher fumbled and roverback Sonny Gordon covered it on the 41. The Bucks moved the ball to Michigan's 36 and then failed to move on two straight plays.

On third and 10, quarterback Jim Karsatos went short to his favorite target, Cris Carter, who was hauled out of bounds two yards short of the first down by Erik Campbell. Bruce then decided to go with Frantz on the 45-yard attempt, which went just left of the mark.

"It was a tough decision, but you have to take that chance," Bruce said.

"I THOUGHT it was good," a tearful Frantz said. "I just hooked it a little to the left. I just can't believe it."

Unlike the Ohio State-Michigan games of old, yesterday's clash before an Ohio Stadium record crowd of 90,674 was an offensive explosion.

JAMIE Morris keyed the offense with a career-high 210 yards, 150 in the second half. He also scored a pair of touchdowns. Jim Harbaugh made good on his "guaranteed victory," hitting 19-of-29 passes for 261 yards.

"Morris did a great job," said Schembechler. "When was the last time any back got more than 200 yards against Ohio State?"

Todd Schulte (41) and Bob Perryman (right) celebrate Michigan's Rose Bowl-clinching, 26-24 victory.

Daily Photo by JOHN MUNSON

Roses are Blue; losing is scarlet

By ADAM MARTIN

The greatest thing about the Michigan-Ohio State rivalry is that neither team expects to lose.

Wait. Make that both teams expect to win.

This fact alone makes losing especially painful. Just ask Ohio State quarterback Jim Karsatos, a Fullerton, Ca. native who expected yesterday's roses to be red — scarlet red.

"I WAS planning on going home," Karsatos said. And now? "I'm thinking about getting dressed, going home, nothing."

Karsatos and the rest of the Buckeyes had only pain in their faces after OSU failed to kick the winning field goal. They were hurting inside. Despite a share of the Big Ten Championship (Michigan and Ohio State finsished tied at 8-1), the Buckeyes will have to settle for a New Year's Day trip to Dallas and a berth in the Cotton Bowl.

INSTEAD of everything coming up roses, OSU came up empty. The Cotton Bowl is no substitute for the Granddaddy of them all. Sure, the Buckeyes will be glad to play Jan. 1, but the past, Michigan 26, Ohio State 24, Nov. 22, 1986, will be particularly hard to forget.

"This is the worst feeling I've ever had," said a teary-eyed Chris Spielman, OSU's all-everything linebacker. "It's gonna take me awhile to get over it, but what are you gonna do? We fell short."

INSIDE

Fun and games ...but no Roses

Roses bloom for Devils, wilt for 'M'

By MARK BOROWSKY
Special to the Daily

PASADENA, Calif. — Blame the turf. Blame the fans. Blame Disneyland. Even blame the weather.

Yes, "blame" was the functional word for Michigan in the 1987 Rose Bowl. But for whatever reason one cites for this year's Big Ten collapse, the final result of this year's Rose Bowl was all too predictable. Michigan took a 12-point lead before 103,168 fans before falling to Arizona State last Thursday in Pasadena 22-15.

Excuses were made, but the reasons for the loss were simple. Football games are usually won on the line of scrimmage, and that's where Michigan lost this one. Arizona State dominated both sides of the line, whether giving Sun Devil running back Darryl Harris (23 carries, 112 yards) gaping holes or constantly harassing Michigan quarterback Jim Harbaugh, who tossed three interceptions.

MICHIGAN finished at 11-2, and ranked eighth by both wire service polls, while Schembechler is now 1-7 in the Rose Bowl.

SCOTT LITUCHY AND JOHN MUNSON/Daily

TOP: Coach Bo Schembechler takes time out to pose with Mickey Mouse, Goofy and Donald Duck at Disneyland in Anaheim, Calif. **LEFT:** Arizona State quarterback Jeff van Raaphorst, the game's MVP, rushes for eight yards during ASU's first touchdown drive. **RIGHT:** Michigan quarterback Jim Harbaugh gets instructions from Bo before scoring the team's second, and final, touchdown.

| SEPT. 12 | No. 9 MICHIGAN | 17 |
| | No. 13 NOTRE DAME | 19 |

Irish win battle of field goals, 19-17

Season opener...
...a thrilling start

SOUTH BEND, Ind. — Michigan head coach Bo Schembechler has spoken against playing night games on numerous occasions, but no one can deny that Saturday's thriller between the Wolverines and Notre Dame deserved its place in the spotlight.

Although the 1988 college football campaign is still in its infant stages, the Fighting Irish's 19-17 victory before 59,075 hysterical fans will rank among the season's finest.

It matched two nationally ranked teams filled with rich tradition.

It was General Bo versus the feisty Lou Holtz. When asked about a call he disputed in the third quarter, Holtz said: "I think that's the only time I lost my poise all day I'm proud to say. I thought I handled myself well."

The players shared their respective coaches' zestfullness. As Michigan ran off the field after its pre-game warmup, the two teams engaged in a minor scuffle.

It was a game of high emotions throughout. In the third quarter, the television camera showed a teary-eyed Ricky Watters on the bench after he fumbled a punt deep in his own end. This game obviously meant something.

— PETE STEINERT

Notre Dame place-kicker Reggie Ho celebrates his game-winning field goal moments before Mike Gillette missed on a 48-yard attempt with no time left.

JOHN MUNSON/Daily

| SEPT. 19 | No. 15 MICHIGAN | 30 |
| | No. 1 MIAMI | 31 |

Hurricanes blow by Michigan, 31-30

Defending national champion and top-ranked Miami made an epic comeback to drop Michigan to a rare 0-2 start.

Last quarter rally drops Blue to 0-2

BY MICHAEL SALINSKY

If Michigan's loss to Notre Dame last week was heartbreaking, then there has to be some other word to describe its 31-30 loss to Miami Saturday at Michigan Stadium.

Deflating? Stunning? Double heartbreaking?

With 9:27 left in the game, the Wolverines held a 30-14 lead over the No. 1 team in the nation and had the ball, first-and-ten, on the Miami 41-yard line.

Less than nine minutes later, Miami had scored 17 points, stunning the crowd and dropping the Wolverines to 0-2 — their first 0-2 start since 1959.

Miami's biggest play on a day of big plays was Cleveland Gary's short reception and touchdown jaunt covering 48 yards on a fourth-and-one pass from Steve Walsh with just over three minutes remaining. The scoring play cut Michigan's lead to two points.

David Arnold who was crushed by a blocker as he went for Gary, intercepted Miami's attempt for a two-point conversion that would have tied the game. It looked like the Wolverines would still hang on to defeat a visiting top-ranked Miami team just as they had done in 1984.

But Carlos Huerta's on-side kick was recovered by Miami safety, Bobby Harden on the Michigan 47,

'Let's face it, (we) are a good team. We can play good with anybody and we'll get better.'

—'M' coach Bo Schembechler

giving the Hurricanes a chance for the victory. Huerta's kick hit right in front of Michigan's front line and bounced high in the air creating a scramble for the ball that Miami won.

"The front wall didn't block," said Michigan head coach Bo Schembechler. "When they go up high, those front guys got to knock 'em out of there."

KAREN HANDELMAN/Daily

Miami fullback Cleveland Gary turns the corner on Michigan's T.J. Osman during the first half of Saturday's game. Gary hurt the Wolverines by both rushing the ball and catching passes for big gains.

1988

'M' win is a heartfelt one for Bo

Michigan coach Bo Schembechler hoists over his head his second Rose Bowl trophy. After three previous losses to Southern Cal in Pasadena, Schembechler finally got his way.

JOHN MUNSON/Daily

Blue topples Trojan empire

BY PETE STEINERT
SPECIAL TO THE DAILY

PASADENA, Calif. — Before Monday's Rose Bowl game, Michigan coach Bo Schembechler told his players to expect the unexpected, to be prepared for anything.

Sure thing, coach. The Wolverines had already encountered their share of surprises during the regular season: the then unknown Reggie Ho and his automatic toe out-kicking Mike Gillette in the season opener; Miami (Fla.) rallying from laps behind; and starting quarterback Michael Taylor breaking his right collarbone against Minnesota.

Michigan learned to deal with the unexpected. And the Wolverines

taught many skeptics that lesson with their come-from-behind 22-14 victory over Southern Cal. Sports Illustrated's Nov. 14 issue said USC would not lose to "a pretender from the feeble Big Ten. A defeat would be unthinkable."

Think again.

"Down 14-3, knowing what's happened to us in the past, this team has great resolve," said Schembechler, now 2-7 in Rose Bowls. "When they came back and played like they did and won the game, I think it was a great tribute to them."

USC coach and former Schembechler assistant Larry Smith said: "I'm not disappointed, I'm just damn angry."

 I must say that I am elated. That's the word – elated.

— Bo Schembechler, *Michigan football coach*

David Arnold, Brent White, and Mark Gutzwiller celebrate their Wolverine Rose Bowl victory.

ROBIN LOZNAK/Daily

The Schef's Specialty

BY ADAM SCHEFTER

PASADENA, Calif. — The maize and blue helmets were raised to the sky, the players waving them proudly. And suddenly the helmets were joined in the air when Bo Schembechler hoisted the Rose Bowl trophy high above his shoulders.

Two forces meeting in the night. Michigan football. Rose Bowl trophy. A match made for the heavens.

What does the fight song say? The champions of the West? Yes. They were. The champions of the West. And that sure as hell beats being the champions of just the Midwest.

WHICH IS all Bo had been seven of his last eight trips out to Pasadena. With the win, Schembechler took the monkey off his back, grabbed him around the neck, threw him to the ground, and kicked him in the face.

Who said Bo couldn't win the Rose Bowl? "Losing just tears your heart out. And I don't have that good a one to start with," Schembechler said with a boyish grin. "I must say that I am elated. That's the word — elated."

No Roses for Bo
Trojans spoil coach's finale

Maybe a foreign ref would have been fair

PASADENA — Maybe Sweden should have refereed the Rose Bowl because they have declared neutrality for over 40 years.

The Swedes know something about football. After all, the NFL has travelled to Stockholm the past couple years for exhibitions, so there has to be a potential line judge named Sven somewhere in the country.

Anybody could have been better than Pac-10 official Charles Czubin, who threw the holding/illegal block below the waist/I don't like you flag on Michigan's fake punt late in the fourth quarter of the Wolverines 17-10 loss to Southern California.

With under six minutes to play in the contest, Michigan first-year punter Chris Stapleton dropped back in punt formation on a fourth-down and two yards. Stapleton, who starred as a wide receiver as well as a punter in high school, faked the kick and ran for 24 yards and an apparent first down to the Southern Cal 31.

But Czubin saw the seemingly perfectly executed play differently and called the infraction on Michigan's Bobby Abrams, who didn't know the flag was on him until he got back to the lockerroom after the disappointing loss. Wolverine coach Bo Schembechler, who last called the fake punt in 1987 when it tallied a 40-yard touchdown against Michigan State, went legitimately crazy.

— Adam Schrager

PHOTOS BY DAVID LUBINER/Daily

Michigan quarterback Michael Taylor (9) keeps the ball against USC.

Michigan found out that Roses also come with thorns

PASADENA — What could have been the most fairytaled moment in the history of Michigan sports turned into some evil, horrifying reality check.

All right. So Michigan doesn't win everything. And Bo Schembechler can't control everything. And he won't ever be around again. And the Wolverines played with the intensity of a milk carton in his last game.

And Bo nearly fell on his behind.

That was the worst moment for me. After an official dared to throw a yellow flag on a beautifully executed fake punt, Schembechler went bonkers. We've all seen what happened, whether we were at the game, watching at home, or viewing the highlights.

The most respected icon in Wolverine football history tripped over his headphone wire during a most vehement protest, and nearly fell on his behind.

Richard Eisen

Get Rich Quick

Had his derriere actually hit the turf, it would have truly ranked as one of the darkest moments in Wolverine history. Thankfully, that didn't happen and Schembechler could leave his beloved game with most of his dignity intact.

The flag sat on the field, ruining everything. It was like dropping a spot of acid onto the Mona Lisa. Cruelty, thy name is holding.

Tailback Leroy Hoard (33) dodges USC linebacker Michael Williams in the second half of the New Year's Day contest. Hoard rushed for 108 yards, the first time this season an opposing ballcarrier surpassed 100 yards against USC this season.

MICHIGAN FOOTBALL

Bo quits

Coach to resign after Rose Bowl

> **No more headset throwing, no more harangues, no more three yards and a cloud of dust.**
>
> — Rich Eisen,
> *The Michigan Daily*

JOSÉ JUAREZ/Daily

Michigan football coach Bo Schembechler will resign his position after the Rose Bowl, Jan. 1. Schembechler's future as Athletic Director is still somewhat hazy.

"I've been a very fortunate coach. I've coached for 37 years, and 27 of them as a head coach. I was given a job to coach Michigan football in 1969.

"That had to be, when I was in this room and appointed by Don Canham as football coach of Michigan, the greatest day of my life.

"Because Michigan is special. And the opportunity to coach here was tremendous. I couldn't ask for a better career. I'm a very happy man today. I'm not here to shed a tear; it's not because I'm sad at leaving. I hate to leave the players, I hate to leave coaching, but it's time to go.

"And yet, who could ask for a greater career than I've had? It's not that I've done everything in football, but I've coached at Michigan."

— Bo Schembechler

Bo leaves Michigan — joins Tigers

by Adam Benson
Daily Football Writer

Before his final game as football coach at Michigan, Bo Schembechler told his players to think of him as "as one of the seniors," just graduating 21 years late.

Well now that he's graduated, Bo has gone pro.

On Monday, Schembechler took a leave of absence from his post as athletic director to become president and chief operating officer of the Detroit Tigers baseball club.

Associate Athletic Director Jack Weidenbach will be the interim athletic director. There has been no announcement as to when a permanent athletic director will be named.

DAVID LUBLINER/Daily

Then 'M' football coach Bo Schembechler talks with his successor, Gary Moeller, before the Rose Bowl.

FEB. 28, 1990

'M' baseball rocked by scandals

Former coach Bud Middaugh arraigned for embezzlement

Big Ten levels two-year probation sentence against baseball program for rules violations

FEB. 12, 1990

Community rejoices over Mandela's release

APRIL 7, 1992

BLUE BEDEVILED
DUKE 71, MICHIGAN 51

MAY 9, 1991

Bush addresses 1991 graduates

FILE PHOTO/Daily

President Bush addresses University graduates at May's campus wide commencement ceremony in Michigan Stadium.

APRIL 6, 1993

'M' drops title game, 77-71, in final minute; Carolina takes NCAA crown

A dejected Chris Webber, upset over his costly last-minute timeout error, leaves the court with head bowed in agony as teammate Leon Derricks tries to console him.

KRISTOFFER GILLETTE/Daily

OCT. 25, 1994

Library namesake reflects on tenure at 'U'

By RONNIE GLASSBERG
Daily Staff Reporter

The namesake of the Harold T. and Vivian B. Shapiro Undergraduate Library said he knew it was traditional to name buildings after past presidents and he is happy they picked the UGLi.

"I'm extremely pleased for a number of reasons: I have a wonderful relationship with Harlan Hatcher; it's also very close to where the Economics Building used to be that burned down; and I have an enormous commitment to undergraduate education," Shapiro said in an interview yesterday.

On Thursday, the Board of Regents named the undergraduate library after the University's 10th president and his wife. While the sign has not yet been changed, the name change took effect immediately.

APRIL 4, 1996

Unabomber suspect held

Kaczynski earned 2 mathematics degrees from 'U'

SEPT. 8, 1998

E-mail becomes a crucial element of student life at 'U'

FEB. 12, 1999

Clinton

Aug. 17, 1998: Clinton testifies before grand jury from his office. Later that day, Clinton addresses American public, admits to an inappropriate relationship with Lewinsky

Today: Clinton acquitted by the Senate. Michigan Senator Carl Levin casts deciding vote on second article

---

703-233-33
MICHIGAN FOOTBALL PROGRAM RECORD

47-34-5
VS. OHIO STATE

54-23-5
VS. MICHIGAN STATE

13-8-0
VS. NOTRE DAME

54-24-3
VS. MINNESOTA

36,306
ENROLLMENT

$3,502
IN-STATE TUITION

$12,010
OUT-OF-STATE TUITION

$483,754,000
ENDOWMENT

Gary Moeller
FOOTBALL COACH

Lee Bollinger
UNIVERSITY PRESIDENT

NOTABLE GRADUATES

1990 Rich Eisen, NFL analyst

1993 Sanjay Gupta, CNN medical correspondent

1994 Selma Blair, actress

1995 Larry Page, Google founder

MOELLER TAKES CHARGE

Acting coach Gary Moeller was victorious in his first bowl appearance as a head coach.

SCOTT LITUCHY/Daily

MOELLER ENTERS SECOND SEASON WITH STRENGTH UP FRONT

JAN. 6, 1988

A win for Mo that counts for Bo

TAMPA, Fla. — His smile stretched farther than the Gulf of Mexico

Acting Michigan football head coach Gary Moeller won one of the biggest games of his career. But at the press conference after the Wolverines' 28-24 victory over Alabama in the Hall of Fame Bowl last Saturday, Moeller kept events in perspective.

"It feels great, but it is still Bo's team and a victory for Bo," said Moeller. "I don't want the win to go in any Mo (win) column. This is a Bo victory."

Sorry coach. The win may not go in the Mo column but it does in this column. For Mo, it was Miller Time.

Mo in command. Confident. Successful. A refreshing change from his head coaching days at Illinois.

"I'm just happy for everyone involved," said Moeller. "I'd be lying to you if I didn't tell you I feel really happy about the way things happened. I'm happy for myself and my family."

— Scott G. Miller

> ❝ The players are a lot more relaxed in practice, Mo's walking around watching everyone practice and he's trying to catch punts and kick punts. The players will be cracking jokes, talking to him, but at the same time, he is the disciplinarian that he is. ❞
>
> — Vada Murray, *Michigan free safety*

NOTABLE QUOTABLE

"Don't shed any tears for Michigan, we don't want your tears. Don't feel sorry for Michigan, we don't want your sorrow. Michigan will be back."

— interim head football coach Lloyd Carr at the press conference announcing Gary Moeller's resignation

Moeller pleads no contest after resignation

Moeller resigned in May 1995 after a drunken incident outside a Southfield, Mich. restaurant. He was arrested and charged with disorderly conduct and assault.

MARK FRIEDMAN/Daily

Mo's debut: 'It hurts'

Blue falls as Irish QB leads late charge

> **"Our kids are down and we should be. We very honestly went into that game with the idea that we were going to win that game. And I'm not speaking from the graveyard, either. That's what hurts."**
>
> — Gary Moeller,
> *Michigan football coach*

JOSE JUAREZ/Daily

Michigan tailback John Vaughn breaks free for yardage in the third quarter of Saturday night's game versus Notre Dame. Despite Vaughn's 201 yards in rushing, the Wolverines suffered a disappointing 28-24 loss.

by Mike Gill
Daily Football Writer

SOUTH BEND — When the Wolverines opened fall practice in August, new head coach Gary Moeller was asked why he and his assistant coaches were watching and hanging out at the Detroit Lions training camp so much.

"Are you planning on using the run-and-shoot offense?" someone jokingly asked Moeller.

Moeller laughed and said "no."

Yeah, sure. The University of Michigan, known for the. Reaganesque bang-the-ball-up-the-middle philosophy for over 20 years, would switch to something risque and innovative.

Mo didn't lie. When Michigan debuted their 1990 version Saturday night to a prime-time audience at Notre Dame Stadium, there was no inkling of the Silver Stretch. But while Moeller didn't borrow any pages from Wayne Fontes and the Lions' playbook, he did borrow one from the Cincinnati Bengals: using their no-huddle offense.

The result: 443 yards total offense and an average gain of 6.3 yards per play. Call it a success.

> **"He coyly sprinkled the run with the pass. Basically, he coached a gutsy, innovative game that has the Wolverines dominating the Irish for most of the contest. But it wasn't enough."**
>
> — Eric Lemont, *The Michigan Daily*

MICHIGAN FOOTBALL

Blue crushes Buckeyes, 31-3

Defense keys rare blowout

by Phil Green
Daily Football Writer

It was supposed to be a tight, hard-hitting affair, but Saturday's Michigan-Ohio State game proved to be one-sided. The Wolverines, paced by Desmond Howard's 213 all-purpose yards and a staunch defense, soundly handled the Buckeyes, 31-3.

"I thought it would be closer," Michigan guard Matt Elliott said. "I don't think Ohio State played as well as they could have. I don't think they played as well as some of the games we had seen on film."

The victory gave Michigan (8-0 in the Big Ten, 10-1 overall) its third outright conference title in four years, during which the Wolverines have not lost to Ohio State. The Buckeyes (5-3, 8-3) remained in third place with the defeat.

"I guess if you're 10-1 you've got to be happy, so I'm happy," Michigan coach Gary Moeller said. "To beat Ohio State, it's very special."

PHOTOS BY KENNETH SMOLLER/Daily

TOP LEFT: On his 93-yard punt return, Desmond Howard breaks away for touchdown. **TOP RIGHT:** Michigan quarterback Elvis Grbac completed 8 of 14 passes for 123 yards against the Buckeyes Saturday. **BOTTOM:** Rookie tailback Tyrone Wheatley pulls away from the Ohio State defense Saturday.

Mo's confidence earns 8-0 season

Michigan's 31-3 victory over archrival Ohio State was the crowning jewel to a very special Michigan football season. Now is the time to savor the season, and dole out all the post-season adulation.

Indeed, there is plenty to go around for the Wolverines. Pick a player, any player. This season's success has been the result of 11 players carrying out their individual tasks on every play. And while several Wolverines have even been nominated for national individual awards, the time has come to pay tribute to someone who has gone largely unrecognized this season — the guy wearing the headset, Michigan coach Gary Moeller.

Matt Rennie

Rennie Lane

Moeller has been the driving force behind the Wolverines all season long, stressing the need to improve with each game and keeping the team focused on its goals. However, that's rather standard fare for any college coach.

But Moeller distinguishes himself from other coaches when it's time to make a crucial decision. Actually, Moeller makes crucial decisions even when it isn't time. And he does it without batting an eyelash.

I don't think there is a decision risky enough to make Moeller sweat. Granted, his risks are calculated, but they are risks. This never seems to faze Moeller, who decides his fourth-down play selections the way most of us decide what we want on our pizza.

Wolverine Des-tiny

Howard draws attention with athletics, knowledge

Pose signifies picturesque season

KENNETH SMOLLER/Daily

Heismond
On his 93-yard punt return, Desmond Howard splits tacklers, and breaks away for his touchdown, before showing his Heismond Trophy pose.

KENNETH SMOLLER/Daily
Desmond Howard leaps to snare his third catch of the game in the fourth quarter Saturday against Indiana. Howard now has 15 touchdowns in six games.

Desmond provides Blue with much-needed Magic

It's Desmond!

KENNETH SMOLLER/Daily

Michigan flanker Desmond Howard outruns the last Ohio State defender on his way to a 93-yard punt return for a touchdown.

FILE PHOTO/Daily

Howard, defense key Homecoming victory

No hype, but still no contest

Howard wins Heisman Trophy

by Theodore Cox
Daily Football Writer

NEW YORK — It's official. To no one's surprise, Michigan receiver Desmond Howard became the 1991 Heisman Trophy winner at the Downtown Athletic Club in New York yesterday evening. Howard finished with 2,077 points, out-distancing runner-up Casey Weldon of Florida State, who had 503.

Howard became only the second Wolverine to win the Heisman in the award's 57-year history. Tom Harmon was the first in 1940.

"It's a great feeling," Howard said. "I felt more comfortable once they made the announcement and the Heisman was in my hands. It was a beautiful feeling inside.

"It's going to go down in history, as far as Desmond Howard goes. It's one of the greatest days of my life."

Howard conceded that he felt he had a good chance of winning the award since the Michigan-Notre Dame game.

"It's very hard to block it out, because you're being reminded of it day in and day out by reporters," Howard said.

Howard took 85 percent of the first-place votes, breaking O.J. Simpson's record percentage set in 1968. But Simpson still holds the widest margin of victory, 2,853 points to Leroy Keyes' 1,103.

What they said about Desmond Howard:

'I'm not saying he's got an 'S' on his chest, but he's damn close'
—Bill Mallory
Indiana coach

'From what I've seen, he does have an 'S' on his chest'
—John Gutekunst
Minnesota coach

'He's as great in person as he is on film'
—Jim Coletto
Purdue coach

'You're going to hear great things from Desmond Howard in or out of football. He will be remembered'
—Erick Anderson
Michigan linebacker

ASSOCIATED PRESS

Yesterday, Desmond Howard became the second player in Michigan football history to win the Heisman Trophy, which honors the nation's top collegiate player.

Huskies turn Blue to mush

KRISTOFFER GILLETTE/Daily

Michigan's Desmond Howard (front) and Elvis Grbac (rear) connected only once, on a 35-yard pass play.

Vogue Bailey strikes own Heisman pose

by Phil Green
Daily Football Writer

PASADENA, Calif. — It all started following a 93-yard punt return against Ohio State late in November. Michigan's soon-to-be-crowned Heisman Trophy winner Desmond Howard struck the famed Heisman stance in celebration.

Just over a month later, Howard's pose appeared all over the Rose Bowl. But this time, he wasn't doing the celebrating.

Following a first quarter interception, Washington cornerback Walter Bailey did his own Heisman shuffle. But unfortunately for Bailey, the cameras all missed it.

But three quarters later, the Huskies' other Bailey, Mario, hauled in a 38-yard touchdown pass

from Mark Brunell. Following the reception, Bailey performed the pose in the end zone for the national television audience.

'He can come over to my house. I'll show him the real thing.'
— Desmond Howard
Michigan receiver

'That's okay, I've got a title.'
— Mario Bailey
Washington receiver

KENNETH SMOLLER/Daily

The Washington Huskies hold up wide receiver Mario Bailey after his 38-yard touchdown reception from Mark Brunell in the fourth quarter of the Rose Bowl. The Huskies went on to win, 34-14, and claim a share of the national championship.

No scapegoat in Rose Bowl mismatch

PASADENA, Calif. — Losing the Rose Bowl has become almost as big a Michigan tradition as the winged helmets and "The Victors." In fact, most Wolverine fans have a rougher hangover from New Year's Day than they do from the night before.

True to form, Michigan lost to Washington, 34-14, in the 1992 edition of the game. However, this somehow was different. This time, Michigan didn't have a scapegoat.

Matt Rennie

Rennie Lane

No phantom touchdowns. No quarterback injuries. No controversial penalties.

When the Wolverines looked for scapegoats after this game, they had to look at themselves. After all, this was not a game that could have gone either way. The only two possible outcomes for this game were: (1) a Washington victory, or (2) an earthquake.

Instead of being left asking, "What if?" Michigan fans were instead asking "Are we punting again?"

Ah, punting. Michigan couldn't even win this battle of offensive concessions. Eddie Azcona often looked like he was kicking a water balloon rather than a football. Azcona's performance undoubtedly had dozens of club soccer players drooling over his scholarship.

But blaming this loss on Azcona or any other single player is like blaming the Johnstown Flood on a leaky faucet in Altoona.

This year, the Wolverines had to resign themselves to the fact that they just weren't as good as their opponents. This was a new experience.

Even after the 20-point beating Florida State handed Michigan earlier this season, the Wolverines could remind themselves that two of the Seminoles' touchdowns were scored by their defense.

This game offered no such consolation.

Sure, Michigan went into halftime trailing only 13-7, but nobody honestly believed the score to be an accurate assessment of the first half. And even though the Wolverines did have three possessions with a chance to take the lead, they could do nothing with any of them.

The Huskies took away the Wolverines' primary offensive weapon, Heisman Trophy winner Desmond Howard, and still managed to contain the Michigan running game, which usually benefitted from the opponents' double coverage of Howard.

No passing. No running. No chance.

Roses are Blue, 38-31

Michigan takes roses, rekindles past glories

Matthew Rennie

Rennie Lane

PASADENA — The sign in the Rose Bowl stands said it all.

Happy Blue Year.

What a start to the new year for this Michigan squad. What an end to the careers of this sensational senior class. And what a relief for Michigan fans, who finally got a break from their usual New Year's Day misery.

Michigan came into this game with something to prove. The Wolverines had not won a game since Nov. 7. And they had not beaten a team with a winning record all season. Plus, their opponents were the Washington Huskies, the same team that humiliated Michigan in this same game last year.

The Wolverines buried all of that, and in the process, may have taught us a lesson — that national championships are not the only reason to play football.

Before this year's clash, both schools had tailgate areas outside the stadium for their fans. The difference between the two programs was evident. Washington fans wore their 1992 National Champions sweatshirts. Michigan fans listened to a 1969 tape of Bob Ufer, the late Michigan football broadcasting legend.

The Huskies celebrated the present. The Wolverines dwelled on the past.

This Rose Bowl rematch inspired the Husky entourage to relive last year's glory. They had photos and shirts and hats and tapes from last year's 34-14 thrashing of Michigan, which gave them a share of the national title.

DOUGLAS KANTER/Daily
Michigan's Tyrone Wheatley celebrates during the Wolverines' 38-31 Rose Bowl victory over Washington.

> " **[Wolverine coach Gary Moeller] achieved in only three years what it took his predecessor Bo Schembechler 12 seasons and six trips to Pasadena to accomplish – a Rose Bowl triumph.** "
>
> — Josh Dubow, *The Michigan Daily*

Superman's Return: Wheatley dons cape in Pasadena

by Albert Lin
Daily Football Writer

PASADENA –– Fred Jackson had an idea. Michigan's offensive backfield coach thought his team needed an extra spark to send it on its way to a victory in the Rose Bowl.

So Jackson looked toward his star pupil, a sophomore running back with a knack for the big play. And he gave Tyrone Wheatley a little history lesson.

Jackson led Wheatley outside the Rose Bowl the afternoon before the game and showed him the plaques affixed to the concrete structure, each bearing the name of a Rose Bowl most valuable player.

Jackson noted that the last Michigan player to earn the honor was a running back, Leroy

Hoard, who ran for 142 yards as a sophomore in a 1989 triumph over Southern Cal.

Then he told Wheatley, "Ty, that could be you tomorrow."

Saturday, Wheatley did everything he could to put his name up there. The sophomore vaulted himself to the head of next year's Heisman class by gaining a career-best 235 yards on just 15 carries, for an eye-popping 15.7 yards per attempt. He also scored three touchdowns, on runs of 56, 88 and 24 yards.

"I thought (showing him the MVPs) would get him focused," Jackson said. "Leroy Hoard, the time he got his name on that plaque was because of big runs. He won the game on the big run. I just wanted Tyrone to get into the mindset that big plays would win this game.

"I told Ty two weeks ago that he had to gain 200 yards for us to win this football game."

How prophetic.

What made Wheatley's accomplishments more remarkable is an injury suffered on the second drive of the game. A helmet to the back brought on back spasms that periodically caused sharp pain to shoot down his left leg.

Would the man once known by the moniker 'Superman' be on his way out, just like the D.C. Comics hero?

"It just kept stabbing me from then on and kept getting tighter and tighter," Wheatley said. "It felt like someone had just taken a muscle in my leg and tied it in a knot."

Blue gives Hall of Fame performance

Wolverines look to Tampa while Bucks' future left in doubt, 28-0

By ADAM MILLER
DAILY FOOTBALL WRITER

Try again, John Cooper.

The Ohio State football coach remained winless against the Wolverines as coach of the Buckeyes Saturday as Michigan shocked the then-No. 5 Bucks, 28-0, at Michigan Stadium. It was Michigan's first shutout of Ohio State since 1976 and the Buckeyes' first scoreless game since 1982.

"It is quite obvious that the best team won today," Cooper said. "This is one of the most embarrassing losses in my coaching career. We were outplayed in every way."

Indeed. The Wolverines (5-3 Big Ten, 7-4 overall) dominated the contest from start to finish, and led, 21-0, at halftime. They accumulated more total yards (421-212), more first downs (22-14), maintained possession longer (36:01-23:59) and intercepted four Ohio State passes, compared to one Buckeye interception.

The victory probably landed Michigan a berth in the Hall of Fame Bowl, played New Year's Day at 11:30 a.m. in Tampa, Fla., though bids will not be made official until today at the earliest.

"Obviously I am very happy with this team," said Michigan coach Gary Moeller, who rode off the field on his players' shoulders.

TOP: Defensive back Chuck Winters sacks Ohio State's Bobby Hoying in Saturday's 28-0 Wolverine victory. The win all but clinched a Hall of Fame Bowl berth for Michigan and stopped the Buckeyes from clinching a spot in the Rose Bowl. **RIGHT:** Michigan cornerback Ty Law intercepted two passes in Saturday's game.

Michigan handed the Buckeyes their first loss of the season. With a win, Ohio State might have earned a trip to the Rose Bowl.

PHOTOS BY DOUGLAS KANTER/Daily

> **It was quite obvious that the best team won today. This is one of the most embarrassing losses in my coaching career. We were outplayed in every way.**
> — John Cooper, *Ohio State football coach*

1993

Buffs' Hail steals one from Victors

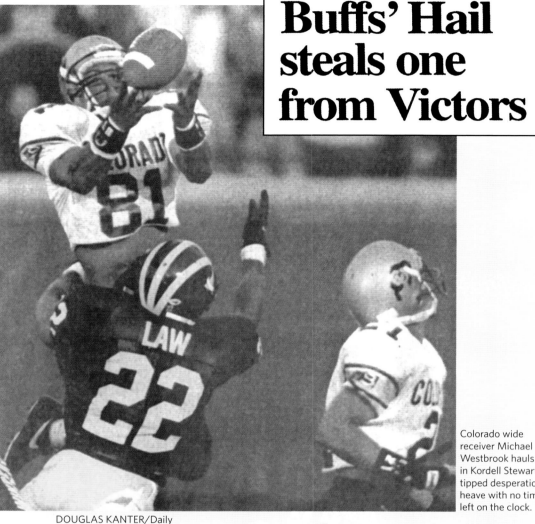

DOUGLAS KANTER/Daily

Colorado wide receiver Michael Westbrook hauls in Kordell Stewart's tipped desperation heave with no time left on the clock.

A loss from above

Stewart's shocking last-second 64-yard pass steals win for Colorado

By MICHAEL ROSENBERG
Daily Football Writer

Football is a game of peaks and valleys and Saturday Michigan slipped off Mount Everest and landed in the Dead Sea.

The decline was as exhilarating as it was quick. Twice in a fortnight the Wolverines played with fire. Two weeks ago they torched Notre Dame. Saturday they got burned.

Michigan, fresh off a shocking 26-24 upset of the Fighting Irish, was beaten by Colorado on a last-second, 64-yard, it-happens-every-decade Hail Mary pass from Kordell Stewart to Michael Westbrook. The pass was tipped out of the hands of Michigan safety Chuck Winters by Colorado's Blake Anderson and pulled from the air by Westbrook. The touchdown gave the seventh-ranked Buffaloes a 27-26 victory over No. 4 Michigan.

"I have never had a feeling like this in my life." Westbrook said. "It was tipped. There was nobody else around. It was just me and the football. All I had to do was catch it."

Stewart's pass was eerily reminiscent of Doug Flutie's touchdown throw to Boston College teammate Gerard Phelan against Miami in 1984.

That pass, which also measured 64 yards, propelled the Eagles past the Hurricanes and Flutie toward the Heisman Trophy.

It remains to be seen whether Stewart will be similarly acclaimed. After the game, he was simply overwhelmed with the events of the final six seconds.

"It has to be one of the greatest wins of my career." Stewart said. "The coach called this so-called play. It worked."

It was not the first time coach Bill McCartney sent in that so-called play, called "Rocket." The Buffalo boss had called for the bomb at the end of the first half.

That pass was intercepted. By Chuck Winters.

"I'm sick." Winters said. "My belly hurts. It never crossed my mind that they would do it."

The play is so seldom-used that nobody in black and gold could decide how often it is practiced or what Westbrook is supposed to do.

"We practice it once a week." coach Bill McCartney said. "Westbrook's job on that play is to position himself for when the ball is tipped."

ON THE SIDELINES

Willy the Wolverine: the debate rages

OCT. 16, 1989

by Judith Droz
Daily Sports Contributor

For 172 years Michigan never has had a mascot. However, now there is a movement to bring the only school in the Big Ten without a mascot a cheerful, smiling Wolverine.

The entrepreneurial team of seniors Adam Blumenkranz and David Kaufman created Willy the Wolverine four years ago. "We've never had a mascot, so we invested in market research and after six different drafts Willy was born," Blumenkranz said.

But who is Willy?

Most students know Willy — the furry guy on the cover of coupon books or the costumed character spotted throughout campus.

Part of the athletic department's complaints about Willy the Wolverine is that it is a commercial venture. "The issue is we have decided that we really don't need a mascot to start off with," said Senior Associate Athletic Director Jack Weidenbach. "If you look at Willy the Wolverine and the ads in the paper, it's a commercial promotion. We have no business being in that. We don't think we should be sponsoring commercial promotions."

Debate is split among throughout campus on whether Willy should receive the support of the University.

"At the football games students await anxiously for the band to play Bullwinkle and stick their thumbs in their ears," LSA junior Sandra User said. "I don't think it is too hard to conceive Michigan fans becoming attached to a cute mascot like Willy."

66 **What can be more annoying than watching some overgrown ball of fuzz named Willy run around Michigan Stadium, acting like a buffoon? ... In Michigan Stadium for crying out loud. Where Bo works. Just say no to Willy.** 99

— Rich Eisen, *The Michigan Daily*

1995-2007

MARK FRIEDMAN/Daily

Carr to coach as interim for '95 season

"He played" "He's competing"

"He's working" "He was outstanding"

"I'm not pleased" "He was tremendous"

The CARR-O-METER was a way the *Daily* measured Carr's level of satisfaction with the team's performance and his energy level during the game.

Doing his best Aretha Franklin, Carr plays the respect card

Lloyd Carr speaks at a press conference yesterday after being named Michigan's permanent football coach. (Nov. 14, 1995)

KRISTIN SCHAEFER/Daily

Carr's preparation produces 'M' vitality

" **No one has done more for Michigan than Lloyd has.** "

— Joe Roberson, *former Michigan athletic director*

WARREN ZINN/Daily

Michigan coach Lloyd Carr receives the Rose Bowl championship trophy from Tournament of Roses President Gary Dom after the Wolverines 21-16 victory. (Jan. 7, 1998)

Coach won, lost with integrity

Carr's contributions extended beyond the field

The Lloyd Carr era is officially over.

Some people are probably rejoicing — and judging by the comments on our website and letters to the editor we received last night, maybe "some" should probably be switched to "most."

But even though he may ultimately be remembered as the guy who couldn't topple Jim Tressel and Ohio State's evil empire in the late stages of his career, Carr's time at Michigan has been anything but unsuccessful.

I could recite his great win-loss record (he's won more than 75 percent of his games for all you haters), but Carr's contributions to this program extend much further than what fans see on the field 12 Saturdays a year.

Carr was a rarity in college football — a coach who aimed to educate his players both on and off the gridiron.

As Michael Rosenberg of the Detroit Free Press wrote: "Unlike a lot of coaches, he actually reads books with letters other than 'X' and 'O.' "

And he made his players read those books, too. In fact, Carr wouldn't allow players in his office until they would recite a word from the dictionary to him.

Athletic Bill Martin raved endlessly of Carr's intangibles following Saturday's game.

"He is so intent on the graduation rates, on these kids' academics," Martin said. "And he always, always brings that up with them at every meeting."

Carr was and will continue to be a pioneer for area charities, like C.S. Mott's Children's Hospital. Fundraising events he's backed have raised tens of millions of dollars for different groups.

Ever go to Carr's Wash for Kids? Not only did it raise money for those who needed it, but it put a positive light on the football team in the community. Could the next coach be another great face for the program? Sure. But he'll have a hell of an act to follow when you consider everything Carr has done.

"He does so much for our hospitals in terms of fundraising, making his time available, that nobody even knows about," Martin said. "He'll get a note from somebody who has a sick second cousin in the hospital. Lloyd goes and sees that person in the hospital."

SCOTT BELL

> ❝ **I wanted to be able to walk out of here knowing that to the very last minute I did my job to the best of my ability. And I know I'll be able to do that.** ❞
> — Lloyd Carr, *Michigan football coach*

Michigan football coach Lloyd Carr will take a job as an associate athletic director after he gives up his coaching duties. The nationwide search for his replacement has already begun.

ZACHARY MEISNER/Daily

Run Away

Biakabutuka's 313 yards ruin Ohio State's title hopes

By Ryan White
Daily Sports Editor

At some point during Saturday's Michigan-Ohio State contest, somebody should have told Tshimanga Biakabutuka that he wasn't supposed to be the dominant runner in the game.

It most likely wouldn't have mattered though. Biakabutuka probably would have just shrugged and broken off another 20-yard run.

The Wolverine tailback powered his way to a monstrous 313 yards and a touchdown, and led Michigan to a 31-23 upset over the No. 2 Buckeyes in front of 106,288 at Michigan Stadium.

The win ended Ohio State's national championship hopes and gave Northwestern the outright Big Ten championship and a trip to the Rose Bowl. It also earned Michigan (5-3 Big Ten, 9-3 overall) a trip to the Alamo Bowl Dec. 29 in San Antonio, Texas.

It was Biakabutuka's best performance in a Michigan uniform, and it overshadowed a 105-yard, one-touchdown game by Ohio State's highly touted Heisman Trophy hopeful, Eddie George.

Michigan coach Lloyd Carr said that Biakabutuka told him last week that Biakabutuka wanted to prove he was the best back in the league, but Biakabutuka gave much of the credit for doing it to his offensive line.

"I've been playing football for six years and even in high school I never saw holes that big," he said. "Anybody here could have run through those holes and gained all those yards."

MARK FRIEDMAN/Daily

TOP: Michigan tailback Tshimanga Biakabutuka ran through the Ohio State defense to lead the Wolverines to an upset of the No. 2 Buckeyes. **RIGHT:** Michigan's Amani Toomer and the Buckeyes' Shawn Springs got in a shoving match.

> " I don't know what (Ohio State wide receiver Terry Glenn) was thinking, to come out and say that he was going to treat us like another team. This is the Michigan-Ohio State game – you can't do that. "
>
> — Charles Woodson,
> *Michigan cornerback*

Bucked Again

> " In a speech to Ohio State Friday night, former Ohio State coach Earl Bruce said the Buckeyes wouldn't be a great team until they beat Michigan. Everyone thought these Buckeyes were great. Guess not. "
>
> — Ryan White,
> *The Michigan Daily*

JOE WESTRATE/Daily

Ohio State's Joe Germaine had a difficult time orchestrating any kind of offense in the second half with Wolverines like James Hall in his face.

Blue slaps Ohio State with first loss of the season

By Barry Sollenberger
Daily Sports Editor

No one thought it could be done.

A Michigan victory over Ohio State? Impossible. After all, the Buckeyes were 17 1/2 point favorites in Columbus over a Michigan team that had the pulse of a mummy in its two most recent games — losses to both Penn State and Purdue.

So what happened?

The No. 21 Wolverines scored 13 unanswered points to shock the second-ranked and previously unbeaten Buckeyes, 13-9, in front of a stunned crowd of 94,676 at Ohio Stadium.

Michigan	**13**
Ohio State	**9**

"No matter what the outside world, other people and the odds said, we thought we could win," Michigan linebacker Jarrett Irons said.

The Wolverines finished the 1996 campaign with a pedestrian 8-4 record, but they dashed No. 2 Ohio State's title aspirations and halted offensive tackle Orlando Pace's Heisman hopes in a defensive struggle.

OCT. 13

Defense will have to carry this team

JOHN LEROI
Out of Bounds

You can hear them now. All the believers counting down until the Penn State game, making plane reservations to California (and Florida, just in case).

But this time, there is no doubt the Wolverines have the kind of defense that can win games all by itself. Two touchdowns allowed all season. The six points that Northwestern put on the scoreboard actually raised Michigan's points per game average from 5.0 to 5.2, still tops in the nation.

Well, if the 5-0 Wolverines want this year to be different from the past four, their defense had better win some games, because the offense probably won't.

OCT. 20

Same old song: Defense earns Blue another win

PAUL TALANIAN/Daily

OCT. 24

Regardless of records, MSU rivalry 'bitter'

Chris Miller (left), an Engineering junior, changes the game day countdown while LSA junior Andy Yosowitz (center) and Engineering junior Bill Reeves (right) watch. Many students view the intrastate rivalry as serious business.

WARREN ZINN/Daily

NOV. 3

Blue moves to 8-0 after rolling over Gophers

By Nicholas J. Cotsonika
Daily Sports Editor

Without the emotion that energized East Lansing last week or the hype that will swirl soon around State College,

M	Michigan	24
A	Minnesota	3

Michigan lived on thoughts of golden rings and roses Saturday. The fourth-ranked Wolverines, flat but focused on the future, took a 24-3 victory from a Minnesota team notorious for deflating overstuffed egos.

Twice in the past 30 years –– 1977 and '86 — the Golden Gophers sullied the season of a previously unbeaten, highly ranked Michigan team.

Knowing that, Michigan coach Lloyd Carr said he told his players they didn't want any part of that history. They then refused to suffer a letdown before 106,577 at Michigan Stadium, though Carr said "there was no emotion before the game, at halftime or after the game."

The Wolverines have captured the Little Brown Jug 11 straight years and 28 of the past 30, but more important, they didn't fumble it at a critical time. With victories at Penn State and Wisconsin the next two weeks, the Wolverines (5-0 Big Ten, 8-0 overall) will go to the Rose Bowl for the first time since the 1992 season and could have a shot at the national championship.

LEFT: Michigan co-captain Joe Jansen holds up the Little Brown Jug, which the Wolverines won for the 11th consecutive time. **RIGHT:** Teammates hoist injured senior co-captain Eric Mayes above the crowd following Michigan's Rose Bowl-clinching victory over Ohio State on Saturday.

NOV. 10

Wolverines annihilate Penn State to take lead in race to Rose Bowl

By Danielle Rumore
Daily Sports Editor

STATE COLLEGE — Chants of "It's great to be a Michigan Wolverine!" bellowed from the winners' lockerroom after yesterday's game, as silence and disappointment seeped from the Penn State side.

	Michigan	34
	Penn State	8

The game between undefeated Michigan and Penn State for control of the Big Ten was anticipated to be the best matchup in the country, but sometimes expectations fall short of reality.

Behind a dominant offensive line and stellar defensive performance, No. 4 Michigan (6-0 Big Ten, 9-0 overall)

rolled to a convincing 34-8 victory over No. 2 Penn State (4-1, 7-1) in front of a record crowd of 97,498 at Beaver Stadium on Saturday night.

The victory, Michigan's first over Penn State in the past three tries, made the Wolverines the lone undefeated team in the Big Ten, gave them the lead in the Rose Bowl race and sent them to No. 1 in the Associated Press poll for the first time since 1990.

"Honestly, it wasn't easy. It was a matter of preparation," Michigan safety Marcus Ray said. "You watch our offensive line, the guys up front — they dominated. If our offense continues to play like that, we'll be very, very successful."

SARA STILLMAN/Daily
Freshman running back Anthony Thomas gave the Wolverines their first touchdown with this run in the first quarter of Saturday's game at Penn State.

> " **Straight out of a Batman episode was the Michigan defense against Penn State, in characteristic form. Pow! Bam! Splat!** "
> — Alan Goldenbach, *The Michigan Daily*

The Victors!

1997	MICHIGAN		OPPONENT
SEPT. 13	27	(No. 14)	3 No. 8 Colorado
SEPT. 27	38	(No. 8)	3 Baylor
SEPT. 21	21	(No. 6)	14 Notre Dame
OCT. 4	37	(No. 6)	0 Indiana
OCT. 11	23	(No. 6)	6 Northwestern
OCT. 18	28	(No. 5)	24 No. 15 Iowa
OCT. 25	23	(No. 5)	7 No. 15 Mich St.
NOV. 1	24	(No. 4)	3 Minnesota
NOV. 8	34	(No. 4)	8 No. 3 Penn St.
NOV. 15	26	(No. 1)	16 No. 23 Wisconsin
NOV. 22	20	(No. 1)	14 No. 4 Ohio St.
JAN. 8	21	(No. 1)	16 No. 8 Wash St. (Rose Bowl)

WARREN ZINN/Daily

NOV. 24

'M' back in Rose Bowl after 5 years

By Alan Goldenbach
Daily Sports Editor

Four consecutive four-loss seasons and a five-year absence from the Rose Bowl had many convinced that the Michigan football program was stumbling into a pit of mediocrity.

Now, the doubts have disappeared and roses have taken their place. Michigan is going back to the Rose Bowl with a chance to win its first national title since the 1948 season. The top-ranked Wolverines capped their first perfect regular season since 1971 with a 20-14 victory Saturday over No. 4 Ohio State before a record crowd of 106,982 at Michigan Stadium.

The Wolverines will face No. 10 Washington State in Pasadena on Jan. 1, in what will be Michigan's 17th Rose Bowl appearance.

With Florida State losing to Florida, the Wolverines and No. 2 Nebraska (10-0 with two games before its bowl game left on its schedule)

remain the only two undefeated teams in the nation. The Seminoles' loss Saturday vaulted Michigan to the top of the USA Today/ESPN Coaches poll.

The victory was highlighted by the grit of the nation's top-ranked defense with a dash of flash provided by perhaps the best player in the country, All-Everything Charles Woodson.

Three big plays from Woodson helped give Michigan a 20-0 lead: a 37-yard reception that set up the game's first touchdown, a 78-yard punt return that put Michigan ahead, 13-0, and an interception in the end zone in the third quarter.

"Great players play big in big games," Michigan coach Lloyd Carr said. "I think Charles Woodson certainly played one of his greatest games in the very, very biggest game that we have at Michigan, in a game that meant everything to us."

'Wood' you believe it?

WARREN ZINN/Daily

Woodson reminds us all how amazing he is

SARA STILLMAN/Daily

NOV. 24, 1997

Woodson may deserve it, but he won't win Heisman

A college football player will win the Heisman Trophy next month, but he won't be the best player in the country.

Tennessee quarterback Peyton Manning will probably win, becoming the 20th quarterback to win the trophy in its 63-year history. His school record 523-yard, five-touchdown effort against Kentucky on Saturday most likely guaranteed him the trophy, although he garnered those numbers against the Southeastern Conference's worst defense.

The trophy, in theory, is designed for the best player in the country, but very rarely is it awarded to that person.

College football's best player this year is a swaggering, multi-dimensional player who, when asked if he is the best player in the nation, responded, "Yeah, I think so," and flashed his trademark cocky smile. He is the same player who reminds everyone that he is the best, especially after he makes a big play.

He is the same player who just two days ago helped Michigan to its first Big Ten title and Rose Bowl berth since the 1992 season and its first perfect regular season since 1971.

Cornerback Charles Woodson is the best player in the country, but he most likely won't win the Heisman. Defensive players never do. Even though Woodson does it all on the field, his natural position is cornerback, arguably the most important and critical position on football teams today. His true position will prove, ironically, to be the reason he will not win.

— Danielle Rumore

Woodson getting offensive but wants the ball even more

Woodson anchors spectacular secondary; if only he could kick

WOODSON'S HEISMAN CASE

DEFENSE

Tackles	Int.	Yds.	TD	PD*
43	7	7	0	5

OFFENSE

Receiving

Rec.	Yards	TD
11	231	2

Rushing

Att.	Yds.	TD
3	15	1

Passing

Comp.	Att.	Yds.
1	1	28

PUNT RETURNS

No.	Yds.	Avg.	TD	Long
33	283	8.6	1	78

*Passes defensed

Woodson's performance against the Buckeyes sealed his Heisman bid. He also claimed the Chuck Bednarik, Jim Thorpe and Walter Camp awards.

JAN. 9, 1998

Woodson leaves 'M' to go pro

By Alan Goldenbach
Daily Sports Editor

With the suave demeanor and cocky smile that he carried his entire Michigan career, Heisman Trophy winner Charles Woodson said that he had accomplished all that he could as a Wolverine.

For the man who continuously takes down one obstacle after another, the next challenge is duplicating his collegiate success as a professional.

Friday morning, Woodson, accompanied by his mother, Georgia, his three roommates and a group of his teammates, announced that he will forego his senior year at Michigan and enter the NFL Draft. Most scouting pundits predict that the first primarily defensive player to win college football's most coveted individual honor will be one of the top five players selected in the April draft. According to Woodson, this was a decision made long before Friday's declaration deadline.

Heisman Trophy winner Charles Woodson and UM head football coach Lloyd Carr address the media following Charles' announcement to enter the NFL draft on Friday, January 9, 1998.

WE'RE NO. 1

WARREN ZINN/Daily

Michigan goes long to stop Cougars

Griese throws for 3 TDs in Rose Bowl

By Alan Goldenbach
Daily Sports Editor

PASADENA, Calif. — Preseason critics said that the 'M' in Michigan stood for "mediocrity."

Twelve stunning performances later, those naysayers can have but one word for which 'M' represents: magnificence.

The top-ranked Wolverines captured their first national championship in 49 years with a 21-16 victory New Year's Day over No. 8 Washington State in the 84th Rose Bowl before an Ann Arbor-esque crowd of 101,219.

"I'm really proud of this team," Michigan coach Lloyd Carr said after the game. "They answered every question asked of them, and they embraced the pressure of being number one. This team has tremendous heart and character, and that's what got us here."

The Wolverines, however, are not undisputed champs. The Associated Press poll deemed Michigan the nation's top team, but the USA Today/ESPNM coaches poll told a different story. Previously No. 2 Nebraska, by way of an overpowering 42-17 victory in the Orange Bowl over No. 3 Tennessee on Jan. 2, leapfrogged the Wolverines in the other major poll to take the top spot, thus spawning the third split national championship this decade.

MARGARET MYERS/Daily

I'm really proud of this team. They answered every question asked of them, and they embraced the pressure of being number one. This team has tremendous heart and character, and that's what got us here.

— Lloyd Carr,
Michigan football coach

TOP: Michigan's Tai Streets, injured for much of the season, overcame a pair of dislocated fingers and hauled in a pair of long touchdown passes, including this 53-yarder in the second quarter to put Michigan on the scoreboard. **BOTTOM:** Michigan fans cheer together in the Rose Bowl on Jan. 1 as they watch the Wolverines beat the Cougars, 21-16, during the 84th Rose Bowl. Fans used their voices and maize-and-blue pom-pons to help cheer the Wolverines to victory.

Unbelievable season ends with perfection

By Nicholas J. Cotsonika
Daily Sports Editor

PASADENA, Calif. — Long after the trophy has tarnished and this newspaper has yellowed, tales will be told with chest-bursting pride of these Michigan Wolverines and this Rose Bowl, of this team's character and its comebacks, of the emotional energy shared by those lucky enough to behold the marvelous magic made on New Year's Day.

The greatest football season in school history ended here as the rosy twilight gleamed off the San Gabriel foothills. Michigan's 118th team won the 84th Rose Bowl, 21-16, and finished No. 1. Nothing can spoil it. Not a controversy about how the game ended, with Washington State begging for one more second, one more play and one more gasp of life. Not a split decision among the voters, who awarded half of the national championship to Nebraska by a miniscule margin.

No, nothing can spoil this. Nothing can top this. Nothing could quell the crowd's cheers, even a half-hour after the game, when the fans were still chanting with the band, "WE'RE NO. 1!"

"I will cherish this game, this university, for the rest of my life," said senior quarterback Brian Griese, who was named the game's most valuable player. "You have opportunities in life, and those who stand out are the ones who take advantage of those opportunities. It's just sweet for us to capitalize on an opportunity to make history."

The Wolverines are the winningest program in the NCAA and won their 32nd Big Ten championship this season, but they finished 12-0 for the first time ever to win their first national championship since 1948. They consider it their 11th national championship; time may consider it their most unlikely.

When this season began, the Wolverines were ranked 14th, and recovering from four consecutive four-loss seasons seemed daunting enough. An unblemished record and a national championship weren't in the picture.

The 84th Rose Bowl

Jan. 1 1998

Pasadena, Calif.

21
16

"If you would have told me then," defensive end Glen Steele said, "I would have laughed." After all, Michigan didn't win a national championship in coaching legend Bo Schembechler's 21-year era of eminence. Bo never went 12-0.

Though coach Lloyd Carr ended up emerging from Schembechler's shadow, standing alone in the bright, California sun as the winner of four of the five major coach of the year awards, Carr's mission simply had been to silence the critics who had hounded him since his hiring three years ago.

"Nobody gave us a chance to be in the Rose Bowl, let alone win the national title," said all-purpose star Charles Woodson, the Wolverines' game-breaker who this season became the first primarily defensive player to win the Heisman Trophy.

> " **We've been the bridesmaids so many times, it's nice to finally be the bride.** "
> — Leslie Sibery,
> *University alum*

WARREN ZINN/Daily

Throwing up his arms in ecstasy, center Zach Adami celebrates the first of two 50-yard touchdown receptions by wide receiver Tai Streets. The victory clinched Michigan's first national championship since 1948.

Voters divide championship

By Nicholas J. Cotsonika
Daily Sports Editor

Triumph was tinged with disappointment following No. 1 Michigan's victory in the Rose Bowl last Thursday. After No. 2 Nebraska throttled No. 3 Tennessee in the Orange Bowl the next night, giving Tom Osborne a victory in his final game as coach, the Wolverines fell behind the Cornhuskers in the USA Today/ESPN coaches' poll and split the national championship.

Michigan (12-0) had been the consensus No. 1 team entering the bowl season and finished first in the Associated Press media poll. Nebraska (13-0), which had been a distant second in both polls, picked up significant ground with its 42-17 victory.

Edging the Wolverines by a narrow margin in the coaches' poll, the Cornhuskers secured a share of their third national title in four years. They were outright champions following the 1994 and '95 seasons. The Wolverines earned a share of their first national title since 1948.

SEPT. 12, 2001

Trade Center collapses after attack

DANNY MOLOSHOK/Daily
In her house just moments after it occurred, LSA student Lis Hyde watches the replayed images of an airplane flying toward the World Trade Center.

MAY 30, 2002

Regents announce Coleman as first female president

"We believe she will prove to be one of the great leaders of the University's history."

— Regent Laurence Deitch
D-Bingham Farms

DEBBIE MIZEL/Daily

NOV. 8, 2006

AFFIRMATIVE ACTION BANNED

SEPT. 6, 2005

Katrina's effects felt at 'U'

NOV. 5, 2008

CELEBRATION
CAMPUS ERUPTS AFTER HISTORIC OBAMA WIN

RODRIGO GAYA/Daily

FEB. 12, 2010

OBAMA TO DELIVER COMMENCEMENT ADDRESS

President Obama and Governor Jennifer Granholm during the 2010 Spring Commencement ceremony held at the Michigan Stadium. (May 4, 2010)

SAM WOLSON/Daily

796-259-36
MICHIGAN FOOTBALL PROGRAM RECORD

54-36-6
VS. OHIO STATE

60-27-5
VS. MICHIGAN STATE

17-11-1
VS. NOTRE DAME

62-24-3
VS. MINNESOTA

38,103
ENROLLMENT

$6,513
IN-STATE TUITION

$20,323
OUT-OF-STATE TUITION

$3,468,623,277
ENDOWMENT

Lloyd Carr
FOOTBALL COACH

Lee Bollinger
UNIVERSITY PRESIDENT

NOTABLE GRADUATES

2000 Tom Brady, New England Patriots quarterback

2006 Peter Vanderkaay, Olympic swimmer

2009 Darren Criss, actor and singer

---

the 2000s

MICHIGAN FOOTBALL

One for the Millennium

LOUIS BROWN/Daily

TOP: Members of the Michigan Football team celebrate their 34-35 victory over Alabama at the Orange Bowl in Miami's ProPlayer Stadium on New Year's Day. **RIGHT:** Michigan wide receiver David Terrell breaks away from Alabama safety Marcus Spencer en route to one of his three Orange Bowl touchdowns. Terrell's Orange Bowl record setting 10 reception performance evoked cheers of "Heisman Trophy" from the hoards of Michigan fans who made the long trip to Miami.

Orange Bowl win comes back to 'M' script

MIAMI— Ian Gold jogged to the Michigan sideline this past Saturday, arm wrapped around a reporter, face beaming, ready to be engulfed by the quickly developing mayhem.

"Amazing," Gold said of the football game that had ended seconds earlier, a 35-34 heartstopping Michigan overtime victory over Alabama in the 2000 Orange Bowl. "That was the best ending to a football game ever."

Maybe it wasn't the best ever, but it was pretty damn close. The final minutes of the 2000 Orange Bowl included a little of everything — a blocked field goal as time expired in regulation, a one-play touchdown drive for Michigan when quarterback Tom Brady found a wide-open Shawn Thompson, a two-play Alabama touchdown drive when Crimson Tide quarterback Andrew Zow took advantage of a defensive mismatch — reserve linebacker Eric Brackins was somehow assigned to cover Alabam wide receiver Antonio Carter — and, finally, a missed Ryan Pflunger extra point, all of which culminated in an incredible 35-34 Michigan vicotry.

In its first game of the new century, Michigan played a game that was all too fitting to end its last season of the last one. Not surprisingly, it was Tom Brady, the senior leader who fought tooth-and-nail just to earn the starting job, who delivered the win.

— Josh Kleinbaum

> **❝ These Wolverines didn't win a national championship. They didn't even win a Big Ten title. … But this team, maybe more so than that great '97 squad , exemplified what being from Michigan is all about. ❞**
>
> — Josh Kleinbaum, *The Michigan Daily*

One for the record books
Orange Bowl records set on New Year's Day

Touchdowns: 10; eclipsed Alabama-Syracuse (9 in 1953)
Receptions: David Terrell (10); three players were tied with nine
Completions: Tom Brady (33); eclipsed Charlie Ward (24 in 1994)
Passing yds.: Tom Brady (369); eclipsed Frank Boyles (304 in 1945)
Pass attempts: Tom Brady (46); eclipsed Steve Walsh (44 in 1989)
Penalties: Alabama (18); eclipsed Tennessee (17 in 1939)
Pts. in a quarter: 35 (3rd); eclipsed Oklahoma-Duke (34 in 1958)
Penalty yds.: 247; eclipsed Tennessee-Oklahoma (242 in 1939)
Most pts. by loser: Alabama (34); eclipsed Nebraska (30 in 1984)

2000 ORANGE BOWL

'A great feeling'

COLUMBUS — Saturday night in this home of Ohio State, Bucks fans filled the airwaves to release their grievances — some sounding despondent, others sounding angry, an even greater amount sounding their resignation to the fact that Ohio State can no longer compete evenly with the Wolverines.

CHRIS DUPREY

Dupe's Scoop

The Buckeyes have been reduced to a "once in four years" team against Michigan. In the typical student's tenure, the Buckeyes will win every other game at the Horseshoe and lose both games in Ann Arbor. The probability of winning in this rivalry is no longer a coin flip.

Once a greater opponent on Michigan's schedule than intrastate rival Michigan State, Ohio State has taken a recess. The Buckeyes are only capable of winning a game in this series in which they clearly have the superior team, such as in 1998.

Reasons are afloat for this downturn. It's a mental issue for the players, some talk-radio respondents say. "2-10-1 since John Cooper arrived in Columbus," others bellow. "That's all there is to say."

Those are fine excuses, but it ignores Michigan's methodical approach to these games. Lloyd Carr knows Ohio State inside and out and his team reflects that mastery.

No one in Columbus wants to give credit to Carr, but that's not a surprise. Nothing the Buckeyes and his counterpart Cooper do surprises Carr in the least. He has the preparedness of an Eagle Scout — matches, knife and compass.

And the Wolverines, like their leader, are impeccably prepared for this game every year.

"It always comes down to preparation and performance," Carr said, noting that this past week of practice was one of Michigan's best all season.

DAVID KATZ/Daily

Henson celebrates his game-clinching touchdown in front of a national television camera and 98,568 fans.

> " When you meet the kind of adversity we had, it's easy to fall apart and make excuses, point the finger or quit trying. To their credit they didn't do that. "
>
> — Lloyd Carr, *Michigan football coach*

Despite a 54-51 defeat at the hands of Northwestern two weeks earlier — Michigan's third loss of the season — the Wolverines secured an unlikely share of the Big Ten title with a win over the Buckeyes. The game was Ohio State coach John Cooper's last against Michigan; his teams beat the Wolverines just twice in his 13-year tenure.

ON THE SIDELINES

WOMAN UP FRONT

DAVID ROCHKIND/Daily

Drum major Karen England does the traditional back bend after leading the marching band onto the field before Saturday's football game. Women were first allowed into the band in 1972, but this year England becomes the first female to serve as drum major. (Sept. 5, 2001)

2000

ALL IS QUIET

'M' rearranges sports events

The Michigan athletic department announced yesterday the changes that will be made to this weekend's schedule. Five teams will be in action with various schedule adjustments, while three other sports — including football — have been canceled.

FRIDAY, SEPTEMBER 14
VOLLEYBALL AT NIKE INVITATIONAL — CANCELED
MEN'S SOCCER AT LOUISVILLE INVITATIONAL — CANCELED
WOMEN'S SOCCER AT HARTFORD — CANCELED

SATURDAY, SEPTEMBER 15
WOMEN'S GOLF AT MARY FOSSUM INVITATIONAL — CANCELED
MEN'S SOCCER AT LOUISVILLE INVITATIONAL — WILL PLAY
VOLLEYBALL VS. ILLINOIS STATE — WILL PLAY
FOOTBALL VS. WESTERN MICHIGAN — POSTPONED
WOMEN'S CROSS COUNTRY AT SPIKED SHOE INV. — CANCELED
FIELD HOCKEY AT CONNECTICUT — CANCELED

SUNDAY, SEPTEMBER 16
WOMEN'S GOLF AT MARY FOSSUM INVITATIONAL — CANCELED
FIELD HOCKEY VS. CENTRAL MICHIGAN — WILL PLAY
MEN'S SOCCER AT LOUISVILLE INVITATIONAL — WILL PLAY
WOMEN'S SOCCER AT CONNECTICUT — CANCELED

The athletic department is attempting to reschedule the Michigan vs. Western Michigan football game. The field hockey team was originally scheduled to play in connecticut this weekend, but have scheduled Sunday's game with Central Michigan instead. Volleyball also rescheduled and will play Illinois State in absence of their original trip to the Nike Invitational.

DAVID KATZ/Daily

Michigan Stadium, and the rest of the nation's stadiums, will be eerily quiet tomorrow. Michigan hopes to reschedule the Western Michigan game later in the season.

NFL cancels weekend slate

The NFL announced yesterday it would not play this weekend. This week's scheduled games:
ARIZONA AT WASHINGTON; ATLANTA AT ST. LOUIS; BUFFALO AT MIAMI; CINCINNATI AT TENNESSEE; CLEVELAND AT PITTSBURGH; DALLAS AT DETROIT; DENVER AT INDIANAPOLIS; GREEN BAY AT NEW YORK GIANTS; JACKSONVILLE AT CHICAGO; KANSAS CITY AT SEATTLE; NEW ENGLAND AT CAROLINA; NEW YORK JETS AT OAKLAND; PHILADELPHIA AT TAMPA BAY; SAN FRANCISCO AT NEW ORLEANS; MINNESOTA AT BALTIMORE

Baseball to start on Monday

Major League Baseball originally was to reopen play on Friday, but also cancelled games this weekend. The plan for right now is to make up the missed games during the first week of October and move the playoffs back a week.

However, due to this announcement, future Hall of Famers Cal Ripken and Tony Gwynn are now expected to end their careers with home games.

Return to normalcy: Michigan takes on MAC team

MARJORIE MARSHALL/Daily
LEFT: This is just one of many American flags that flew at Saturday's Michigan-Western Michigan game. The pregame and half-time ceremonies paid tribute to those killed in the horrific terrorist attacks on New York City and Washington, D.C. **RIGHT:** Before Saturday's football game, Michigan players Chris Perry, Larry Stevens, Jonathan Goodwin and Jeremy Read stand for a moment of silence to honor victims of the Sept. 11 terrorists attacks in New York and Washington. (Sept. 24)

Time runs out on Blue

Spartans win in last second, but did they beat the clock?

By Jon Schwartz
Daily Sports Editor

EAST LANSING — Early Saturday evening on the Spartan Stadium turf, a chaotic finish to the Michigan-Michigan State football game may have handed the game to the wrong team.

With 17 seconds left in the game and Michigan State at the Michigan three-yard line, quarterback Jeff Smoker rolled out to his right and made a run for the endzone. When he was tackled after gaining only a yard, the clock kept ticking.

Out of timeouts, Smoker had to get his team to the line and spike the ball before time ran out. He did that — the ball hit the turf before the scoreboard clock struck zero — but it seemed as though the clock was stopped earlier than it should have been.

The ending even left ABC commentator Brent Musberger musing about the apparent result of the Spartans' "home-field advantage," and Michigan Radio announcer Frank Beckman screaming, "That was criminal!"

On the next play, Smoker found T.J. Duckett in the endzone for the touchdown and a 26-24 win.

Inside
Wild ending seals Wolverines' fate; Spartans destroy Michigan's rush defense, *Page 1B.*

TOP: Eric Brackins and the rest of the Wolverines had a tough time bringing down Michigan State's T.J. Duckett, who ran for 211 yards and scored two touchdowns, including the game-winner with no time left on the clock..
RIGHT: Michigan State players surround T.J. Duckett after he caught the game-winning touchdown pass after time ran out Saturday. The Spartans had time to run the play after Jeff Smoker spiked the ball and the clock stopped with one second left.

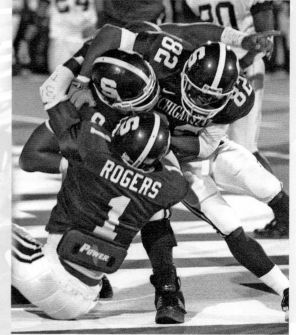

PHOTOS BY DANNY MOLOSHOK/Daily

Brabbing rights

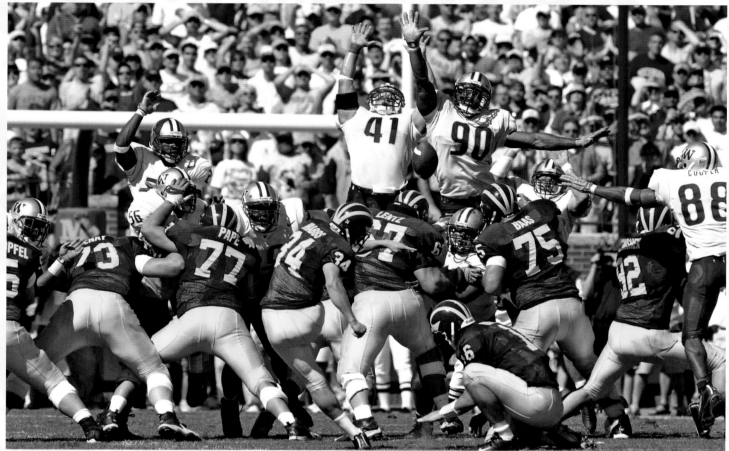

LEFT: The Michigan faithful looked on Saturday afternoon as kicker Philip Brabbs nailed the game-winner to give the Wolverines a 31-29 victory. Brabbs had missed two field goals earlier in the game.
BOTTOM: Michigan tailback Chris Perry led the Wolverines' rushing attack with 123 yards and 2 touchdowns, including a 57-yard touchdown run in the first quarter.

Blue kicker Brabbs makes amends via last-second heroics

By David Horn
Daily Sports Editor

"That's what I'm talking about Brabbs! That's what I'm talking about!"

Michigan receiver Tyrece Butler's barks at the end of Saturday's win at Michigan Stadium were perhaps in reference to something the Wolverines have gained a keen appreciation of early in this 2002 campaign: Second chances.

Saturday's rematch with Washington (0-1), in which the Wolverines looked to

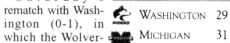

	WASHINGTON	29
	MICHIGAN	31

avenge last season's spectacular 23-18 loss in Seattle, was the first of three opportunities the team has to make up for the 2001 season's failures. One Wolverine in particular — kicker Philip Brabbs — learned about second chances (third and fourth chances, actually) when he kicked the game-winning field goal with no time remaining to give Michigan (1-0) a 31-29 win in its first game of the season.

PHOTOS BY DANNY MOLOSHOK/Daily

Red zone Fiesta

DANNY MOLOSHOK/Daily (stadium), clockwise from top left,
DAVID KATZ/Daily, DANNY MOLOSHOK/Daily, DAVID KATZ/Daily
Michigan's Chris Perry (top left) looked on as Ohio State fans celebrated on the field. Many fans tried to bring
down the goal post (right). Ohio State's Will Allen (left), who had the final interception, celebrates with his team.

Loss to Ohio State makes season a failure

COLUMBUS - Several minutes after the Wolverines second straight loss to Ohio State, junior tailback Chris Perry fought back tears and fits of rage as he continued to keep his eyes glued on the thousands of Buckeyes' fans rushing the field in massive celebration.

As the last Wolverine to walk off the field — and be escorted by police officers — Perry kept looking back at the mayhem. He'd probably still be standing there if running backs coach Fred Jackson didn't push him along into the lockerroom.

"I wanted to see all the celebration," said Perry. "I wanted to see them all celebrating, because I want to live with it and remember it."

Officially, Michigan will now have to celebrate another season that failed to meet expectations.

Michigan had the kind of season in which it could very well have been playing for a national title berth on Saturday in Columbus. Then, it would have been Perry basking in glory while trash-talking snake-bitten Ohio State fans watched.

But the flipside is that this Michigan team could just as easily have been 6-6: If a miraculous Philip Brabbs' field goal had missed wide right against Washington, a Penn State completion had not been called out of bounds and a Brooks Bollinger pass to Jonathan Orr had connected in the final minutes, the Wolverines could be heading for the Motor City Bowl.

— Joe Smith

> ❝ **I wanted to see them all celebrating, because I want to live with it and remember it.** ❞
>
> — Chris Perry,
> *Michigan running back*

Freaky Friday

The Wolverines overcame a 28-7 fourth-quarter deficit to beat the Gophers on the 100th anniversary of introduction of the Little Brown Jug.

Can you believe it? Wolverines' stunning comeback saves season

When did you start thinking the Wolverines could win? Did you let the thought creep in after they scored in the third quarter? Or did you push it away still?

For many of the players, it was Jacob Stewart's interception at 13:30 in the fourth that made them think they could really do this. The cornerback stepped in front of a receiver and ran the ball back, making it 28-21 and giving the porous defense a little redemption.

The defense hadn't made a play all night, it seemed. They flailed their arms while the Gophers ran for 424 rushing yards.

"Of course we had to turn it around," defensive end Larry Stevens said emphatically. "I mean, the team's jamming it down our throat. What (are) you going to do? You going to lay down? That's your manhood right there. That's your pride. That's what you stand for."

So the defense started making tackles, and the offense had switched to the hurry-up and they were only down by seven. Did you believe in Michigan yet?

Not so fast.

Sure, it looked like the Wolverines could win now, but they've been close at the end before. Remember Oregon? How about Iowa? And sure enough, just as soon as Michigan pulled close, Minnesota pulled away again, 35-21.

But like some game of tug-of-war, Michigan pulled back, harder. A touchdown bomb to Braylon Edwards. A Chris Perry 10-yard touchdown run. 35-35.

Did you let yourself think it could happen then? Even with the way the Wolverines had fought back, you had no reason to believe they could finish it. You had every reason to think that they'd come up short again. You'd seen it before.

So had the Wolverines. What were they thinking on the field?

"Don't let this be (like) the last two games." That's what Braylon Edwards was thinking. "I'm tired of hearing about how we fought hard, but yet we didn't make the plays. 'You guys did good, you guys didn't give up, but you just didn't come up with it.' We said, 'To Hell with that. We're going to come up with this one. We're going to make this one work.'"

So they advanced down the field, and they fumbled the ball. Perry dropped it, and you must have been crushed. But wait — there was Tim Massaquoi, finishing a block, spotting the ball, falling on it, saving Michigan's chances.

And those chances now rested on the leg of a true freshman. Michigan took a knee on third down, and Garrett Rivas came out to kick the 33-yard field goal.

Did you trust him? Stevens, Edwards and John Navarre — they all said they knew Rivas would make it. And he did.

Did it take a while to sink in? Was it hard to believe that the Wolverines had completed the biggest comeback in Michigan history, scored 31 points in the fourth quarter? Imagine how the players felt.

"That's probably the most emotional lockerroom I've ever been in in my life," Edwards said. "You had guys that were crying, coaches that were crying. I even cried a little bit. I don't even cry, but I cried a little bit."

After the game, Stevens said he still didn't know what happened. How *did* it happen? How did a team this talented get itself in that position anyway — 4-2 and staring down loss No. 3? How did Michigan dig itself such a deep hole and then overcome so much so quickly?

"We're not a great football team," coach Lloyd Carr said, "but we've got great heart, I'll tell you that. We've got great heart."

You know that now, don't you? Or maybe you knew it all along.

— Courtney Lewis

TONY DING/Daily

The Wolverines celebrate their 15th straight victory over Minnesota by raising the Little Brown Jug. Friday's game was the 100th anniversary of the Jug's introduction to the rivalry.

> **That's probably the most emotional locker room I've ever been in in my life. You had guys that were crying, coaches that were crying. I even cried a little bit. I don't even cry, but I cried a little bit.**
>
> — Braylon Edwards, *Michigan wide receiver*

No. 5 MICHIGAN 35   No. 4 OHIO STATE 21

A ROSE FOR 'U'

Michigan senior running back Chris Perry, surrounded by media and fans, proudly holds a rose in the air. Perry and the Michigan seniors clinched their first outright Big Ten title with a 35-21 win over Ohio State Saturday.

TONY DING/Daily

Varsity overcomes early-season woes to capture Big Ten

By J. Brady McCollough
Daily Sports Editor

Sitting in the visiting lockerroom at Kinnick Stadium after their 30-27 loss to Iowa Oct. 4, the Michigan football team's seniors were in the midst of some major soul searching.

The Wolverines were 4-2 and had lost their chance at a national championship. With one more loss in their remaining six games, the seniors would likely leave Michigan without playing in a Rose Bowl.

"We never thought we'd be 4-2 at that point in the season," Michigan fifth-year senior captain Carl Diggs recalled. "I never imagined that."

But celebrating their 35-21 win over Ohio State Saturday on a rose-covered field with an emotional student body, the Wolverines were a long way from their somber lockerroom in Iowa. With six straight wins, three over top-10 teams, Michigan rewrote the script of its season, clinching its first outright Big Ten title and Rose Bowl berth since 1997.

"It's like a storybook (ending)," senior tailback Chris Perry said. "It feels surreal right now, but after I get home and sit down and think about it, it'll feel even better."

Perry better have gotten some ice before he sat down. Struggling with pain in his right hamstring throughout the 100th meeting between Michigan and Ohio State, Perry ran for 154 yards and two scores on 31 carries. The Heisman Trophy candidate also caught five passes for 55 yards, giving him his fifth game this season with more than 200 total yards (209).

Perry and quarterback John Navarre benefited from a determined offensive line, which shut down one of the nation's most dominating defensive fronts. The Buckeyes, previously leading the country allowing just 50.5 rushing yards per game, gave up 170 to the Wolverines. The Michigan line also gave Navarre ample time to throw, holding the Buckeyes without a sack.

"It's a great eeling," Michigan offensive tackle Tony Pape said. "That was the number-1 defense in the nation. They're the defending nation champions, and they were a great defense."

> ## "It's like a storybook (ending). It feels surreal right now, but after I get home and sit down and think about it, it will feel even better.
> — Chris Perry,
> *Michigan running back*

MICHIGAN FOOTBALL

Blue loses Rose Bowl

COURTNEY LEWIS
Full Court Press

PASADENA, Calif. — Well, that didn't last long. John Navarre's leave of absence as resident punching bag is officially over.

He temporarily gave up that position after beating Ohio State in the Big Ten title-clinching game that should have defined his legacy.

But in the stands during the Rose Bowl game, in the airport on the way home and in my inbox, Michigan fans grumbled about the 28-14 loss to Southern Cal., placing the blame squarely on the senior quarterback. *He's slow. He should've thrown the ball away. It's all his fault.*

My response to all of this jumping on the Navarre-sucks bandwagon?

Get off Navarre's back. The Southern Cal. players were there enough on Thursday.

The Trojans sacked Navarre nine times. They hurried, harassed and hit him all afternoon.

Navarre spent nearly as much time on the ground as on his feet. He fumbled twice, although he recovered the ball both times. He was taken down by guys he never even saw coming. He threw an interception, albeit on a fluke play. He did not, to state the obvious, have a good game.

> " Southern Cal was like the big kid that holds the little guy by the head to keep from getting punched. Michigan kept swinging, but it couldn't get any closer than an arm's length away. "
>
> — Courtney Lewis, *The Michigan Daily*

Michigan seniors Carl Diggs (43, left) and John Navarre
of Southern California Trojans in the Rose Bowl on New
year played in Pasadena, Calif. in the 90th game in the

PHOTOS BY TONY DING/Daily

Buried alive

TOP: Michigan seniors John Navarre steps off the field after Michigan's 28-14 loss to the University of Southern California Trojans in the Rose Bowl on New Year's Day. It was Michigan's 18th appearance in the Rose Bowl this year played in Pasadena, Calif. in the 90th game in the bowl's history.
LEFT: Doak Walker Award winner Chris Perry was buried by Southern Cal. defenders all day, and when he was hit, it was usually by multiple unblocked Trojans.

Blue tops State in overtime comeback

By Gennaro Filice
Daily Sports Editor

With just under nine minutes left on Saturday, the Big House was as quiet as it has been in years. DeAndra Cobb's 64-yard touchdown run gave Michigan State a seemingly insurmountable 27-10 lead. But the Wolverines weren't quite ready to fold in the 97th meeting with their in-state rival.

"One of the things that we always talk about around here (is) the things that it takes to be a championship team," Michigan coach Lloyd Carr said. "There's a lot of things you have to be able to do: You have to continue to believe in yourself when things look bleak."

True freshman quarterback Chad Henne, who finished 24-of-35 for 273 yards and a career-high four touchdowns, adhered to Carr's demands for optimism: "We were sitting on the sideline and everybody was down, and I was thinking in my head, 'There's still a chance.' "

And following an unbelievable finish to regulation, three Braylon Edwards touchdowns and three overtime periods, the Wolverines had completed one of the most improbable wins in school history, prevailing 45-37.

Braylon's Late Show

> 66
> **One minute, Michigan State was well on its way toward its first win in Ann Arbor since 1990. The next, it was holding on for dear life.** 99
> — Bob Hunt,
> *The Michigan Daily*

TOP: The Michigan football bench erupts in celebration after the Wolverines' 45-37 (3 OT) victory over Michigan State on Saturday. **BOTTOM PHOTOS:** Braylon Edwards caught two touchdowns in the fourth quarter to lead Michigan back from a 27-10 deficit. In the third overtime, he caught another touchdown for the win.

TONY DING AND RYAN WEINER/Daily

2004

The Horn supremacy

Texas won with a last-second field goal — thwarting the Wolverines' Rose Bowl chances for a second-straight season.

'M' unable to stop Young, drops heartbreaker to Texas

By **Sharad Mattu**
Daily Sports Editor

PASADENA, Calif. — When its regular season ended, Michigan's Achilles heel was clear. Mobile quarterbacks such as Michigan State's Drew Stanton and Ohio State's Troy Smith had given the Wolverines fits with their ability to scramble and throw.

Texas quarterback Vince Young is made of the same mold, and, since it was announced on Dec. 5 that Michigan and Texas would square off in the Rose Bowl, the Wolverines knew that to win they would have to contain him.

But in the end, four weeks of preparation made no difference.

Young put together a performance for the ages — running for 192 yard and four touchdowns to go along with 180 yards passing and a touchdown — and Dusty Mangum kicked a 37-yard field goal as time expired to give Texas a 38-37 win.

The ball deflected off safety Ernest Shazor's elbow and just missed linebacker Prescott Burgess outstretched arms, but Mangum was able to eke the ball over the crossbar.

"We knew this game would come down to defense," Burgess said. "Defense wins championships, and we just weren't able to get the job done."

The defensive struggles overshadowed a strong showing by Michigan's offense. The Wolverines were led by senior Braylon Edwards, who caught 10 passes for 109 yards and three touchdowns and set Michigan's all-time record for career touchdowns receptions with 39.

Sophomore Steve Breaston, who took on an increased role because Jason Avant was out with an injured knee, caught a 50-yard touchdown pass and consistently gave Michigan a boost in field position, returning six kickoffs for 221 yards.

RYAN WEINER/Daily
LEFT: Sophomore Steve Breaston looks on in disbelief after the Wolverines' loss. Breaston set a Rose Bowl record with 315 all-purpose yards. **RIGHT:** Texas players celebrate after Dusty Mangum kicked a game-winning field goal with no time left to give the Longhorns a Rose Bowl victory.

A second to none

'THAT'S THE BEST GAME I'VE EVER SEEN OR PLAYED IN.' — ALAN BRANCH, MICHIGAN DEFENSIVE LINEMAN

By Ian Herbert
Daily Sports Editor

Mario Manningham wasn't the first option — that was Steve Breaston in the slot.

But with one second left in the game, Manningham beat Penn State's best cornerback, Alan Zemaitis, on a 10-yard post to finish off the upset of No. 8 Penn State. With more than 111,000 people screaming in Michigan Stadium and who knows how many more watching on TV, it was Manningham who made the game's most important catch in the game's most pressure-filled situation.

And then he was off.

After Manningham made the catch to seal Michigan's 27-25 win over No. 8 Penn State, he dropped the ball and took off running. And like much of the afternoon against Penn State defensive backs, no one could catch him.

"I was trying to chase him down, but he's just too fast," sophomore running back Mike Hart said. "He was running away from everybody."

Twice this season — against Notre Dame and Minnesota — the Michigan players have had to watch visiting teams end games in the Big House by celebrating with their fans. This time, it was Michigan's turn. The Wolverines ran from there to the student section and jumped into the stands — to sing and dance with their Maize-clad peers.

"That's the best game I've ever seen or played in," defensive end Alan Branch said. "It was an unreal feeling."

RYAN WEINER/Daily
Freshman receiver Mario Manningham caught a 10-yard touchdown pass as time expired to give the Wolverines the victory over previously unbeaten Penn State.

MAKING EVERY SECOND COUNT

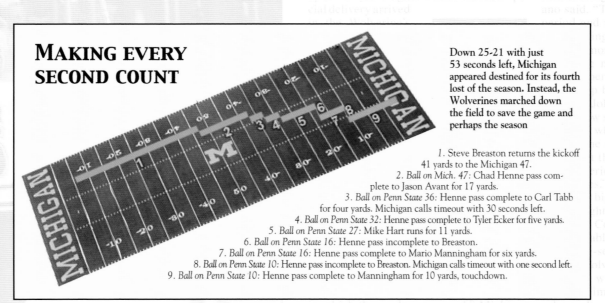

Down 25-21 with just 53 seconds left, Michigan appeared destined for its fourth lost of the season. Instead, the Wolverines marched down the field to save the game and perhaps the season

1. Steve Breaston returns the kickoff 41 yards to the Michigan 47.
2. Ball on Mich. 47: Chad Henne pass complete to Jason Avant for 17 yards.
3. Ball on Penn State 36: Henne pass complete to Carl Tabb for four yards. Michigan calls timeout with 30 seconds left.
4. Ball on Penn State 32: Henne pass complete to Tyler Ecker for five yards.
5. Ball on Penn State 27: Mike Hart runs for 11 yards.
6. Ball on Penn State 16: Henne pass incomplete to Breaston.
7. Ball on Penn State 16: Henne pass complete to Mario Manningham for six yards.
8. Ball on Penn State 10: Henne pass incomplete to Breaston. Michigan calls timeout with one second left.
9. Ball on Penn State 10: Henne pass complete to Manningham for 10 yards, touchdown.

SECOND TO ONE

THE ONE THAT GOT AWAY

ALEX DZIADOSZ/Daily

RIGHT: The Wolverines dejectedly walk off the field following their disheartening 42-39 loss at the hands of No. 1 Ohio State. **LEFT:** Antonio Pittman breaks away for a touchdown during Ohio State's 42-39 win in Columbus on Saturday.

Game was good, but OSU was better

COLUMBUS —

Some way, somehow, The Game lived up to all of the hype.

The two teams that met in the newly sodded Ohio Stadium were clearly the top two squads in the nation.

Michigan and Ohio State fought until the very end, with the Wolverines exchanging blow after blow with the nation's top-ranked team.

But as clear as it was that the two were the cream of the NCAA crop, it was even more transparent who the better of those teams was.

Scarlet-and-gray clad students walked away after storming the field with much, much more than just the 10-yard chunks of grass they grabbed in the post-game celebration.

There was a trip to the National Championship game, just one of the many incentives on the line Saturday afternoon.

There were bragging rights, something the Buckeyes have claimed for nearly the entire Jim Tressel era. The Buckeye coach now holds a 5-1 advantage over Michigan.

And of course, there were the other prizes on the line. When you factor in a Big Ten title and a Heisman trophy for quarterback Troy Smith, I'd say the Buckeye faithful left their stadium with a little more than just large patches of sod.

Michigan? Well, they left Columbus with the dubious task of having to play the waiting game.

Will there be a rematch? Should there be a rematch? Is a rematch fair?

— Scott Bell

B-S?

The BCS chose Florida over Michigan to play Ohio State in the title game.

	1	2	3	4	5
BCS STANDINGS Dec. 3, 2006					
	.9999	.944	.934	.8326	.7953

Game was good, but OSU was better

SPECIAL EDITION

BO SCHEMBECHLER | 1929-2006

Michigan Man

STEVE KAGAN/Daily

" **We have lost a giant at Michigan and in college football. Personally, I have lost a man I love.** **"**

— Lloyd Carr, *Michigan football coach*

2006

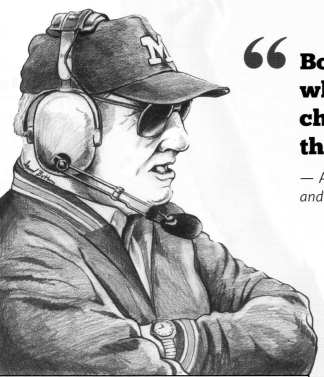

ILLUSTRATION BY SAM BUTLER

Bo and Woody made the rivalry what it is. There's a decent chance they'll be watching the game together today.

— Adam Schefter, *NFL network analyst and former Daily sports editor*

Bo Schembechler was an outstanding citizen in every respect. He was a dear friend of ours and will be greatly missed by his numerous friends. It is a great loss to the University of Michigan in particular and football in general.

— President Gerald Ford, *former Michigan lineman*

After Bo's passing, Varsity presses on

By **STEPHANIE WRIGHT**
Daily Sports Editor

COLUMBUS — On Saturday, Michigan coach Lloyd Carr faced a task far tougher than trying to beat Ohio State.

He had to coach just one day after his mentor, legendary coach Bo Schembechler, passed away at age 77.

At his press conference following Saturday's game, Carr struggled to fight back tears when asked to describe how difficult the past 24 hours had been for him.

Most of the time, he seemed unable to put his pain into words.

Carr found out about Schembechler's death just minutes before the team's noon meeting on Friday. In addition to dealing with his own grief, Carr had to pass the sad news along to his players, a duty he called hard and emotional.

Even though most of Michigan's players are too young to remember Schembechler's coaching days, nearly all of them had developed a close relationship with the coach, who maintained an office in Schembechler Hall long after he retired.

"He was a great man," running back Mike Hart said. "He started the tradition of excellence in the classroom and on the football field at Michigan. And it continues to this day. No one's ever going to forget about him on this team and what he did for this team. He was still a big part of this program."

Bo Schembechler

Coach embodied — and strengthened — football tradition

Michigan's game against Ohio State today marks the 103rd time the two teams have met on the playing field. It is an important game in its own right, with both teams undefeated, ranked number one and two. Today's game is big, but it is not bigger than Michigan tradition — year after year of winning seasons and sold-out games, fans scattered across the world with their eyes and ears turned to every football game. Bo Schembechler was that tradition.

By KEVIN WRIGHT
Daily Sports Editor

Put aside the different subdivisions and throw out preseason rankings.

It came down to execution.

Plain and simple, Appalachian State's 34-32 upset win over No. 5 Michigan in Saturday's home opener, a feat labeled as the greatest upset in college football history, was decided on the field.

"They just outplayed us," Michigan tight end Mike Massey said. "They executed better than we did, and we had a lot of penalties that hurt us too."

Appalachian State wide receiver Dexter Jackson brought reality home for the Michigan faithful with his post-game comments.

"By coming in here and beating Michigan, it's a big statement to represent every team that's in our division," Jackson said. "This opened a lot of doors for a lot of teams."

Saturday's loss to Appalachian State more than likely locked the door to a national championship bid and opened floodgates that could drown what's left of the Wolverines' 2007 campaign.

Michigan's home opener was supposed to be their first step to a National Championship run, but all it took was a two-time national champion from a lower subdivision of college football — the Football Championship Subdivision (FCS), formerly Division I-AA — to dash those hopes.

"When you lose to a team like that — they're a I-AA team — how can you go for a National Championship?" said Mike Hart, who rushed for 188 yards and three scores despite a bruised thigh sidelining him for roughly two quarters. "I believe, personally, it's out of the picture. I'm not going to give up on it. It's in everybody else's hands now."

Blue suffers historic upset

RIGHT: Left tackle Jake Long walks off the field after Michigan's loss to Appalachian State on Saturday. Long is part of a trio of Michigan seniors who put off their NFL aspirations for a year in hopes of capturing a national championship. Now those hopes are all but gone.

BOTTOM: Senior quarterback Chad Henne and the Wolverines couldn't elude losing 34-32 to Appalachian State, a Football Championship Subdivision team.

RODRIGO GAYA/Daily

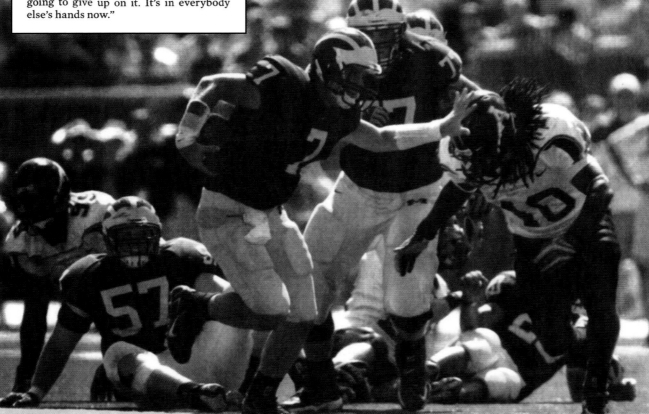

> 66 **We were very confident. We studied a lot of film, and what we saw was a lot of holes.** 99
> — Armanti Edwards,
> *Appalachian State quarterback*

2007

In upset, team gives Carr his last hurrah

By DANIEL BROMWICH
Daily Sports Editor

ORLANDO, Fla. — It was a perfectly fitting end to a season where nothing fit at all.

After a year in which the pieces of the Michigan football puzzle were beaten (twice), humbled, torn, sprained, dislocated and then beaten (twice) again, the pieces finally came together and created an everlasting image for anyone who cares about Wolverine football: Michigan coach Lloyd Carr riding victorious off the field on his players' shoulders after a more-impressive-than-it-looked 41-35 upset of the defending National Champion Florida Gators.

"It was a great ride," Carr said. "A great ride by a bunch of great guys."

Carr was talking about being carried off the field, but he could have just as easily been referring to the game that had just finished or even to his final season as the Michigan football coach.

After an up-and-down season finished with losses to Wisconsin and Ohio State, critics predicted that the Wolverines would be outmatched and outclassed by Florida (5-3 Southeastern Conference, 9-4 overall). Michigan (6-2 Big Ten, 9-4) foresaw a different ending to its coach's final season.

"You hear all throughout the weeks that it's not even going to be close, it's going to be a rout, they're going to beat us by 50," wide receiver Adrian Arrington said. "Even their players were saying that. We had a big chip on our shoulder, and we came out here and played."

RODRIGO GAYA/Daily

Michigan coach Lloyd Carr ended his coaching career with a win in Tuesday's Capital One Bowl.

UPLIFTING EXIT

RODRIGO GAYA/Daily

> " **They were a hungry team, they came out ready to go, ready to fight, and they heard a lot about the SEC and wanted to get a piece of it. And they did, unfortunately.** "
>
> — Tim Tebow, *Florida quarterback*

The Michigan defense pressures Florida quarterback Tim Tebow as he releases a ball from his own end zone.

It may look different, but it's still Michigan

RODRIGO GAYA/Daily

Michigan fans show their support for incoming head coach Rich Rodriguez. (Jan. 3, 2008)

" **We're not a very good football team right now. That's obvious. ... I'm mad, and I'm mad beginning with me.** "

— Rich Rodriguez, *Michigan football coach*

After loss to Toledo, it can't get much worse. Can it?

RICH ROD-EMPTION

MAX COLLINS/Daily

'M' wins Rodriguez's way

It's time for the Rich Rodriguez era to end

Michigan head coach Rich Rodriguez on the sidelines during the team's 21-10 loss to Ohio St. at Michigan Stadium on Saturday.

SAID ALSALAH/Daily

2008-2010

NCAA: MICHIGAN BROKE RULES

Five violations cited for 'U'

JAKE FROMM/Daily

University President Mary Sue Coleman and Michigan football coach Rich Rodriguez look on as incoming Athletic Director David Brandon discusses the NCAA's allegations about the Michigan football program at a press conference.

The NCAA's Notice of Allegations released yesterday states that the University violated NCAA regulations in five main areas.

ALLEGED VIOLATION 1

The University's football program exceeded the number of hours coaches may work with student-athletes and that five quality control officers illegally engaged in activities reserved exclusively for team coaches.

ALLEGED VIOLATION 2

The University's football program violated regulations that prohibit staff from monitoring student-athletes in voluntary, off-season workouts and conditioning — activities for which they are accused of having exceeded time restrictions on.

ALLEGED VIOLATION 3

Alex Herron, a graduate assistant football coach, provided misleading, and at times false information about his role in the allegations of misconduct during the NCAA's investigation into the Michigan football program.

ALLEGED VIOLATION 4

Rich Rodriguez acted in a manner that "failed to promote an atmosphere of compliance with the football program" and failed to properly monitor the activities of his program with regard to the allegations set forth by the NCAA.

ALLEGED VIOLATION 5

The athletic department did not properly oversee the activities of the football program to ensure full compliance with NCAA rules and regulations as they relate to the allegations set forth by the NCAA.

> ❝ **Rodriguez's stock continues to fall in an awful bout of bad karma and questionable decision-making.** ❞
>
> — Ryan Kartje, *The Michigan Daily*

Robinson leads comeback in legendary performance

NOTABLE QUOTABLE

I'm wearing my shoelaces untied in honor of Denard."

— Michigan coach Rich Rodriguez at the beginning of Saturday's postgame press conference.

MAX COLLINS/Daily

Can the one-man show keep going?

SOUTH BEND, Ind. —

Before I say anything, it should be noted that the fans who watched Saturday's win against Notre Dame watched what could have been the greatest individual performance by a Michigan player ever.

It was truly a special occasion. Denard Robinson's feats of speed and agility and moxie were so unbelievable that to try to describe them with mere words seems almost to cheapen them. Michigan fans — not to mention all the Irish fans who packed into Notre Dame Stadium — should consider themselves extremely lucky to have witnessed such an incredible player's ascent into national superstardom.

That being said, prepare to get your buzz effectively killed.

I really hate to play this role, but I have to. On Saturday, Robinson accounted for 502 yards of offense (I'm sorry, just writing that makes my jaw drop. Re-affixing it ... now).

Michigan's total yards, as a team? 532.

Any way you phrase it — he did, in fact, account for more than 94 percent of the offense — that number is either amazing or terrifying, depending on your view. For now, feel free to be amazed, and that's perfectly okay.

— Joe Stapleton

By RYAN
Daily Spo...

...TH BEND, Ind.
...es remaining on th...
... Denard Robinso...
... Seconds before,
... Dayne Crist had g...
...redible 95-yard tou...
...udolph.
...Robinson's poise
...s had been praising

...ne met his te...
...to put it in,
...he Wolverin...
...ay."
...ird down on
...to redshirt
...Roundtree w...
...plays," Roun...

...smiled back
...r center.
...mages of fellow sophomore quarterback

See **ROBINSON**, Page **3B**

502
TOTAL YARDS

258
RUSHING YARDS

244
PASSING YARDS

3
TOUCHDOWNS

THE LAST STRAW
GATOR BOWL 2011

RICH ROD OUT

52-14

MARISSA MCCLAIN/Daily

> **There was a good number of fans who were excited for the change and wanted to see what [Rodriguez] could do. They were there, but I guess they just weren't quite as loud as some of us who disliked him before he ever stepped foot on campus. We said he wasn't a 'Michigan Man.'**
>
> — Joe Stapleton, *The Michigan Daily*

Rodriguez officially fired as head coach

A.D. David Brandon: 'Michigan fans expect more than this'

By TIM ROHAN
Daily Sports Editor

The Michigan coach who led the Wolverines to their worst three-year span in Michigan football history was fired yesterday afternoon. Rich Rodriguez's 15-22 record and plenty of off-the-field drama resulted in a tumultuous tenure that will not be forgotten anytime soon.

"Michigan is not used to this," said Uni-

versity Athletic Director David Brandon in a press conference yesterday afternoon. "Michigan fans expect more than this — so do Michigan athletic directors. And so we need to put ourselves in a position where we get ourselves competitive again."

No coach has recorded a worse record in Michigan's 131-year football history and no other Michigan football team has performed worse in a bowl game — leaving the 52-14 Gator Bowl loss as Rodriguez's lasting impression in his lone bowl appearance.

His offense, led by sophomore quarterback Denard Robinson, re-wrote the record books this season. But the Wolverine defense was as bad as the offense was good.

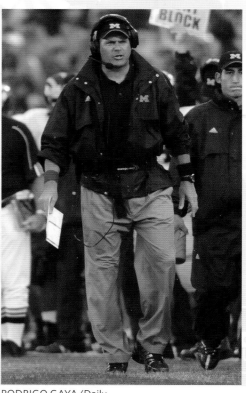

RODRIGO GAYA/Daily

HIGH HOPES FOR HOKE

Players back Brandon's decision, embrace Hoke

> 66 **I love him. He's a great coach. He's a great mentor. He's a great friend. He's every single thing you want a college coach to be and he does it flawlessly.** 99
> — David Molk, *Michigan center*

MARISSA MCCLAIN/Daily

Michigan Athletic Director Dave Brandon and Hoke at yesterday's press conference. (Jan. 13, 2011)

MARISSA MCCLAIN/Daily

Michigan coach Brady Hoke has focused on winning the Big Ten since his introductory press conference back in January.

DEC. 1, 2011

Hoke named Big Ten Coach of the Year

STEPHEN J. NESBITT
Daily Sports Editor

After leading the Michigan football team to a 10-2 season, Michigan coach Brady Hoke was named the Hayes-Schembechler Coach of the Year and and the Dave McClain Coach of the Year on Wednesday.

"It's a great honor, it's humbling and all those things," Hoke said in a video released by the Athletic Department. "But there are so many people involved with awards, whether it's the Heisman Trophy or the balloon toss, it's one of those things that (goes to) ... everyone who assists us in the football program. That's an award for everybody."

Hoke inherited a 7-5 team from former coach Rich Rodriguez in January and, with the help of offensive coordinator Al Borges

and defensive coordinator Greg Mattison, transformed the Wolverines into a conference contender. This season's Michigan team collected its first-ever 8-0 record at Michigan Stadium.

"He deserves (Big Ten Coach of the Year)," said senior captain David Molk of Hoke on Monday. "I love him. He's a great coach. He's a great mentor. He's a great friend. He's every single thing you want a college coach to be and he does it flawlessly."

Hoke was the first Michigan coach since Fielding H. Yost in 1901 to win 10 games in his first season. Hoke was also just the fifth Big Ten coach to win 10 games or more in his first season as coach, joining Wisconsin's Bret Bielema (12-1, 2006), Ohio State's Earle Bruce (11-1, 1979), Yost (11-0, 1901) and Minnesota's Henry Williams (10-0-2, 1900).

Hoke gained the respect Rodriguez never had

> 66 **This is Michigan, for God's sake.** 99
> — Brady Hoke,
> *Michigan football coach*

A DECADE LATER, SPORTS ARE THE PERFECT UNIFIER

MARCH 19, 2010

Michigan to host Notre Dame under the lights

Monday, September 12, 2011

Junior quarterback Denard Robinson overcame a poor first half to lead Michigan to a 35-31 win over Notre Dame. Robinson accounted for 98.7 percent of the Wolverines' offense.

PHOTOS BY MARISSA MCCLAIN/Daily

How it ended: The Last 5 Minutes

4:57 — Robinson to Hemingway, jump-ball for 45 yards.

4:32 — Robinson throws interception in the endzone.

3:14 — Jake Ryan stops Cierre Wood on third down, forcing a punt.

1:22 — Vincent Smith takes screen pass 21 yards for go-ahead touchdown.

UM 28-24

1:05 — J.T. Floyd called for pass interference on Michael Floyd.

0:36 — Rees hits Theo Riddick for a 29-yard touchdown.

ND 31-28

0:22 — Robinson finds Gallon wide open on wheel route for 64 yards.

0:08 — Robinson hits Roundtree for a 16-yard touchdown.

UM 35-31

A NIGHT YOU'LL NEVER FORGET

Robinson & Co. stole the show

By TIM ROHAN
Daily Sports Editor

One-hundred fourteen thousand, eight hundred and four pairs of eyes slowly turned toward Jeremy Gallon. They widened when they realized no Notre Dame jerseys were in the picture they'll remember forever.

"Oh my god. Where did he come from?" said one man standing in the South endzone.

From his vantage point, Denard Robinson just threw a pass to no one in particular down the right sideline.

Gallon blended in with his teammates on the sideline, until a blue blur came streaking out of nowhere. Just like Michigan had.

The crowd was roaring, woken up from its slumber by a team that needed waking itself. Every maize pom-pon beat the air in unison. The event — the first night game ever, the largest crowd ever, the anticipation building because it seemed everyone who had ever called Ann Arbor home was back in town this weekend — felt larger than life. Under the lights.

And the game was outshining the

event.

Now Gallon was wide open, running free.

But Robinson and Gallon had been working on this play all summer. Down by three points. Thirty seconds left. Ball on the 20-yard line.

Gallon runs the slow wheel route, leaking out to the sideline and up the field. If the play is run perfectly, he could surprise everyone. This time, the only defender that could've disrupted everything ran to cover Roy Roundtree, who was streaking across the field.

Eight seconds were left on the clock

when Gallon ended his sprint at the 16-yard line. Michigan was in field-goal range. Brady Hoke wanted to go for the win.

Why the hell not?

This game, by all possible logical explanations, should have ended horribly wrong for the Michigan Wolverines.

Here was a chance to get Hoke a signature win, add a chapter to a rivalry.

One hundred thousand-plus people would never forget this if Hoke did it right.

And Notre Dame was handing him the game.

The Michigan Daily | michigandaily.com | November 28, 2011

FINALLY

Hoke's first team tastes redemption

> "We put Team 132 in the books forever. I think this team will always be remembered as the team that set a new standard and re-established what Michigan is supposed to be about."
>
> — Ryan Van Bergen,
> *Michigan defensive end*

MARISSA MCCLAIN/Daily

Michigan halts seven-year skid in The Game

In complete team effort, Team 132 holds off Buckeyes in final minutes

By MICHAEL FLOREK
Daily Sports Editor

Fifth-year senior defensive end Ryan Van Bergen was crying as he emerged from the crowd gathering by the student section.

Senior defensive tackle Mike Martin stood in front of the tunnel taking photo after photo with students he didn't know.

Senior tight end Kevin Koger was sur- rounded by a group of fans who had rushed the field along with thousands of their friends, hugging and patting him, preventing the Tole- do native from making his way up the Michi- gan Stadium tunnel.

This is what beating Ohio State looks like. How does it feel?

"If I could put it into words, I would," said fifth-year senior wide receiver Junior Hemingway.

After seven long years of waiting, the Mich- igan football team finally figured out that feel- ing, with a dramatic 40-34 victory over the Buckeyes at the Big House on Saturday.

The 17th-ranked Wolverines (6-2 Big Ten, 10-2 overall) didn't do it easily or gracefully

— they needed a last-minute overthrow and a final interception from the defense to seal the game — but they did it.

"What satisfies you is when you see those kids in that locker room and when you saw them on the field, how (happy they are)," said Michigan coach Brady Hoke. "It's fun as a coach to see how they responded."

It doesn't matter how it's added up, it equals one thing, the thing Hoke has said since he got here, the reason for his countdown clocks. Michigan finally "beat Ohio."

"It was a team win," Molk said. "It wasn't just an offensive victory, it was a team victory against Ohio State."

Days since Michigan beat Ohio State: 0.

EXTRA SWEET

MARISSA MCCLAIN/Daily

" **We've been through so much. Nobody understands that. But to come out here and win this bowl game, today, with these people I worked hard with from day one, it feels so good. There's nothing like it.** "

— Junior Hemingway,
Michigan wide receiver

Michigan outlasts Virginia Tech in Sugar Bowl

By TIM ROHAN
Daily Sports Editor

NEW ORLEANS — Brady Hoke leaned in, hugged Junior Hemingway and gave him a kiss on the forehead. Hemingway's Most Outstanding Player Trophy sat on the table in front of him, and Hoke wore a smile as he took his seat.

Earlier, Hemingway cried on his mother's shoulder while celebrating Michigan's 23-20 overtime victory in the Sugar Bowl over No. 13 Virginia Tech. Hoke always said he'd lead with his seniors, and a fifth-year senior had capped the coach's blessed first season with a win.

"You've got to have guys who can make those plays, and when (Denard Robinson and Hemingway) are the ones doing it, you feel pretty good about it," said Hoke, whose team became just the fifth in modern Michigan football history to win 11 games.

On a day Michigan amassed just 184 yards of offense, it wasn't Denard Robinson or Fitzgerald Toussaint that saved the day, it was "Big Play" Hemingway, as Robinson calls him. No one will be quick to call Michigan's win pretty, but the few plays Michigan did make came at the most crucial of times, when the game was in the balance.

The first half had belonged to Virginia Tech, but Michigan held the lead. The second half belonged to the Hokies too, but Michigan had overtime. When overtime came, Virginia Tech's third-string kicker — who had was a perfect 3-for-3 to that point — missed a 37-yard field goal. Michigan's Brendan Gibbons made his 37-yarder.

Michigan wills itself to victory, capping improbable season

MARISSA MCCLAIN/Daily

From 1890 until Michigan's most recent victory in the Sugar Bowl, *The Michigan Daily* has reported on the games fans remember and the ones they have tried to forget.

We hope readers will keep reading the *Daily* as student journalists at the University of Michigan continue to cover the tradition of the nation's most winningest program.